THE STORY OF
THE BAND

FROM BIG PINK TO THE LAST WALTZ

THE STORY OF
THE BAND
FROM BIG PINK TO THE LAST WALTZ

Harvey Kubernik & Kenneth Kubernik
With select photographs by Elliott Landy and John Scheele

STERLING
New York

STERLING
New York

An Imprint of Sterling Publishing Co., Inc.
1166 Avenue of the Americas
New York, NY 10036

STERLING and the distinctive Sterling logo are registered trademarks of Sterling Publishing Co., Inc.

Interior text © 2018 Harvey Kubernik and Kenneth Kubernik
Cover © 2018 Sterling Publishing Co., Inc.

All rights reserved. No part of this publication may be reproduced, stored in a retrieval system, or transmitted in any form or by any means (including electronic, mechanical, photocopying, recording, or otherwise) without prior written permission from the publisher.

This is an independent publication and is not associated with or authorized, licensed, sponsored, or endorsed by any person, entity, or product affiliated with The Band or their music. All trademarks are the property of their respective owners, are used for editorial purposes only, and the publisher makes no claim of ownership and shall acquire no right, title, or interest in such trademarks by virtue of this publication.

ISBN 978-1-4549-2890-4

Distributed in Canada by Sterling Publishing Co., Inc.
c/o Canadian Manda Group, 664 Annette Street
Toronto, Ontario M6S 2C8, Canada
Distributed in the United Kingdom by GMC Distribution Services
Castle Place, 166 High Street, Lewes, East Sussex BN7 1XU, England
Distributed in Australia by NewSouth Books
University of New South Wales, Sydney, NSW 2052, Australia

For information about custom editions, special sales, and premium and corporate purchases, please contact Sterling Special Sales at 800-805-5489 or specialsales@sterlingpublishing.com.

Manufactured in Canada

2 4 6 8 10 9 7 5 3 1

sterlingpublishing.com

Cover design by Igor Satanovsky
Interior design by Kevin Baier, KJWork Design Co.

Picture Credits—see page 211

Dedication

For Rick Danko, Levon Helm, Garth Hudson, Richard Manuel, and Robbie Robertson

ii–iii: The Band recording in Rick Danko's basement, Woodstock, New York, 1969; photograph by Elliott Landy.

vi–vii: Rick Danko, Robbie Robertson, and Levon Helm onstage during The Band's performance at the Woodstock Festival, August 17, 1969.

CONTENTS

Prologue 1

1. Igloos, Eskimos, and Dogsleds 9
2. The Hawk Spreads His Wings 19
3. Leaving the Nest and Preparing to Fly 33
4. The Basement Tapes 57
5. Which One Is Big Pink? 69
6. Something Was Delivered 83
7. Faithful Servants 93
8. Right Creek, Right Paddle 117
9. Life Is a Sideshow 137
10. Out in Malibu with a Different View 153
11. The Band Has Left the Building 177

Acknowledgments 194
A Selected Discography 195
Show List 1960–1976 199
Sources 206
Bibliography 209
Picture Credits 211
Index 212

PROLOGUE

SUCH A NIGHT

On Thanksgiving Day 1976, The Band was going to perform live onstage for the very last time, at the Winterland Ballroom in San Francisco. Producing the landmark show was Bill Graham, and Martin Scorsese was scheduled to direct a documentary.

For the event, which was billed as *The Last Waltz*, Rick Danko, Levon Helm, Garth Hudson, Richard Manuel, and Robbie Robertson of The Band were joined by an all-star group of recording artist friends, including Paul Butterfield, Muddy Waters, Van Morrison, Eric Clapton, Neil Diamond, Bob Dylan, Neil Young, Dr. John, Bobby Charles, Joni Mitchell, and Ronnie Hawkins.

I had previously seen three Bob Dylan and The Band concerts in mid-February 1974 at the Fabulous Forum in Inglewood, the last leg of a two-month tour. After the first night, I had a soulful encounter at the Beverly Wilshire Hotel with Richard Manuel, a tortured soul whose voice could steer you through the light and the dark.

Now, after sixteen years on the road, The Band was going to call it quits.

I made immediate plans in Hollywood with my pals—drummer Paul Body, filmmaker Michael Hacker, and photographer Lester Cohen—to catch the action and to report on the event for *Melody Maker*. It wasn't easy to book a last-minute plane from the Los Angeles airport on Thanksgiving to fly up to San Francisco.

I knew I was gonna eventually get a £25 check ($40.00) in the mail for a review that was gonna get published in the December 11, 1976, issue of *Melody Maker*, so how could I miss this?

Five thousand ticket holders paid $25 each (well worth it) for a Thanksgiving dinner of turkey, mincemeat, or fresh Alaskan smoked salmon with rolls, candied yams, potatoes, gravy, cider, and pumpkin pie.

OPPOSITE: Marquee of the Winterland Ballroom, San Francisco, in November 1976, announcing *The Last Waltz* concert.

The doors opened at 6:00 P.M. I already had a connection to a publicist at the Winterland box office, and she quickly steered my squad to the entrance. We copped a table right in front of the stage.

At 9:00 P.M., promoter Bill Graham strolled out and introduced the evening. He mentioned that the concert was being filmed and recorded for posterity.

During the intermission, when several poets read—including Michael McClure, Lenore Kandel, Lawrence Ferlinghetti, and Diane di Prima—I saw Graham hurriedly pacing around Winterland and said a brief hello. I had recently conducted an interview for *Melody Maker* with Bill, Carlos Santana, and Jerry Garcia inside Graham's Mill Valley home. At the time, I asked Bill where the Rolling Stones were lodged when they played Winterland for him in 1972. Graham confided, "We put them up at the Miyako Hotel." Bill also volunteered that over the years the Who, Traffic, and the Kinks had been lodged at this Asian hotel near Japantown.

Several hours later, at 2:00 A.M., the dazzled crowd stomped and The Band alone came out for the last number, "Don't Do It," a cover of Marvin Gaye's "Baby Don't You Do It," penned by the Holland-Dozier-Holland songwriting team.

Then Robertson said "Thank you very much. . . . Good night. Good-bye." Bill Graham came back out and thanked everyone and that was it—the end to an incredible night.

I immediately suggested to my friends, "Let's get a drink at the Miyako bar!" We hoofed it over to the Miyako while still dazzled from the near-religious experience our congregation had just witnessed and heard at the Winterland shul.

As we walked into the elevator, our group was immediately greeted by a grinning Levon Helm on his way to the piano lounge in the Osaka Room. The singing drummer extended his hand. "Did you enjoy the show, boys?"

"Yes, Mr. Helm."

We couldn't afford to actually stay at this swanky hotel, so we took a 6:15 A.M. flight back to LAX after devouring at least a dozen iced teas to caffeinate while waiting for the flight.

On the plane back home, I was flashing on the late summer of 1968, when I'd first met singer and songwriter Jackie DeShannon at the Laurel Canyon Country Store. She was doing a new album called *Laurel Canyon* for Imperial Records.

I recognized Jackie from a 1965 *Shindig!* ABC-TV appearance and newspaper coverage in the *KRLA Beat*. After I complimented her on "When You Walk in the Room" and "Needles and Pins," Jackie said "Have you heard the new LP of The Band? I just recorded 'The Weight' from *Music from Big Pink* at Liberty Studios. Harvey! Have you heard their songs?"

BELOW: Rick Danko and Robbie Robertson onstage during *The Last Waltz* show, November 25, 1976. OPPOSITE, TOP: Danko, Bob Dylan, and Robertson at *The Last Waltz*. OPPOSITE, BOTTOM: Bill Graham during his speech winding up *The Last Waltz*.

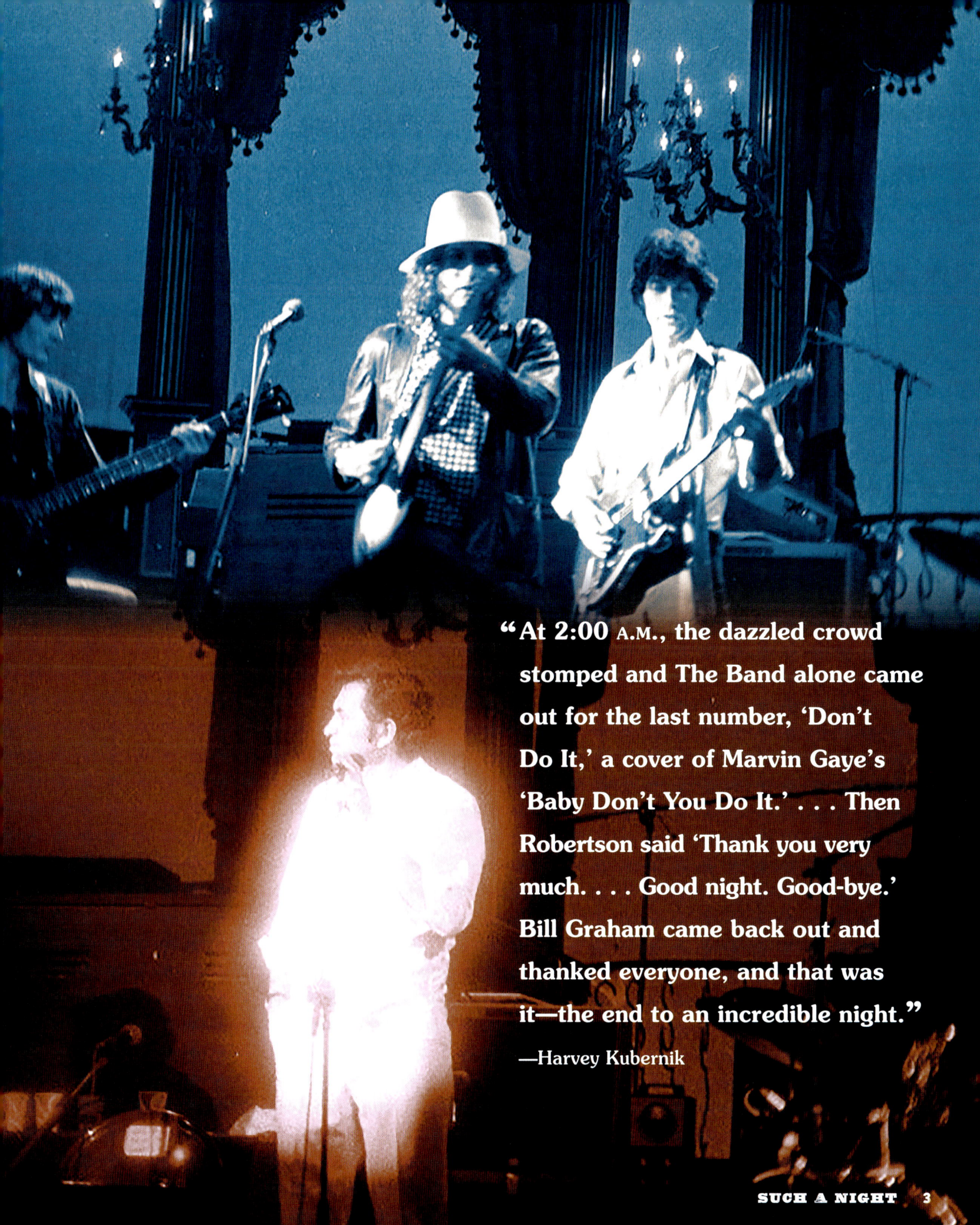

"At 2:00 A.M., the dazzled crowd stomped and The Band alone came out for the last number, 'Don't Do It,' a cover of Marvin Gaye's 'Baby Don't You Do It.' . . . Then Robertson said 'Thank you very much. . . . Good night. Good-bye.' Bill Graham came back out and thanked everyone, and that was it—the end to an incredible night."
—Harvey Kubernik

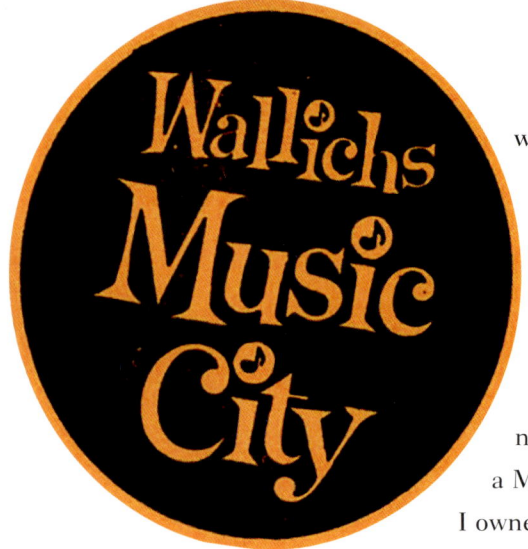

This was a woman who knew Elvis Presley and Eddie Cochran, opened for the Beatles on an American tour, and had songwriting credits with someone named Jimmy Page on a Marianne Faithfull LP I owned. I had heard her voice for half a decade on local AM radio stations KHJ, KRLA, and KFWB.

In her alluring Southern drawl—she was born in Kentucky, as Sharon Lee Myers—Jackie DeShannon gave me a stern directive I never forgot: "Boy, you need to go to Wallichs Music City and get this album!"

"The Weight" was on the KHJ playlist, while the regional FM stations, KPPC and KMET, blared The Band's LP constantly. I got paid from my after-school job at Clinton Laboratories and purchased *Music from Big Pink* at Wallichs. It sounded ancient, yet modern, and I wore the grooves out. One afternoon I even schlepped out to Encino in the San Fernando Valley to Make-A-Tape on Ventura Boulevard, and for a few bucks got a copy transferred to an eight-track cartridge.

In 1970, producer Denny Bruce, arranger/producer Jack Nitzsche, and noted session guitarist Ry Cooder saw The Band at the Pasadena Civic Auditorium. The outfit looked like they'd stepped out from a Civil War western on the Warner Brothers Burbank studio backlot. Bruce told me they were marvelous. On the way home to Hollywood, Cooder had remarked "I like them because they look and play like men, not boys."

Denny also checked out The Band and Miles Davis concert at the Hollywood Bowl in July '70. "They were very much at home on stage, and didn't do anything but simply play all of *Music from Big Pink*. No trying to move around the stage, like 'We're rock stars now.'"

I remember sitting with drummer Bruce Gary in 1971, next to drummer/percussionist Jim Keltner at Lucy's El Adobe Cafe on Melrose Avenue in Hollywood. Jim kept touting The Band's drummer, Levon Helm. "Harv . . . check out The Band on your headphones and dig Levon's work."

Keltner had been to a couple of recording sessions for the group's self-titled second album, *The Band* (1969),

ABOVE LEFT: Logo for Wallichs Music City; the iconic L.A. store closed in 1974.

LEFT: A KHJ radio survey of the top songs of the week of September 4, 1968; "The Weight" was number 3.

when his friend bassist Carl Radle took him to one at Sammy Davis Jr.'s home in the Hollywood Hills, which The Band had rented. They turned the pool house into a recording studio, which was where just about all the basic tracks for the second album were recorded.

I saw Jackie DeShannon in 1977, when Led Zeppelin played the Inglewood Forum. Afterward, Jackie invited me over to her home in L.A. and I subsequently interviewed her for *Melody Maker*. During our conversation, I learned that Jackie, Donna Weiss, and Cher had visited the Village Recorder studio in West Los Angeles in 1973, when Dylan and The Band cut *Planet Waves*. DeShannon sang background vocals on some tracks that were never issued.

Planet Waves was completed in three days. "We knew the technique very well," Robertson recalled. "We'd been playing with Bob for years. There were no surprises involved. We did it, and it was over before we knew it. We managed to get several things off very well for such a short time."

I spoke with Robbie Robertson in 1975 and '76 for a *Crawdaddy* magazine cover story at Shangri-La recording studio in Malibu while The Band was recording their new album, *Northern Lights–Southern Cross*. Robertson, as usual, emphasized that The Band is a group and refused to be singled out, even though he had written all the songs on *Northern Lights–Southern Cross*. "It's just a particular time when one of the guys has more songs written than other times. It just fell that way this time and will probably change again.... We've been together for fifteen years and it would be unnatural and forced all of a sudden if we were going to be rock symbols or rock stars. That's all meaningless to us. It's never been part of our style to chop off heads onstage for extra applause," he laughed.

TOP RIGHT: Ad for a concert featuring The Band with special guest Miles Davis, at the Hollywood Bowl, July 10, 1970.

BELOW: The Hollywood Hills hosted The Band in 1969, where they recorded their eponymous album at a studio built in Sammy Davis Jr.'s pool house.

For six months in 1977, I worked for Albert Grossman, former manager of Dylan and The Band, and his Bearsville Records label. Grossman not only had an ear for talent, but his savvy business instincts always kept him one step ahead of the wolfpack hoping to poach his stable. He was soulful and a son-of-a-bitch; you wanted him negotiating your deal. I was a tour and product publicist, writing bios for artists Jesse Winchester, Paul Butterfield, Todd Rundgren, Utopia, Elizabeth Barraclough, and Foghat. It was an ideal preparation for a sit-down interview I taped in 1977 with Rick Danko for *Melody Maker* at the offices of Arista Records in Century City. We discussed his self-titled solo album and *The Last Waltz*. "The Band really came alive that night," enthused Danko, reflecting on *The Last Waltz*. "We were cruising the last year and it was obvious. No way was I gonna walk out on stage and wing it next to Joni Mitchell. And Muddy Water…."

I was also present on March 1, 1978, when Danko and his group (promoting his eponymous solo album) headlined the Roxy Theatre in West Hollywood. After "What a Town" and "This Wheel's On Fire," all the other members of The Band sat in for "Stage Fright," "The Shape I'm In," and "The Weight."

In April 1978, my brother, Kenny, joined me at the premiere of *The Last Waltz* film held at the Cinerama Dome in Hollywood. (I'm shown onscreen during "Don't Do It.") Almost twenty years later, I co-produced and co-curated an installment in the *Great Writer Series* at LA's MET Theatre, along with the creator of the series, actor and director Darrell Larson. The program, titled *Rock 'n' Roll in Literature*, ran from July 5 to 28, 1995. One evening, the three surviving members of the Doors reunited for a few songs onstage. Another night, Doors drummer John Densmore, along with

RIGHT: Harvey Kubernik doing a reading during the MET Theatre shows in East Hollywood, July 1995. RIGHT, BOTTOM: The Doors' John Densmore and Harvey at one of the MET shows. OPPOSITE PAGE, CLOCKWISE FROM TOP RIGHT: A book inscription to Harvey Kubernik from Robbie Robertson, 2016; an invitation and ticket to an autism benefit show featuring Garth Hudson and the Wild Honey Orchestra playing The Band's music at the Alex Theatre in Glendale, California, March 25, 2017.

some musical associates, performed selections from the widely circulated 1967 Bob Dylan and the Hawks' *Basement Tapes*.

There was also a celebration of works by playwright and actor Sam Shepard. Actors Ed Harris, a longtime Shepard friend and collaborator, and Beverly D'Angelo were among the participants. During sound check, Daniel Weizmann, Paul Body, and I chatted with Beverly. We asked if it was true that she once had been a backup singer in the mid-'70s with Band mentor Ronnie Hawkins in Canada. "I sure was!" she exclaimed. Ms. D'Angelo then serenaded us with a partial rendition of Hawkins's "Mary Lou." During the MET run, I read a few of my stories and interviews on The Band, Charles Bukowski, and Motown Records.

I interviewed Robertson in late 2016 for a March 2017 cover story in *Record Collector News* about his new autobiography, *Testimony*; his solo album of the same name; the release of *The Basement Tapes Complete* in 2014; his early-'60s visits to the Brill Building in New York City—famous for housing music industry offices, studios, record producers, music publishers, managers, and booking agents; the 2016-released *Bob Dylan: The 1966 Live Recordings*; and the now-fortieth anniversary of the celebrated Thanksgiving show. Robertson explained that he wrote the book because the "stories got so heavy from carrying them around all these years that when I got to this place I thought 'I can't carry them all anymore. It's too much.' And writing this book I felt like 'I can unload this.' I feel lighter."

Just last year, my brother Kenneth and I attended two Southern California Band-related tribute events in Glendale and downtown Los Angeles. Garth Hudson's keyboard graced both stages.

During the last decade, I kept hearing Band airplay on FM, Internet, and satellite radio, particularly on Little Steven Van Zandt's *Underground Garage* and on the *Outlaw Country* channels on Sirius XM. Americana and college radio formats spun Band selections on compact disc reissues and vinyl re-releases from Universal Music Enterprises. There were numerous multi-artist Band-themed album collections devoted to them.

A book acknowledging the ongoing impact and cultural influence during their 1966–76 existence, coinciding with the fiftieth anniversary of *Music from Big Pink* and the fortieth one of *The Last Waltz* film—considered by most to be the greatest concert film ever made—needed to be written.

I hope my mission, assembled witnesses, and narrative provide new details about and revealing insights into the glorious backstory and the saga of The Band.

Harvey Kubernik
Los Angeles, California
July 14, 2018

CHAPTER 1
IGLOOS, ESKIMOS, AND DOGSLEDS

That vast expanse of polite cold known as Canada is routinely overlooked as a source of cultural disruption. But back in the halcyon gleam of the 1950s, the distant thunder of a *be bop a lula* of a beat was beginning to shake American youth out of their crew-cut conformity, reverberating beyond borderlines.

Canadian teens were equally susceptible to those heathen rhythms, playing host to a brigand's parade of mannish boys and hoochie coochie men prospecting for rock 'n' roll glory. They brandished Fender Stratocasters instead of pickaxes, styled their spit-curled coifs with switchblades, and roused every little sweet-sixteen to get up and dance, dance, dance.

These were barbarians at the gate, shaking the foundations of the Anglo-Saxon gentility that characterized postwar Canada. Virtually untouched by the struggles and privations afflicting their English motherland, Canada experienced rising prosperity, and, for many young people, a stifling air of moral rectitude.

The youthquake that rock 'n' roll helped unleash shook the entire North American continent, cleaving along a fault line of social, political, and economic contentiousness. Though spared the galvanic ruptures that faced America, Canadians still felt the full brunt of that weaponized rhythm, like an ominous drumbeat.

In June 1956, Vancouver was the first to experience the tumult. Bill Haley and the Comets generated an otherworldly frenzy among the thousands of kids in attendance. Other, more circumspect observers were less than enthused.

OPPOSITE: Ronnie Hawkins and the Hawks, c. 1958; from left to right: Levon Helm, Ronnie Hawkins, Jimmy Ray "Luke" Paulman, and Willard "Pop" Jones.

"**M**usical depravity," wrote the music critic for the *Vancouver Sun*. "One could scarcely conceive that adult entertainers could lower themselves to perform such weird contortions and degrading movement to a so-called musical background as these presented Wednesday evening."

On April 2, 1957, Elvis Presley performed afternoon and evening concerts at Toronto's Maple Leaf Gardens arena before twenty-three thousand delirious teenagers driven to distraction by the locomotive thrust of his wantonly buoyant body, all lips and hips, lubricated by the momentousness of being the right person at the right place at the right time. Even the guys were swooning.

The audience goes wild at Elvis Presley's April 1957 performance at the Maple Leaf Gardens arena, Toronto.

MIKE STOLLER
songwriter and record producer

"Jerry [Leiber] and I actually produced—without credit—the records, our songs in particular, that were in the film *Jailhouse Rock*. And, Elvis asked for us to be there. We had never met him before. He was a very good-looking young man, very energetic. It was his singing. Pure talent. I mean, he just kept going and going in the studio. He'd say, 'Let's do another one.' And it would go on and on until he felt he had it. The studio was booked for the day, and we were used to three-hour sessions."

JERRY LEIBER
songwriter and record producer

"He loved doing it. He wasn't someone who was doing it and wanted to go home, like a lot of people. Elvis had more fun in the studio than he did at home. He was very cooperative and a workhorse. I thought he was the greatest ballad singer since Bing Crosby. As far as I'm concerned, nobody cuts Little Richard on rhythm tunes. You have to go far and wide. But Presley was the ultimate in the ballad."

Acclaimed songwriting duo Mike Stoller (left) and Jerry Leiber (right) flank Elvis at MGM Studios in 1957.

From Ottawa to Vancouver and from Calgary to Edmonton, rock 'n' roll was ringing a rapturous bell and there wasn't a damn thing the community burghers could do about it except pray for the innocent souls of their sons and daughters.

The music, of course, had been hiding in plain sight, lurking on the periphery of middle-class propriety, in the shadowlands. Like a vapor trail it streamed out of the cotton fields of the sun-scorched Mississippi Delta, heading out on any mystery train that promised liberation from the weight of "feelin' half-past dead."

By the time it settled in the urban centers of the Yankee North, a rambunctious young cohort of true believers was bathing in the muddy waters of an authentically black cultural experience, transposing it into a key that chimed with their own class privileges.

Toronto in the late '50s was cloaked in a soft-spoken conservatism, which it wore with blushing pride like a new suit from Canada's famed Eaton's department store. That amiability masked a mean judgmental streak as redoubtable as the St. Lawrence waterway.

Once known as the "Queen City"—statues of Victoria dot the city's landscape—Toronto was Canada's center of finance, home to museums and prestigious universities, as well as a sports capital, a growing metropolis that called such celebrated musical icons as Glenn Gould and Oscar Peterson local heroes.

In the 2011 three-part documentary miniseries *Yonge Street: Toronto Rock & Roll Stories*, Canadian musicologist Jan Haust observed that Toronto was "uniquely perched on the north side of Lake Ontario in a line that included Chicago and Detroit. So it truly was the farthest outpost of this music—black American music—that came up from New Orleans, up the Mississippi into these towns. And it took a lot longer to reach Toronto."

> **"From Ottawa to Vancouver and from Calgary to Edmonton, rock 'n' roll was ringing a rapturous bell and there wasn't a damn thing the community burghers could do about it except pray for the innocent souls of their sons and daughters."**

Canadian Roots

SHARRY WILSON, AUTHOR

"Southwestern Ontario, in particular, was a bustling manufacturing area in the 1940s, '50s, and '60s. The large automotive sector was important to the economy during this time. Garth Hudson, Richard Manuel, and Rick Danko all hailed from this part of the province.

"In Windsor, Ontario, Garth Hudson was born August 2, 1937. Due to its proximity to Detroit directly across the US border, Windsor became the home of US automotive branch plants and an extension of the huge Detroit automotive market. Windsor thrived in this role for many years.

"Richard Manuel was born April 3, 1944, in Stratford, Ontario, made famous by the live-theater Stratford Festival that began in 1952. Prior to that time, Stratford was principally known as a railway industry town. Richard's father worked at the Chrysler® plant, so the automotive industry was yet again an important component of the city's fabric.

"On December 9, 1943, Rick Danko was born in a small rural community near Simcoe, Ontario, not far from Hamilton, where Ronnie Hawkins first came to Canada to play. Steel manufacturing was the largest industry in Hamilton back then.

"Robbie Robertson was born July 5, 1943. His mother was of Mohawk and Cayuga descent and was a member of the Six Nations reserve near Grand River, Ontario, the largest First Nations reserve in Canada. She moved to Toronto to live with her sister and find work.

"She married Jim Robertson in 1942, shortly after he returned from serving a tour of duty with the Canadian Army. The family settled into a bustling downtown neighborhood filled with immigrants of various nationalities.

"Robbie's mother later told him that his real father was Alex Klegerman, a man of the Jewish faith she had shared a close relationship with while Jim Robertson was overseas. Robbie's mother arranged for him to meet his two uncles, Alex Klegerman's brothers, since Alex had predeceased both of them. They immediately included him as family and Robbie maintained a close relationship with both uncles.

"In this way, Robbie became more familiar with his Jewish roots and heritage. It was an unusual mix for someone who was also a member of the First Nations, but Robbie embraced the situation and made it work for him. It made him seem all the more exotic."

Radio proved to be the essential cog connecting all those anxious adolescents eager to embrace the new sound of the city. More often than not, it was that latest hip invention, the portable transistor—easily hidden like some illicit contraband from the prying eyes and ears of aggrieved parents—that provided this pulsating Pandora's box of enticements. Under bedroom coverlets or on the school bus, the radio—and its attendant disc jockeys—became essential characters in shaping the "Teen Age."

Garth Hudson, organist, keyboardist, and saxophonist of The Band, explained to journalist Nick DeRiso of *Something Else!* webzine in October 2012 how influential rock-and-roll radio was to him as a teenager: "The basement [of our house] had a darkroom where my dad did his photography. I would go down there, and eventually I put a radio in with a copper wire. I drilled a hole through the floor of my bedroom and out into the back porch . . . that was the aerial. I was picking up Alan Freed when I was about fourteen or fifteen. Suddenly, I realized that somebody over there was having a lot more fun than I was!"

> "Richard Manuel and I got all of our R&B education from across the water because we were closer to Cleveland. Over there in the east, where Rick and Robbie came from, they picked up 'The Hound' from Buffalo. We were tutored by different radio announcers."
>
> —Garth Hudson to Nick Deriso, *Something Else!*, August 2015

LARRY LEBLANC
music journalist, writer, radio broadcaster

"Canadian radio in the '50s and '60s largely played what was on American Top 40 radio. There was a smattering of Canadian recordings, but few. Most of the music scenes in Canada were local. A number one band in Toronto meant nothing in Montreal or Winnipeg and vice versa. The national Canadian acts were Bobby Curtola, and Chad Allan & the Expressions [which] became the Guess Who. . . . CKLW in Windsor was regarded as a Detroit radio station.

"If Canadian radio took its cues from any station, it would be CHUM-AM in Toronto, the flagship of the CHUM chain, which had a half-dozen AM stations across the country. CHUM could make or break a hit across the country.

"At the same time, people in Southern Ontario and in Toronto could pick up R&B [broadcasting] giants like John R. out of Memphis and George 'Hound Dog' Lorenz out of Buffalo. They were popular in Toronto. Many of us would go to Buffalo in the early '60s, and I bet some of the Hawks did too, go down to Audrey and Del's record store in Buffalo to get the newest R&B and soul records. Most of those records, and certainly blues records, were not available in Toronto."

Portrait of music journalist and radio broadcaster Larry LeBlanc, c. 2015.

TOM WILSON
booking agent

"I started as an agent with Ron Scribner in 1959, when there were not very many agents booking Canadian rock 'n' roll bands anywhere in Canada. We had to literally force Canadian rock on the market. We would always try to have Canadian artists as the opening act. We also worked with Dick Clark on his *Caravan of Stars* concerts in Canada. He liked and used Canadians such as the Five Man Electrical Band and Richie Knight and the Mid-Knights.

"Most of the Canadian acts we were booking in the late '50s and on were playing at high schools, summer dance pavilions, church dances, movie theaters, matinees and, of course, the bars. For rock and rhythm and blues there were dance clubs. The most famous was the Bluenote, where you would see, hear, and mingle with the cream of the Toronto musical community: Dianne Brooks, Steve Kennedy, Domenic Troiano, Grant Smith, Doug Riley, Jay King, Wayne St. John, Shirley Matthews, Kay Taylor, Pentti "Whitey" Glan, Jack Hardin, Shawne and Jay Jackson, Prakash John, Eric Mercury, George Olliver, Duncan White, Sonny Milne, Jon and Lee, Terry Brown, Roy Kenner, and David Clayton-Thomas."

JULIETTE JAGGER
music journalist

"Toronto's Yonge Street—cutting north to south in the heart of the city—was a racy little hotbed of local culture in the sixties. Lined with gaudy emporiums, grimy bookstores, leather shops, and cheap movie theaters, it was the sort of place that seemed to come alive at night.

"In those days, it wasn't uncommon to hear the music of raucous rock 'n' rollers or of howling bluesmen pouring out of the windows and doors of local venues like the Brown Derby, the Colonial Tavern, Friar's Tavern, and the Hawk's Nest. But, it was the notorious Le Coq d'Or Tavern at 333 Yonge that was the main attraction on the strip.

"With its dark red walls, western-themed décor, and white-booted go-go dancers, Le Coq d'Or became the place to be seen in the late 1950s—largely based on the rockin' antics of Arkansas-born Rompin' Ronnie Hawkins and his band the Hawks. The club ultimately served as the backdrop for what would eventually become known as the celebrated 'Toronto Sound.'"

A promo piece from 1956 of the influential American disc jockey Alan Freed, who brought rock and roll to the youth of North America, including a young Garth Hudson.

Just as be-boppin' New Yorkers congregated around 52nd Street like moths to a scriptural flame, Toronto's nightlife ignited along Yonge Street. There was no night on the town quite like a night on Yonge Street. It was a little bit of Broadway and a whole lot of the O.K. Corral. Bodies and beer bottles often went flying across the dance floors, fueled by a toxic brew of country boys in search of city girls. You could escort your date down the street to a more dignified setting, where jazz pianist Oscar Peterson was holding court, or catch Ray Charles and his orchestra at some swank hotel.

The Yonge Street strip—the heart of the Toronto Sound—c. 1960. The infamous Le Coq d'Or Tavern is visible at left.

IGLOOS, ESKIMOS, AND DOGSLEDS 17

CHAPTER 2

THE HAWK SPREADS HIS WINGS

Ronnie Hawkins wasn't just a hell-raiser who kept a step ahead of the law. He had an uncanny ability to spot talent. Like others in the burgeoning pop music world of the time, he knew he needed to keep upping the quality of his material and the players around him.

The competition on Yonge Street was brutal, ass-kicking soul-style revues and other young bucks with windswept hair and itchy guitar licks were vying for his gig, his audience, and, most importantly, his ladies. Over the course of four years he kept trading out players, like a ball club drawing from its farm club, to find the right combination. By 1961, he had them, a murderer's row of talent that kept the Toronto music scene buzzing with excitement and anticipation. Ronnie had assembled a team to match his wildest ambitions . . . maybe they were too ambitious for their own good.

Hawkins and the boys were at the eye of a hurricane; all hell was breaking loose around them, the tempo punishing. He practiced the band during the days, striving for a level of perfection in a music celebrated for its rough, gnarled edges. And no one in the band was safe from being replaced by someone better.

OPPOSITE: Ronnie Hawkins and the Hawks tear up the stage, likely at the Le Coq d'Or, c. 1964.

At this time, Hawkins was scuffling for gigs around Memphis; a few session dates and the promise of a career seemed tantalizingly within reach. He decided to form his own band to put his own spin on rockabilly, and that required a special kind of drummer: Levon Helm. An Arkansas razorback to his very marrow, Helm was raised in the implausibly named hamlet of Turkey Scratch.

In 1958, Levon was about to graduate from high school, which was a big deal for his family; no one in his clan had ever earned that diploma. His parents were never going to agree to let him on the road with a seeming reprobate like Hawkins without that parchment. But after graduation, Helm's real education began, playing roadhouses and juke joints—"every shithole-and-a-half"—the kind of places where if they didn't like you, you used your guitar like a bayonet to get out alive. When the word came down that the show was heading north, to Canada, it sounded crazy.

LEVON HELM
drummer, singer, the Band

"Growin' up, I couldn't have had a better place for music. In the Delta there was Jerry Lee [Lewis], Elvis, Muddy [Waters], Sonny Boy [Williamson]. It was a hybrid [of] gospel influences, hillbilly influences, blues influences . . . it all got mixed up.

"My main order of business was to get over to the radio station and sit in the corner and watch Sonny Boy and the *King Biscuit Time* band do their radio show.

"The first time Elvis came to Helena [Arkansas] there was Bill [Black] playin' this doghouse bass, Scotty Moore had his Gibson plugged into an amplifier, and Elvis was strummin' his Martin acoustic that was picked up by his vocal mic. And it tied the sound all together like a sock cymbal and a snare drum ties the rhythm all together. I saw 'em a couple of times later and they added [drummer] D. J. Fontana, and he's doubling everything they're doin' and he's knockin' the lights out of his drums. It was Elvis . . . sure, but it was the Elvis Presley Band—that's what you wanted to see."

LARRY LEBLANC
music journalist

"For those growing up in Southern Ontario in the '50s and '60s, Ronnie Hawkins was the top of the local music ladder. The absolute connection to Southern rockabilly and all of the music was fantasized about."

ABOVE: Larry LeBlanc and Ronnie Hawkins.
OPPOSITE: Ronnie Hawkins and the Hawks onstage at the Le Coq d'Or Tavern, Toronto.

RONNIE HAWKINS

"Robbie's mother, Dolly, said her son had dropped out of school and was afraid he was gonna get in some trouble because he was running with these musicians. And that's when I brought him in as a roadie. He doesn't like to remember it that way, but I paid him $50 a week and room and board."

RICK DANKO
bassist, songwriter, singer, The Band

"I'd never seen a rockabilly show the likes of Ronnie Hawkins. I was so impressed that I booked myself to be his opening act."

ROBBIE ROBERTSON
lead guitarist, songwriter, The Band

"I remember being in a group that opened for Ronnie. It was the first time I heard the Hawks, and it was an extraordinary experience because I never heard music played so fast, so violently, so explosively. I tried to pick up whatever I could and asking questions without getting on anybody's nerves. I tried, over the years, to swindle my way in."

"THE HAWK WAS SOMETHING ELSE. HE LOOKED THE PART, TALKED THE PART, AND WALKED THE PART. HE LIKED TO FIND REAL GOOD PLAYERS AND PIT 'EM AGAINST EACH OTHER. ONE OF THEM CUTS THE OTHER UNTIL HE'S BLEEDING."
— LEVON HELM

In the Beginning
RONNIE HAWKINS

In 1965, at age seventeen, Larry LeBlanc conducted an interview with Ronnie Hawkins for the *Ajax News Advertiser* and the *Hit Parader* while attending Dunbarton High School, about 35 miles northeast of downtown Toronto. He interviewed Ronnie in the lobby of Le Coq d'Or club, portions of which are excerpted here:

"When I was young, I listened to a lot of country and a lot of country blues—B.B. King out of Memphis, Lightnin' Hopkins, Lightnin' Slim. Muddy Waters hadn't moved to Chicago yet. I picked cotton with Ellas McDaniel, who later changed his name to Bo Diddley.

"Well, I first cut in 1952, when I was sixteen—but it was only in the Memphis circuit, one of those little fly-by-night companies—I cut a country tune, Eddy Arnold's 'I Really Don't Want to Know' and 'Bo Diddley.' I cut 'Bo Diddley' six times in the old days. . . .

"Music was a little more country then, what we called rockabilly. Carl Perkins was the one that started to swing. All he did was add a drummer to a hillbilly band, kinda jazz it up a bit. Elvis was copying Carl. Then, of course, Colonel Tom [Parker, Presley's manager] came in and took over and Elvis skyrocketed to the top. I came out of the army in '58. Jimmy Ray Paulman called and told me he'd like to start a little band and [asked if I] would like to front the group. I didn't have anything to do until the second semester was over in school.

"On our first night [in Canada] there were three people in the club. 'Man,' the owner said, 'this is a jazz place. You can't play that racket here.' But we did. Tuesday, there were about ten people. I phoned around to some people Conway [Twitty] knew and we got a few more in Wednesday. Friday we were nearly full and the same Saturday. So the owner gave us another week. The crowd on Monday beat Saturday, and by Wednesday they were lined up outside the club.

"I brought the first blues here. Nobody had ever heard of Bo Diddley, Muddy Waters, B.B., or anyone in Canada. But for the first three or four years, we only played up here a bit. Then as time went by, we played more and more and more—staying a month at one club.

"Without Yonge Street, none of us would've been any good, you'd never have heard of any of us. . . . That whole strip was the only place you could get any entertainment or booze at the time. Our music was brand new. They hadn't seen that Memphis style of rockabilly. Over time we chiseled out a little circuit between Windsor, Montreal, and Toronto."

Ronnie Hawkins onstage at the Le Coq D'Or Tavern with mic in hand, Robbie Robertson playing guitar, Jerry Penfound on saxophone, 1963.

OPPOSITE: Ad for a Ronnie Hawkins and the Hawks gig at Le Coq d'Or, Toronto, c. 1963.

"The first time I saw Levon in action was in Woodstock, Ontario, about thirty-five miles from London, where I grew up. Ronnie and the Hawks were playing in a Legion Hall," keyboardist and organist Garth Hudson told author and Band scholar Barney Hoskyns in the July 2012 issue of *MOJO*. "We were impressed, all of us young rockers. They were good-looking fellas and moved well; they had the girls looking at 'em all the time. I remember our manager saying that no one could follow the Hawks.

"When I first joined the group, they already had the rhythms together. They would say, 'That's official!' and that would mean that it sounded in the groove. At the beginning of rehearsals, Levon would very quickly have the rhythm. He had the subtle ornamentation—the takeup notes and the little interjections, and the use of tarps. I would look over at him many times when he played the intro, because we wanted to make it as precise as possible," Hudson explained to Hoskyns, now helming www.rocksbackpages.com. "We always tried to make the track fit the words and the voices. I never used a sound that was close in harmonic structure to Levon's voice. I would try and complement it."

ABOVE: Cars stream into downtown Toronto, 1992.

RONNIE HAWKINS

"Levon had his own band [in high school]—Levon Helm and the Jungle Bush Beaters. He was actually a guitar player, but he didn't have that rhythm, so he said he'd go on drums. . . .

"Then I picked up Rick Danko. He was an apprentice meatcutter who was playing polkas down around the Simcoe [Ontario] area. Rick had the potential, a good-looking young kid about sixteen, playing lead guitar in his little band."

ROBBIE ROBERTSON

"With Ronnie Hawkins, after all the guys from the South left, each time another Canadian comes in. And another Canadian comes in. And Levon and I encouraging Ronnie to hear Richard Manuel singing with a group who opened for us. 'That piano player. . . . There's something about that guy. He's really gifted. We should consider him.'

"Not that Ronnie needed a lot of pushing or anything. But with each guy once Garth, Richard, and Rick were with Levon and me, I felt, 'OK. Here we go. Now we're there.' We didn't feel like we had in the past where 'this guy is gonna be here for a while and then we're gonna find somebody else.' Everybody else felt temporary, for sure. And this no longer did feel temporary. And that's when you know you are together and you got something."

LARRY LEBLANC

"In the early 1960s, as rock and folk was beginning to take hold in North America, Toronto was still a... backwater city.

"The scene changed when Ronnie Hawkins, backed by Levon and the Hawks, began holding court nightly at the Concord Tavern, and especially later at the Le Coq d'Or club on the city's downtown Yonge Street strip. . . . Clubs alongside Le Coq d'Or [and] on Queen Street nearby began buzzing with nightly entertainment."

JOHN WARE
session drummer

"In '64, Jesse Ed and I made a road trip in the summer—a spiritual journey to the mecca of our aspirations—to Toronto to hang with Ronnie and the Hawks. It was high adventure for two eighteen-year-old Okies.

"In Canada, the law had weird twists and turns when it covers who can be in an establishment that serves alcohol. The clock and food are the deciding factors, but Levon and Ronnie made some kind of deal with the management at Le Coq d'Or, allowing us to stay in the club proper after 8:00 P.M. We absorbed that music, very up-close, for a few crazy nights . . . Eddie trying to grok Robbie Robertson and me with the Levon backbeats. Hell of an education."

A Drummer's Inspiration

JOHN WARE

"Oklahoma City was a good music town . . . good enough. It was not steeped in the blues as was Tulsa, just ninety minutes to the northeast. The prime element for young bands (beyond radio hits) was a sort of rockabilly (not yet named) and real country. There were a few good venues for bands on the road, and I frequented all I could get into.

"I first saw Ronnie Hawkins and the Hawks in 1959. Hawkins was a real draw in beer joints (Oklahoma was essentially dry). His highly athletic stage antics were exciting, but by the time I was first introduced to his music, he had shifted personnel (again) to young players from Toronto and Hamilton, Ontario, Canada. He'd had talked-about lineups in the past (including some tumultuous years with Roy Buchanan on Tele), but the Hawks I saw in Oklahoma City were young and very musical.

"But at the center of the stage was a singing drummer from Arkansas with the charm of an elf who really got my attention. He played with ruthless abandon and managed to put his backbeats in a slightly different place than others I had seen and heard live. It was the music I wanted to play.

"Just a little over a year later my high school band, including the now legendary and late Jesse Ed Davis, was playing a party in Tulsa. As we were packing up, we were approached by a man who complimented and engaged us by offering a chance to play Ronnie Hawkins's club in Fayetteville, Arkansas. That man was Ronnie's manager, Dayton Stratton. The Rockwood (great name) was famous in that part of the country, and the opportunity to play it seemed like the chance of a lifetime. Plus, it was the home of a bar band that was essentially the Mid-America Beatles (long before the Fab attack).

"That booking was real, and there, in Fayetteville, I met Levon Helm for the first time . . . met him and had the chance to worship at the altar of the 'Geist' that changed my approach to drums forever. I did not have the chance to interject requests for 'how' and 'why' that beat placement worked. He wasn't in the business of mentoring. He was in the business of being Levon, and, as he was only three years my senior, it was enough to yearn . . . and learn.

"Ronnie and the Hawks didn't put out albums and singles regularly. My band learned their songs and mimicked their approach by hearing them live. We expanded our band to get more and bigger sound, adding a second keyboard and a sax wizard at one point, but we were high school kids without much in the way of paying gigs."

OPPOSITE: Drummer John Ware, c. 1968.

Guitarist Fred Carter Jr. had been holding center stage for the Hawk when Robbie Robertson came in to the Hawks on bass in 1960. Soon enough, Robertson was itching to take on this local legend. After sharing a few "trade secrets," Carter recognized that this youngster was coming on too strong and had way too much moxie; the veteran was forced to turn his back on Robertson during performances so that he couldn't copy any licks.

By 1961, the lineup was changing and so was their sound. The hillbilly hayride whoopin' and hollerin' was giving way to a more sophisticated blend of soul, R&B, and blues. The Hawks were emerging as the vital engine of the enterprise, elevating the local music scene in their wake. More than simply background players, they were becoming a band.

Pianist Richard "Beak" Manuel couldn't play that finger-bustin' style of his predecessor, Stan Szelest; his approach was a simple exposition of the melody, embellished with a tender heart that sounded at cross purposes to the more theatrical elements in the music. But boy, could he sing R&B; he had, in Hawkins's words, "a throat."

Organist Garth Hudson was thoroughly trained in classical music as well as in jazz, his great passion. He was subtle and supple, extending the harmony with an Ellingtonian élan, adding a celestial tint with his arpeggiated runs, digging deep in the "amen, brother" well of spirituality with his well-tempered, churchlike chording.

His people were old school, and looked askance at him for abandoning his formal musical path to play with, well, heathens. But Hawkins, as slick as Canadian winter ice, spun a tall tale about how Garth was being hired to teach the other boys in the band the finer aspects of music-making. Amid a symphony of raised eyebrows, Hudson received their blessing.

Above all else, the defining characteristic of rock 'n' roll is the wail of an electric guitar. Every band in Toronto had its twangy fingerprint; in Robbie Robertson, the Hawks had a monarch butterfly who stung like a king bee. While still in his teens, Robertson stood out with his seasoned blend of Southside blues and Chet Atkins–style pickin'. His phrasing was often oblique, all angles and wrought edges, a slurry of glass and gravel that implied a lifting clarity, if only you tilted your head just so.

There wasn't a single guitarist around town who didn't covet his tone, didn't stand in awe before him during the last set when all the real players gathered to pay tribute and hope for a fleeting insight. The secret was cutting slits in your amp's speaker (preferably a Fender Deluxe Reverb) with a razor until it starts to distort. But that's as useful as having Picasso telling you that to paint well, you must start with the right easel.

LEFT: Ronnie Hawkins, c. 1960.

LARRY LEBLANC

"Up to that time, every musician in Toronto was trying to copy Levon and the Hawks, specifically Robbie, whose guitar sound would define what became known as the Toronto Sound for years. Robbie had a Fender Telecaster, so everybody in Toronto R&B bands had a Fender Telecaster and tried to play like him. Among the leading musicians who followed in his style were Domenic Troiano [Mandala, Bush, and the James Gang], Freddie Keeler [David Clayton-Thomas and the Shays], and Larry Leishman [Jon and Lee and the Checkmates]. Colin Linden plays in that style to this day, and he played with a later version of The Band.

"Also, and this is very important, Robbie was taught guitar by Peter Traynor while both of them were in the Rhythm Chords. Traynor [began working as a part-time amplifier repairman] at Long & McQuade music equipment store in midtown Toronto, where he'd work on modifying Robbie's guitar (of course, other guitarists wanted Peter to do the same for them). In 1963, this led to Peter founding Yorkville Sound [the parent company of Traynor] with Jack Long [of Long & McQuade], to build amps, speakers, etc. Every band had Traynor amps in the '60s and '70s and the company is still popular today."

> "Ronnie appealed to the band about how much better we could all be with Garth, givin' us lessons, music to study. And we had to let Garth's family know that we weren't just there to play in every club and drink everything in every club."
>
> -Levon Helm

Oh, Canada!

GARY PIG GOLD

"While innocently, not to mention proudly, nicknamed 'Toronto the Good' by vast majorities of its citizens even as the 1950s became the '60s, those who instead dared venture out after the streetlights went on usually found themselves gathered with wide-eyed mischief along the city's fabled Yonge Street strip. And it was there, for several high-decibel decades, that most of North America's sharpest action, musical or otherwise, could often be found . . . at prices far beneath those in New York City or much closer, in Detroit.

"Now when the rightfully legendary Ronnie Hawkins and his ragtag gaggle of Arkansas rockabillies found themselves, on the recommendation of Conway Twitty, booked to play Southern Ontario circa 1958—"Canada? What state is *that* in??" Ronnie apparently asked the former Harold Jenkins before driving northward—the first thing to impress the skeptically shivering Hawks was realizing club owners would always, and happily at that, pay the band in full immediately after each engagement concluded . . . *without*, as was usually the case in the USA, any firearms being brandished whatsoever! Not only that, but those curious young cats 'n' kittens who were drawn Yonge-ward to dance and drink soon lovingly crowned Ronnie their very own King Elvis—despite the fact he was in truth no more 'Canadian' than the Memphis Flash on even his best-behaved nights.

"So utterly hospitable, both onstage and off, did they soon find Toronto that Ronnie and faithful drummer Helm decided to unpack, unwind, and stay on in the Great White Northlands; in fact, Ronnie remains there to this very day! And while some may question why this supremely talented man decided to settle on *that* side of the Pine Curtain, making money as opposed to touring the globe making history—he was, after all, the first man to moonwalk across national television, a good quarter-century before Michael Jackson's *Motown 25* [1983 television special] exhibition—Hawkins and his Hawks had an incalculably inspirational effect upon the Canadian rock-and-roll scene.

"Besides helping develop Toronto into a musical hotbed every inch the equal of those concurrently cookin' in, for example, Liverpool or Hamburg, Rompin' Ronnie ran one tough and rumble r 'n' r boot camp which went on to produce not only The Band, but *so* many other fine musicians, arrangers, singers and/or songwriters you can probably find scattered throughout your very own record collection.

"Yes, Ronnie's renowned eye for trouble was matched only by his ear for talent. Ontario was indeed filled beyond capacity with world-class musicians, but only the Best of the Very Very Best were ever allowed, under Ronnie's expert tutelage, to become bona fide Hawks. Such was an honor equaled only by one's apprenticeship alongside John Mayall or James Brown."

OPPOSITE: Canadian singer-songwriter, record producer, filmmaker, and author Gary Pig Gold.

ABOVE: The lights of Toronto's Yonge Street at night, 1965.

CHAPTER 3
LEAVING THE NEST AND PREPARING TO FLY

In the early 1960s, Robbie Robertson sometimes accompanied Ronnie Hawkins to the legendary Brill Building on Broadway in New York City, where music publishing companies, songwriters, and record labels were based. The duo would visit the office of Roulette Records' Morris Levy.

Hawkins had minor hit singles in 1959 with "Mary Lou" and "Forty Days," a remake of Chuck Berry's "Thirty Days," and a 1963 cover of Bo Diddley's "Who Do You Love," informed by Robertson's searing guitar. Robbie also wrote two songs for Hawkins, "Hey Boba Lou" and "Someone Like You."

In the 2016 interview I [Harvey] conducted with Robertson for *Record Collector News* (see page 7), I noted that in reading his memoir, it was insightful to read about his foundational experiences at the Brill Building. Robbie explained, "I thought, who would think in their wildest imagination that Tin Pan Alley was a real place? The Brill Building. And then Donnie Kirshner's thing. All of it was actually in a place you could go. And the doors were golden when you walked in. And inside there in all these rooms were people who wrote songs and sent them out to the whole wide world.

"I had such a respect for and a [connected] feeling to these people," he added. "Doc Pomus and Mort Shuman, Jerry Leiber and Mike Stoller. Otis Blackwell. Titus Turner. So to say none of that rubbed off on me just wouldn't be true. And I recorded with John Hammond Jr. [blues guitarist and son of noted producer John Hammond Sr.] on an album that Leiber and Stoller produced. And I knew Doc and Mort all of their lives. Doc and Mort remained friends. I was friends with Jerry and Mike."

OPPOSITE: Bob Dylan and the Hawks at Santa Monica Civic Auditorium, December 19, 1965.

Robertson, Danko, Manuel, and Hudson—who had previously toiled in bands with names like Robbie & the Robots and Thumper & the Trombones (Robertson), the Rockin' Revols (Manuel)—and Helm (borrowed from a group called the Jungle Bush Beaters), had finally hit pay dirt with Ronnie Hawkins. They appeared on some of Ronnie's early records, among them his *Mojo Man* LP (released in 1964).

Five sets a night, seven nights a week, it was a fine madness, careening from the sweltering stage to the ramshackle Warwick Hotel in downtown Toronto to grab some clean clothes and an hour's rest, and back again.

Eventually the Hawk, the Captain Bluebeard of this rapscallion horde, started to fray, sensing that even *he* had limits. In 1962, he married, cut back on his schedule, and considered what it meant to actually breathe. This opened a space for the Hawks to find their own voice, enjoying the spotlight and exploring material that better suited their increasingly singular sound.

The party wasn't over—exactly—but it was starting to groove to a different tempo that caused, unsurprisingly, "creative differences" to surface, as well as a break from rigorous leadership. As Levon noted in his 1993 autobiography, *This Wheel's on Fire*, "In the end it came down to Hawk's feeling that more discipline was the best thing for the situation." Combined with the age-old demands for more money, the seeds soon bloomed into a full-blown breakup in early 1964. Levon became the group's new leader while they built up a small reputation as a disciplined roots rock band. Along the way, they changed their name from the Hawks to the Crackers to the Canadian Squires and then back to the Hawks (or rather, Levon Helm and the Hawks or sometimes Levon and the Hawks).

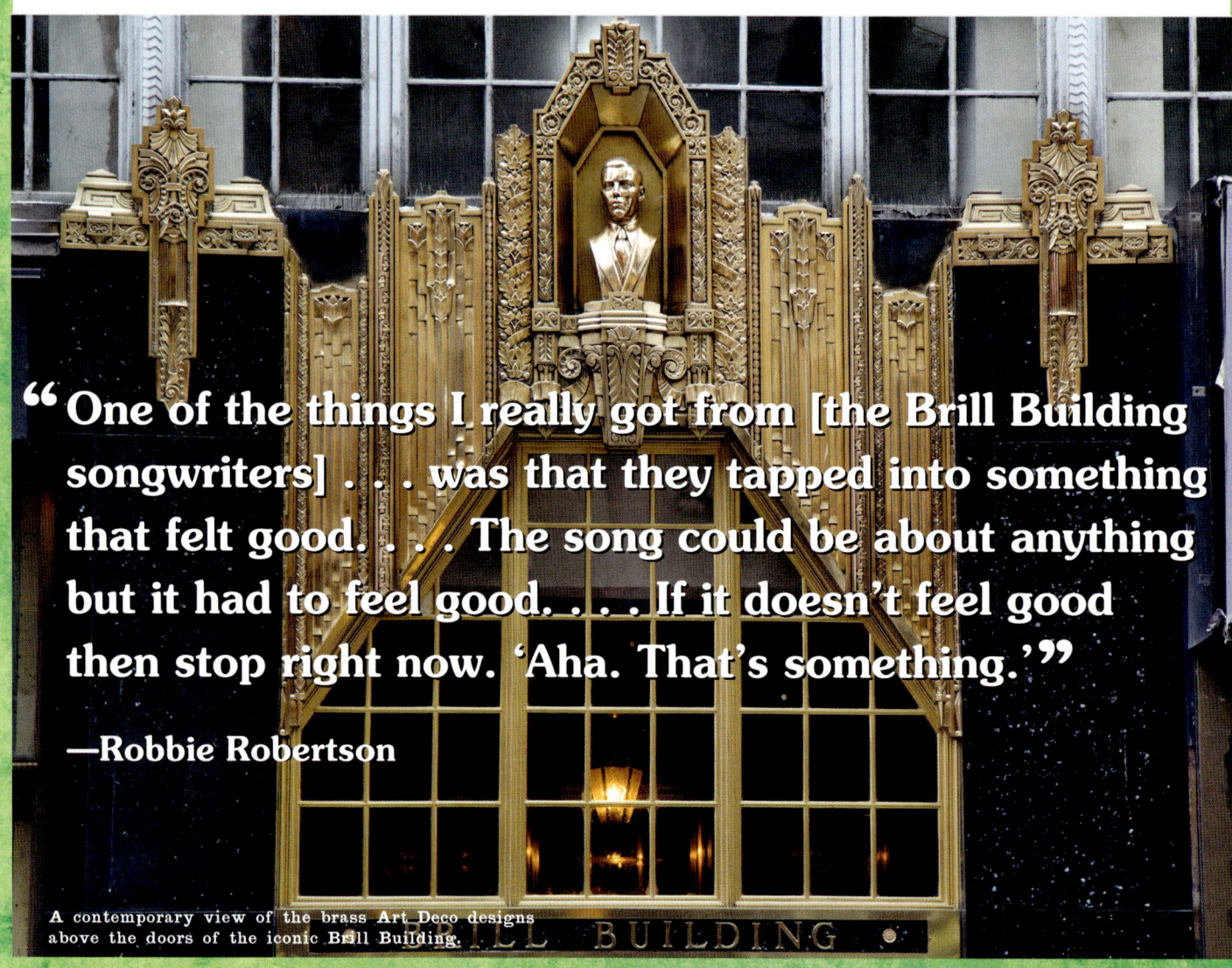

"One of the things I really got from [the Brill Building songwriters] . . . was that they tapped into something that felt good. . . . The song could be about anything but it had to feel good. . . . If it doesn't feel good then stop right now. 'Aha. That's something.'"

—Robbie Robertson

A contemporary view of the brass Art Deco designs above the doors of the iconic Brill Building.

Levon and company also cut a couple of obscure singles under their various names, including "Leave Me Alone" and "The Stones I Throw (Will Free All Men)" in 1965, and "Go Go Liza Jane" in 1968.

Free to pursue their collective muse, the group found steady employment in Toronto, Montreal, and Quebec City. There were a few excursions south—gigs around the Jersey Shore and a memorable show in Arkansas at the Marvell High School prom. And then there was the disastrous booking at New York hot spot the Peppermint Lounge, home of the dance craze known as the Twist. Given that the group was more committed than ever to following its own eccentric musical orbit—Rick referred to this time as their "Cannonball [Adderley] period," in honor of the renowned soul jazz saxophonist—a less apt booking could hardly be imagined. Needless to say, those eager to bust a move on the dance floor found themselves twisted in knots.

LARRY LEBLANC

"To truly understand The Band you have to understand that they were a Toronto band that spread its wings after they left Ronnie Hawkins. But the musical essence of Levon and the Hawks could be heard in Toronto bands that followed them."

MIKE STOLLER

"Back in 1965, Jerry Leiber and I were producing an album with John Hammond Jr. The band was cooking.

"We had Charlie 'Honeyman' Otis on drums, we had the Stones' Bill Wyman playing bass on a couple of tracks, and there was this cat named Rick Danko who played bass on the rest. That was the first time I met Robbie Robertson. He was a great guy, and I was really impressed by his guitar playing. Robbie and Rick were in Bob Dylan's band at the time, and Dylan came in to watch the session."

ABOVE: Leiber and Stoller, 1959.

BELOW: Levon and the Hawks' song "The Stones I Throw (Will Free All Men)" hit No. 22 on the December 13, 1965 CHUM Hit Parade.

There were some covers—blues legend Bobby "Blue" Bland was a staple of their live set. Clearly they weren't playing to the Top 10; there was nothing teenyboppish about these young men playing adult music, showcasing their protean ability to bend and shape their earthy, bourbon-soaked sound.

They had long bitched and moaned about the whole "front man, sideman" dynamic that had prompted the move from Hawkins. Suddenly, a new mentor appeared, and his vision wasn't limited to merely rockin' the room: he was poised to set the world on fire.

1964 was the year the British Invasion arrived. The Beatles conquered America with a seismic push from Ed Sullivan; in Hollywood, Sunset Strip nightclubs transformed from folk and jazz rooms to rock and pop venues.

The entire music and cultural landscape was about to unfurl in ways that previously seemed unimaginable. New York's Greenwich Village, with its irresistible gravitational pull, became the place for young sojourners in search of the next new thing. There, they collided with another transformative presence, resplendent in a halo of translucent curls.

With his air of folksy wisdom and adenoidal grandeur, he represented something both unprecedented and inevitable: a seething current of contrariness animated by a healthy dose of wiles. He was the moment, and he needed a band to help carry the load, which was proving too much for any individual, even one named Bob Dylan.

SHARRY WILSON

"Mary Martin encouraged Bob Dylan, who seemed to be ready for a change musically, to visit the Hawks in Toronto and watch them perform. 'Like a Rolling Stone' had been recorded in June 1965 and was released with much fanfare in August.

"Dylan came to see Levon and the Hawks perform at the Friar's Tavern in Toronto on Thursday, September 16, 1965. Robbie and Levon had already been recruited into Dylan's electric band and had played a few gigs with him, but the other members of the Hawks were recruited soon after Dylan witnessed their performance. They immediately began to rehearse together after the show and played the night away until 6 A.M."

LEVON HELM

"Good friends in the right places. Mary Martin, a friend of ours from Toronto, was one of Albert Grossman's right-hand people, there in his office in New York. She knew Bob [handled his publishing] and put a word in. She knew he was ready to have a band and play some music."

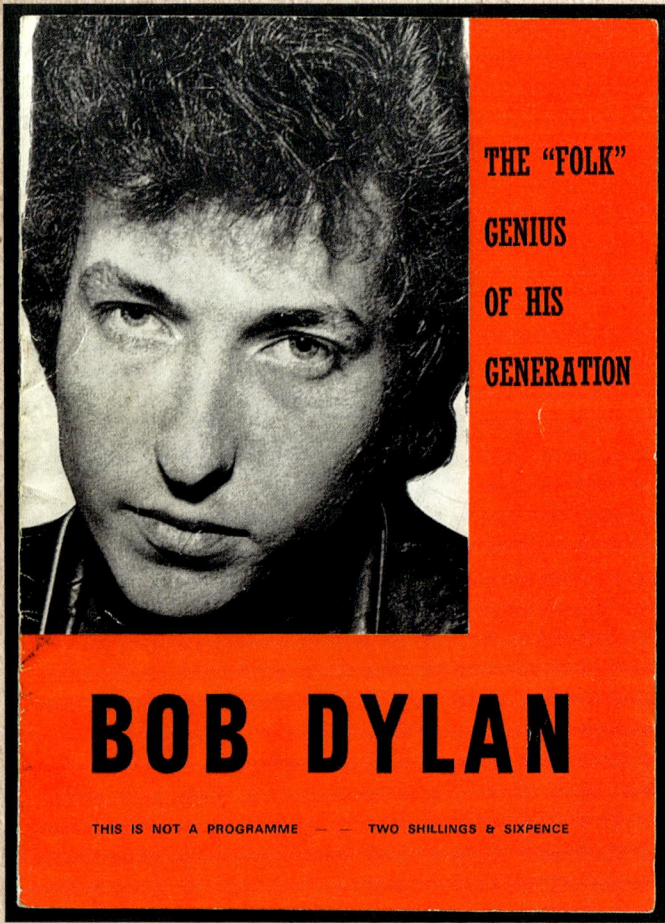

A promo piece for Dylan's 1966 tour touting him as "THE 'FOLK' GENIUS OF HIS GENERATION."

GARY PIG GOLD
singer-songwriter, record producer, author

"It's no coincidence or accident whatsoever that Bob Dylan, himself a product of a *cold,* as opposed to *cool,* upbringing in his own North Country, would quickly discover much common socio-musical ground with Messrs. Hudson, Danko, Manuel, and Robertson after they and Levon finally flew Ronnie Hawkins's coop to seek fame and fortune in, um, Tony Mart's—and I quote—the "Giant Showplace" on the Jersey Coast in Somers Point.

"Already craving a road-worthy reproduction of his Michael Bloomfield–driven *Highway 61 Revisited* attack, Dylan was no doubt delighted to guide, then watch, his adopted Hawks transition with little difficulty within a mere year or three from bar band to *The* Band, creating along the way some of the absolute best thin wild mercury ever heard.

"But nothing prepared listeners for the surreal ecstasy that was Bob Dylan's 'Like a Rolling Stone,' six minutes that shook the pop music worald to its mop-top core. Part global anthem, part lyrical fantasia, Dylan's audaciousness was rewarded with his canonization as the 'spokesman of his generation.' It was a title he disparaged with a sneer and a smirk. His public persona toggled between elusion and illusion; the more inscrutable he appeared, the more attentive, more obsessive his fans acted in response."

"We had our buddy [blues guitarist] John Hammond Jr. show up. I thought we had the best band in the country. The guy down at the Lounge said, 'This blues shit will never get you anywhere.' It's a 'Twist' joint; play 'The Twist!'" —Levon Helm

Levon and the Hawks, 1964. Left to right: Jerry "Ish" Penfound, Rick Danko, Levon Helm, Richard Manuel, Garth Hudson, Robbie Robertson.

Albert Grossman

If it is true that behind every great fortune lies a great crime, it may also be said that behind a great artist's success looms the shadow of an equally promiscuous talent, one that navigates that treacherous intersection between personal trust and professional expediency. Part shepherd, part hustler, it is the manager, that most reviled of creatures, who rides shotgun on the road to the top, brandishes it with deadly intent when things go south, all the while keeping a gimlet eye on the licensing and publishing contracts.

Elvis Presley became "the King" because of the shrewd—some might say self-serving—machinations of his manager, Col. Tom Parker, a onetime carnival barker turned pop culture impresario.

Brian Epstein was running a small family business in the port city of Liverpool when he happened upon a scruffy band of locals making a cellarful of noise. Instantly captivated, he dedicated himself to promoting their joyful sound to the world. The Beatles would have been nowhere without "Eppie's" blind faith.

Andrew Loog Oldham was nineteen, already on the prowl 'round Swinging London, a hunter in search of a trophy. He was one step ahead of the pack when he bagged a group of howlin' R&B enthusiasts—the Rolling Stones—and turned them into every parent's worst nightmare, every daughter's wildest dream.

Albert Grossman drew from all of this in constructing his portfolio; he had the passion, the vision, the moxie, the concrete fortitude that could

Albert Grossman (with glasses, second from left) at the Monterey International Pop Festival conferring with the festival co-organizer Benny Shapiro (in sunglasses, center) and promoter Bill Graham (right, in tan cap), June 1967.

weather even the most lawyered-up assault on him and his. He didn't so much enter a room—let alone open a negotiation—as seize the high ground, surveying the landscape like General Patton landing in Sicily. No grievance, real or imagined, was too small to squash, no contest of wills too incidental to not fight to the finish.

Grossman's Promethean character was nurtured in his hometown of Chicago. An administrator of public housing by day, he circled around the music scene at night, slowly repurposing himself as a club owner and star-maker with a conscience, the best friend of the earnestly downtrodden minstrel.

Grossman had owned a folk club called the Gate of Horn. It was the dawn of the sixties, the advent of the "New Frontier." Folk music was all the rage, chiming with Grossman's own beliefs.

Relocating to New York, he quickly established his bona fides with his guileful marketing and packaging instincts; for example, he introduced Mary Travers to Peter Yarrow and Paul Stookey.

Flush with their success, Grossman turned his attention toward a shy, gangly young voice on the scene, whose capacity for disruption played perfectly into the impresario's gambit to become the biggest *macher* in the industry. Bob Dylan was hiding in plain sight, and Grossman was going to work him for all he was worth.

By 1965, their inscrutable partnership had propelled them not only to the top of the charts, but into the very fabric of the American experience. They were both larger than life: Dylan, lurching unsteadily on his Cuban-heeled boots, while Grossman cast his gaze toward some grander, more golden horizon.

It was only a matter of time before Grossman took control of Dylan's brooding charges; the Hawks were too talented, too hungry to remain minions. Robbie Robertson, in particular, was taking notes, eschewing the more lustful caprices of life on the road in exchange for a master class with pop music's most deliberative minds.

> **"[Albert Grossman] had the passion, the vision, the moxie, the concrete fortitude that could weather even the most lawyered-up assault on him and his. He didn't so much enter a room—let alone open a negotiation—as seize the high ground."**

ANDREW LOOG OLDHAM
record producer, manager, author, radio host

"I was doing PR in January 1963 and hustled Grossman at the Cumberland Hotel [in London]. His client Bob Dylan was in London to play a background music role in a BBC2 television drama, *Madhouse on Castle Street*. . . . He would eventually perform two songs: 'Blowin' in the Wind' and 'Ballad of the Gliding Swan.' I think the BBC wiped the tape so that they could record something else.

"The twenty minutes I spent in the room with Grossman and Dylan that day were life-giving. I knew where I wanted to be. That conspiracy. That marriage. That finishing of sentences of the other. This was a totally different floor of life than I'd ever been on. And I wanted it. It's very good that I already had that gas in my car when I met the Rolling Stones in 1963.

> "Albert Grossman was the gatekeeper to a world of talent he had personally cultivated out of a belief in genius and profitability, both his own and that of his clients."
>
> —Andrew Loog Oldham

Andrew Loog Oldham in March 1966, when he was managing and producing the Rolling Stones.

D.A. PENNEBAKER
documentary filmmaker

"Albert was the right guy to handle the client. There's a line [in the film *Don't Look Back*] where Dylan says, 'You're very salty today, Albert.' Just a fantastic line. They had such a marvelous way that they dealt with each other. On a father-and-son level."

ANTHONY SCADUTO
music journalist, author

"If you are going to get into a superstar level, you have to be hard. In the beginning, Dylan had the bodyguards, the Albert Grossmans. You're an idol, and it's the kind of thing they put you on the crucifix for. You have to be protected, or it's going to destroy you."

LARRY LEBLANC

"Albert spent considerable time over the years in Toronto, which I think led to him being comfortable with dealing with many of the people in the city. By the time he started working with The Band he had also worked with Ian & Sylvia and Gordon Lightfoot, who were both from Toronto. Of course, his assistant, Mary Martin, who worked in his office handling Odetta and Ian & Sylvia, was from Toronto. She convinced Bob Dylan to come to Toronto to see Levon and the Hawks play at the Friar's Tavern on Yonge Street."

Promotional photograph for the D. A. Pennebaker documentary on Bob Dylan's 1965 tour, *Dont Look Back*.

Bob Dylan during his controversial performance at the Newport Folk Festival, July 25, 1965.

For all his self-styled opacity, Dylan was keenly aware of his value in the marketplace, a witting accomplice to his manager, the owlishly opportunistic Grossman. In the aftermath of his controversial performance at the 1965 Newport Folk Festival—going "electric" was heresy to die-hard folkies, catnip to Bob's guileful rebelliousness—Dylan was booked to play at New York's Forest Hills Tennis Grounds and the prestigious Hollywood Bowl.

"In the early '60s I was up at the Brill Building a lot," volunteered songwriter and multi-instrumentalist Al Kooper in a 2017 telephone interview.

"Robbie was up there but in the shadow of Ronnie Hawkins. Aaron Schroeder was my music publisher. I worked for him. Robbie did some things with him. Robbie was at the 1965 Dylan 'Like a Rolling Stone' recording session I played organ on.

"I then played live in 1965 with Robbie, [bassist] Harvey Brooks, Levon Helm, and Dylan—[including shows at the] Forest Hills [Tennis Stadium, August 28, 1965] in New York and the Hollywood Bowl [September 3, 1965]. [The latter] was the only place Bob played where he wasn't booed. How 'bout that?"

Dylan needed a tight group, one that could squeeze out notes that would ring at the back of any hall, players who had the stomach for the parlous road less traveled. For all his perceived aloofness, Dylan had a special affinity for kindred spirits, particularly those with talent and ambition. Guys like Robbie Robertson and Levon Helm.

More shows were scheduled as Dylan was prodded by Robbie and Levon to hire the remainder of the Hawks, who were waiting back in Canada for the call they knew was coming. After a brief rehearsal in Toronto, the reconfigured group debuted on October 1, 1965, at Carnegie Hall in New York.

The Hawks onstage at Festival Hall in Brisbane, Australia April 15, 1966. Rick Danko, Bob Dylan, and Robbie Robertson shown.

LEAVING THE NEST AND PREPARING TO FLY

Dylan and the Hawks at Massey Hall

JOHN DONABIE

Canadian DJ and radio show host John Donabie recalls a memorable concert on the first night of a two-show stretch (November 14–15) in Toronto during Dylan's 1965 tour:

"In the fall of '65 I ordered three tickets to see Bob Dylan and the Hawks at Massey Hall. I did it through mail order. I was working part-time in radio in my hometown of Oshawa, Ontario, about thirty miles east of Toronto. I mentioned I was working in media—a bit of a stretch—and hoped for the best. A few weeks later an envelope came to my home and, lo and behold, there were three front-row seats. Front-row!

"Just my friend Robert and I attended, which left a seat in the middle to put our coats. Eventually the lights went down and out came Bob Dylan. I had seen the Rolling Stones twice and other major acts before, but this is what my best friend and I had waited for.

"The first half of the concert was Bob acoustically. You could hear a pin drop in that incredible hall. I seem to remember he was wearing a hound's tooth suit, which I've read he bought at Lou Myles clothing store on Yonge Street, just near Le Coq d'Or and the Friars Tavern.

"At that point I didn't think it would get any better. After a short intermission, Dylan returned with the Hawks: Robbie Robertson on guitar, Rick Danko on bass, a clean-shaven Garth Hudson on the Lowrey organ (no [Hammond] B-3 for him), Richard Manuel on piano, and Levon Helm on drums.

"I went the first of two nights and found the crowd's acceptance of the Hawks pretty good. Some booing, but not to the extent that I have read happened in other cities. The sound was wild and unleashed. I had never seen a band play this way before. I would say that they were the tightest, loosest band I had ever seen.

"At this point I should mention that I was a few years too young to have seen Levon and the Hawks. You had to be age twenty-one to get into bars.

"Robbie and Rick would catch each other's eye. From time to time they would look back to Levon, who was driving the band with his opening downbeats.

"I had never witnessed anything like it. It would be the first time I would have to get used to Dylan doing some of his old acoustic tunes with a rock band. 'It Ain't Me Babe' stood out to me.

"I would not know it then, but it was only a few weeks after those two concerts that Levon left the group to work on an oil rig. He didn't really care for the material at the time and the constant booing."

Bob Dylan and the Hawks at Massey Hall, Toronto, November 14, 1965.

"The controversy of us playin' with Bob brought on a lot of stuff . . . like standing ovations of booing! You play a song and get through it and everybody just boos, 'The worst, just awful, get out!' It'll make you fightin' mad. It'll get under your skin . . . or it did me. I knew that what we were creating—for even the ones that hated it—was a lot bigger than the band or Bob or all of us put together. It was a helluva thing. . . . You could feel that." — Levon Helm

Newspaper reviewers gave mixed opinions of the Massey Hall performance. Antony Ferry of the *Toronto Star* described Levon and the Hawks as a "third-rate Yonge Street rock 'n' roll band" whose noise drowned out Dylan's message. Robert Fulford, also a reviewer from the same newspaper, thought the acoustic set was boring but the electric set offered "great waves of sound roaring off the stage in marvelously subtle rhythms." Fulford added, "It's Dylan's own new thing. I love it." Barry Hale, a reviewer with the *Toronto Telegram*, felt that it wouldn't be such a bad thing for Dylan to lose his folk purist fans and that their performance at Massey Hall proved that his new sound was picking up new fans.

Peter Gzowski, reviewing their Toronto performance for *Maclean's* magazine, was equally roused. "At Dylan's signal, Levon and the Hawks exploded into sound like a squadron of jet planes, a leaping, rising, crushing wave of sound that pulled the air and rocked the floor. In the balcony I could feel the bass notes through the soles of my shoes."

It was awkward at first; Dylan's folk roots deflected the others from their natural rattle and hum.

SHARRY WILSON

"Their two gigs at Massey Hall, on November 14 and 15 [1965], were seen as a homecoming for the Canadian members of the mostly Canadian band. They were proud of what they had accomplished, and playing Massey Hall was seen as a sign of making it. However, many of the audience were in the same unreceptive mood that characterized the Newport Folk Festival when Dylan first went electric.

"These two concerts took place a mere few months after that landmark concert. The audience was composed largely of folk purists who weren't quite ready to embrace the electric second half of Dylan's shows. Someone yelled out 'Elvis' when the electric set began, and some members of the audience walked out in protest."

There was an attempt to lay down some tracks at Columbia Studios during a break from the tour, but nothing really captured the vibe. Dylan's catch-as-catch-can approach stymied the Hawks' more rigorous, more methodical preparation.

Nonetheless, they soldiered on. Audiences were well informed about the brouhaha surrounding Bob's transition from hobo to popinjay. They greeted him with the faux outrage of young idealists feeling betrayed. Yet amid the catcalls, there were cries of "sellout."

Levon was an early casualty, bailing out after one too many hostile receptions. He was replaced by Sandy Konikoff for a few dates and then, most decisively, by Mickey Jones, a fireplug whose piston precision anchored the increasingly chaotic scrum that passed for a front line of jangly guitars, loping bass, and keyboard reveries.

Perhaps no tour in rock music history has been more written about, more forensically dissected, than this one. The entire carnivalesque journey was on full display here: Dylan as iridescent balladeer, beguiling the worshippers with his acoustic guitar, his rococo wordplay, stretching and straining poor "Johanna" each night to the breaking point. And then, in the second half, unleashing the amphetamine rush of electricity, taunting the crowd to voice its misapprehensions, like it's all just a game and the rules are as pliable as his vocal phrasing. The Hawks, meanwhile, were catching hell and giving it right back, as if "Remember the Alamo" were on the set list.

Dylan featured the piano and organ on his hit album *Highway 61 Revisited* to great effect, the swirling wash of the Hammond adding a hymnal grace to those recurring Baptist block chords, most often courtesy of pianist Paul Griffin, which framed many of the songs. Garth Hudson and Richard Manuel provided a similar gravitas, Hudson, hunched over his keyboards like a mad Matisse, conjuring an array of colors as bright and nervy as a Fauvist painting while Manuel penciled in the telling detail. Amid the rising din, one sensed that the Canadians were shouldering the most weight.

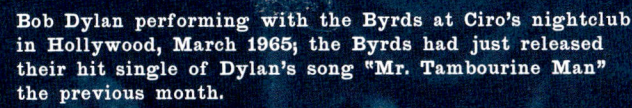

Bob Dylan performing with the Byrds at Ciro's nightclub in Hollywood, March 1965; the Byrds had just released their hit single of Dylan's song "Mr. Tambourine Man" the previous month.

ANDREW SOLT
producer, director, screenwriter

"1965 was the year my life changed. I graduated Hollywood High School, started college, and I discovered the Byrds at Ciro's on the Sunset Strip. It was the year Bob Dylan's musical poetry captivated. In the parlance of the day, it totally blew my mind.

"One day late that fall, I think I heard it on the radio. Probably KRLA or KFWB. Dylan would be appearing during one weekend at three L.A.-area venues December 17–19 at the Santa Monica Civic Auditorium, Long Beach Municipal Auditorium, and the Pasadena Civic Auditorium. What fantastic news. Almost immediately, my brother John and I headed out to buy four tickets to the three upcoming Dylan concerts. We just had to be there.

"At the Santa Monica concert, the first set was acoustic and thoroughly entertaining, but when Dylan strutted out after the intermission with the Hawks, the world seemed to stop spinning for a couple of hours. I was even more transfixed by Dylan live onstage with his electric guitar. I was thrilled by his every move, his delivery and the way he cocked his head and sidled up to the microphone. His confidence and charisma were undeniable. He may have been an unlikely rock icon, but he definitely was one.

"There I was, finally experiencing Bob Dylan live, and it was even more exciting than I could ever have imagined. It was loud, energized, and the musicians backing him (I knew none of their names yet) were all business and super tight. All six of them were totally in sync. Each of the three nights Dylan gave us electrifying and electrified performances of 'Mr. Tambourine Man,' 'I Don't Believe You,' 'Tom Thumb's Blues,' 'Desolation Row,' and probably the greatest rock 'n' roll song of all time, 'Like a Rolling Stone.'

"It couldn't have been any better. It was transformative. I was immersed in something groundbreaking that felt raw and vibrant as Dylan and his group were taking the audience and rock 'n' roll on a magic carpet ride to a whole new level. I didn't want those nights to ever end. It was undoubtedly one of the most exciting weekends of my early life."

LEFT: An ad for three Dylan shows in California in December 1965 attended by Andrew Solt and his brother.

LEAVING THE NEST AND PREPARING TO FLY

Journal Entry – Dylan and the Hawks at the Pasadena Civic Auditorium

Saturday, December 18, 1965, Paul Body

Dylan and the Hawks onstage at the Santa Monica Civic Auditorium, December 19, 1965.

Joe, Evelyn, and I went to see Bob Dylan tonight. He was too much. He came out dressed in a brown-and-black hound's tooth suit, all by himself, with just his guitar and harmonica, strapped around his neck. His skin looked like the color of sour milk and I have never seen anyone so skinny before. Evelyn was really digging it. I was so glad. He ended the first part of his show with a song called "Desolation Row." It was really BEAUTIFUL. I haven't any idea what it is about. His songs are hard to pin down because they mean so many different things. . . . When he got through you could hear a pin drop.

Then there was an intermission and then he came back on with a group, about five guys. . . . They were all dressed in black; they looked like a bunch of Southern preachers.

They started off with a song about Juarez, Mexico, and once they started, the weirdest thing began to happen—people started getting up and leaving. They were offended by the guitar and drums. What a bunch of chum because Dylan was rocking. There were these two guys who really stood out because they were sitting in front of me, one of the guys was tall and skinny and he looked like a jealous bird. He looked real grim. The other guy wore glasses too but he looked like he was just following. How could they walk out like that?

Meanwhile up on the stage, Dylan was moving around like he was plugged into a high-tension wire. BUZZ BUZZ BUZZ. The last song he did was "Like a Rolling Stone." He kept shouting the refrain over and over, and then he left. Him and his Southern preachers.

I was moved. Evelyn was moved too. As we were going out we ran into [some friends]. Everyone was going to smoke some pot; hell that stuff Dylan was singing about got me high enough.

The first portion of the Dylan and the Hawks world tour of February 4–May 27, 1966 took place in North America. The next stops included Australia, Scandinavia, Sweden, Denmark, Ireland, Paris, and the United Kingdom. Leaving the continental United States, Dylan first traveled to Honolulu, Hawaii, and from there to Australia, where he performed seven concerts over ten days.

FRANK NEILSEN
photographer

"On the evening of April 15, 1966, the Dylan fans of Brisbane were about to undergo a major reevaluation of their hero's music. The four thousand-seat Festival Hall was jumping with anticipation at the first chance of hearing and seeing Dylan live.

"With his characteristic harmonica holder around his neck and acoustic guitar, each song he played during the first set was greeted with thunderous applause. . . .

"I had taken my camera along, but I only had a fairly short lens, and had to use direct flash in order to get some shots. Flash really kills the atmosphere of stage lighting, so I didn't expect much of a result. An intermission was called, and the fans spilled into the streets to rave about what they had been hearing.

"When everybody was seated for the second half, there was much discussion about the stage setup. There was an electric organ, a piano, a drum kit, huge speakers, and lots of microphone stands spread across the stage. Out came Dylan with a Fender electric guitar, followed by the 'cowboys' I had met that morning, with more Fenders. The audience was stunned into silence.

"From the first notes they played, it was obvious that something absolutely revolutionary was happening. . . . This was something totally new, and excitingly loud. Those cowboys could really play."

Bob Dylan and Robbie Robertson perform during Tour '66.

Australia Revisited

DAVID N. PEPPERELL

"The major revelation to me of seeing Bob Dylan in Australia in 1966 was not Bob himself—I had followed his career via all his album releases and expected the best, although I have to say that I thought his vocal vivacity on stage was far superior to the performances on his recordings—but rather the five young men he brought to Australia to back him on his electric set. This group gave this country a whole new view of what rock music could achieve.

"We were so excited at the prospect of finally seeing and hearing Bob Dylan in Australia that we didn't notice he was on the stage until the first few strums of his acoustic guitar, apparently loaned from a Sydney musician after Bob's own guitar was damaged in transit, rang out through the old Sydney Stadium, more used to wrestling and boxing than musical genius. He cut an amazing figure on that stage, dressed in an orange-and-brown hound's tooth suit, floral shirt, and Cuban-heel boots whilst his hair was teased out in an afro reminiscent of the corona of the sun. At certain times when the light struck his hair you could see right through it and it resembled a halo.

"From the opening strummed chords of 'Mr. Tambourine Man,' the whole room was hanging on every word. What was interesting was that despite everyone in the audience knowing the words, no one sang along; the song was accepted with deference and awe. Still the applause was deafening as Bob left the stage for the interval.

"Following the interval things got dark. After we got back to our seats . . . he walked back onto the stage, again with no introduction, a Fender Stratocaster electric guitar hanging around his shoulder and accompanied by five musicians playing piano, organ, guitar, bass, and drums. From the moment after the count-in 'one, two, three,' when they deluged the stadium with gorgeous sound, the Hawks made all the previous groups we had seen—including the Beatles, the Kinks, and the Rolling Stones—sound like amateur outfits, almost kids' bands. This was an aggregation of *adults*, people who understood dynamics as much as volume, tapestry of sound rather than just harmonics, and the way that playing less can be playing more.

"As Bob said in a speech from the stage of his last concert of the 1966 world tour, 'This is not English music we're playing. This is American music,' and he certainly proved that onstage in Australia. Many folkies booed and walked out of the second half of the show, complaining that the band was too loud. This was untrue.

"The band just played with an amazing dynamic sound that fully engaged anyone listening and colored the night with magic. To this day I will still say that Dylan and the Hawks was the greatest music concert I ever attended. . . . Bob's singing was full of fire and light, he whooped up to the top notes and growled the low ones, but the main aspect of his vocals was the immediacy and meaning he put into those wonderful words. The band added so much to his performance by filling in the empty spaces between the lines of poetry and illustrating them with power and maybe even exultation.

"Having the unusual combo of piano *and* organ gave the group so much rhythmic and harmonic variety and the songs lived with a wall of sound filled with excitement,

madness, and ecstasy—all the things that make rock music the miracle that it is. Richard Manuel and Garth Hudson formed a keyboard juggernaut anchored by Mickey Jones's skittering drums [Jones had replaced Levon Helm just for the world tour], Rick Danko's bedrock bass, and Robbie Robertson's guitar, which howled keening cries in the thin, wild, mercury sound of it all.

"This event provoked a furious response from a section of the crowd who began catcalling and booing. Dylan ignored them and started the electric half with 'Tell Me, Momma,' another new tune. However, it wasn't the tune that was so surprising but the volume of his backing band, who played louder than I had ever heard a band play, including the Rolling Stones and the Kinks. It was wonderful music, though, that swept you up in it, and it was obvious Bob loved playing like this as he was dancing around, sometimes raising one arm up in the air in a kind of mad joy. I looked at the people with me and they reacted the same way as I did, enraptured by the best music we had ever heard.

"At the end of that song the noise, was horrific. Again booing, shouts of 'Traitor! What happened to Bob the folkie?' and a slow handclap, although I could see that this response came from one section of the audience who seemed to be organized in some way. Dylan's response was to look more bemused as the stage rotated and go into a rocked-up version of another oldie, 'I Don't Believe You,' which again seemed to gain so much from the electric backing compared to the rather spare version on *Another Side*. 'Baby, Let Me Follow You Down' was rocked up next . . . and Bob had me and practically everybody else in his sway, except of course the yahoos.

"This was amazing, inspiring music played brilliantly and sung by a singer whose ability was only half shown by his records. Dylan sang and whooped and hollered and hit notes right off the scale. My heart was beating so loud I felt it could almost be heard above the tornado of Bob and the band's music. . . .

"Regrettably the detractors, many of whom had symbolically walked out, yelling epithets and insults, were still booing and slow-clapping after every song—the band were far too loud to hear them during songs, which was a blessing. It seemed obvious they were some kind of folk purists/leftie dogmatists who had decided that Dylan was a fake and a sellout—I heard these words often used—and they were determined to disrupt and destroy his performance.

"How they were unaware of Bob's two most recent, electric albums, I couldn't work out. They failed in their intent anyway, as the bulk of the audience was totally enraptured with the music and only wanted to hear more, so there then began screaming matchews between the pro- and anti-Dylan forces in the audience, which didn't make being there any easier.

"Undeterred, the group and Bob continued with a comic 'Leopard-Skin Pill-Box Hat,' which really drove the 'folkies' into a frenzy, followed by a beautiful rearrangement of 'One Too Many Mornings.' The harmony on the last line of the verses sung by Bob and the group's bass player was just gorgeous. On 'Ballad of a Thin Man,' Dylan crossed to the piano and, seemingly annoyed at the naysayers' response, really spat the words in the direction of the section of the crowd still catcalling. They couldn't wreck the show—it was far too good for that—but they were so annoying you just wished they would either stop or get out.

"Those elements must have got under Bob's skin, because instead of ending the show with 'Like a Rolling Stone,' as we all had expected, he finished with a vicious 'Positively Fourth Street,' again aimed at the goon squad, then stormed off the stage despite the tumultuous applause from most of the people there. It was a sad end to a magnificent show, but it could not spoil it for me—I was just dazzled by Dylan's performance. I had never heard musicianship like that and had never heard such a cavalcade of extraordinary songs and could not remember ever hearing a greater singer.

"I left the concert hall in a state of almost perfect bliss, believing that a new world was possible and I was seeing its beginning in the music of Dylan and his Band. After we left the show to walk to our car, my four friends and I did not say anything for about half an hour. What we had experienced was really beyond words."

I n a July 2, 1966 review of the European leg of the tour by Tony Barrow for *KRLA Beat* and *KYA Beat*, it is evident that the controversy had followed Dylan and the Hawks to the Old World:

> Dylan ran into the same sort of resistance from his audiences. The Paris L'Olympia was a complete sell-out. However, Dylan's Paris audience was as shocked as his British audience when Bob took roughly a ten-minute break between each song, utilizing the time to tune his guitar.
>
> As expected, Dylan was crucified by the French press. One paper carried the banner headline "Bob Dylan, Go Home" while another and more conservative paper described Dylan's concert as "the fall of an idol."
>
> Bob Dylan's British concert tour ended with a mighty bang at London's Royal Albert Hall. Dylan seemed determined to break off between items and deliver a series of pungent speeches to his audience on subjects from rock 'n' roll to "drug songs."
>
> At one point, Dylan declared that he would never play any more concerts in England. Matters came to a head at the start of his second segment when the star brought on his group and the crowd objected to the over-loud instrumental backings from the two guitars, thundering organ and pounding drums.
>
> In *Disc and Music Echo*, critic Ray Coleman stated "Dylan is great but with that sort of row going behind him he insults his own talent."
>
> During the second half of the show a section of the audience yelled and booed. Many stormed out of the hall while Dylan fought back with angry words from the platform.
>
> We've never seen anything like it before. Nor had the Beatles, who were amongst the concert audience that night.

NEAR RIGHT: Bob Dylan backstage at the Paris L'Olympia, May 24, 1966; Robbie Robertson, smiling, is visible in the background, right.

FAR RIGHT: Ticket to May 11, 1966, Dylan show at the Capitol Theatre in Cardiff, Wales.

PETER ALAN ROBERTS
author and translator

"I [grew up] in a Welsh-speaking coal mining village in southwest Wales. For my fourteenth birthday my parents bought me a ticket for the May 1966 Bob Dylan performance in what was then faraway Cardiff, the capital of Wales, about two hours drive. Since buying me a record player the previous Christmas, they'd had to listen to him pretty much every day. They dropped me off and walked around the streets, till it was time to come and get me. I had a seat in the gallery and I may have been the youngest person in there.

"The second half he was with a band. If anyone was upset about it, I was oblivious. I wasn't even familiar with the earlier Dylan music at that time. Dylan didn't introduce the band, and I thought they were deliberately nameless, were just 'the band.' . . . Later when they put out their records as 'The Band' I thought, well of course, that was always their name. I didn't know about the Hawks name till decades later.

"The drummer had stood out, blonde, on a higher elevation behind the others. I didn't know he was a temporary substitute. They didn't seem to be playing to the audience, seeking our approval—they didn't seem to need it.

"When my parents came to pick me up, they were ending with 'Like a Rolling Stone.' The doorman said, 'What an awful noise!' but he opened the door so they could look in and see them.

"That summer their live version of 'Just Like Tom Thumb's Blues' from the Liverpool concert came out as the B-side of 'I Want You,' and the astonishing magic of their playing was available to listen to over and over again."

JAMES CUSHING
poet, English professor, deejay

"On the 1966 tour, Mickey Jones was the drummer. . . . Jones is a propulsive drummer, a straight-ahead rock drummer that the jazz, swing, R&B, blues aspects of Levon we would later hear when he rejoined the group. Again, no invidious comparisons please, but it may help to think of Mickey Jones and Levon Helm in a Mitch Mitchell and Buddy Miles situation here. Mitch Mitchell brought a certain jazz element to Jimi Hendrix's work, whereas Buddy Miles was more straight-ahead. And both of those have their tremendous advantages. Mickey Jones hits harder as a drummer and less subtle as a jazz guy. He's kind of more aggressive and gives the music a bit more push.

"Also, Robbie Robertson's mathematical guitar genius has to do with the way he layers the notes and the phrases in and among the piano and organ and also rubbing up against the drums, but Robertson preferred to offer well-chosen accents that highlighted moments in a song without dominating it. His guitar essentially makes interpretive comments on the lyrics, and hearing that conversational impetus evolve.

"On the tour, set after set, we hear Robertson stretch, revise, reorder, and insert his parts of the conversation into the larger 'wild mercury' vortex of organ, harmonica, and voice. His guitar accents fit so naturally into Garth Hudson's organ swells that, at times, the instruments and Dylan's voice become elements of one larger unity."

Robbie Robertson reflected on the 1966 Dylan/Hawks stage relationship during a 2002 interview [with Harvey] published in *Goldmine* magazine:

"There was a thing that happened between Bob and The Band that, when we played together, that we would just go into a certain gear automatically. It was like instinctual, like you smelled something in the air, you know, and it made you hungry. . . . Whether we were playing in 1966 or 1976, or when we did the tour together in 1974, we would go to a certain place where we just pulled the trigger. It was like 'just burn down the doors 'cause we're coming through.' And it was a whole other place that we played when we weren't playing with him. It was a whole place that he played when he wasn't playing with us, so it was like putting a flame and oil together, or something. . . .

"In 1966, we were just some musicians working with Bob Dylan. Then the people came to the concerts with their minds made up and booed us. At least on the '74 tour we didn't get any bottles thrown at us," he added, laughing.

In 2016, I [Harvey] interviewed Robbie inside his office in West Los Angeles. During our two-hour dialogue for *Record Collector News* magazine, we further discussed the Hawks' 1966 trek with Dylan.

"The world revolved, and everybody came around and said, 'This is brilliant.' That was very interesting to see everything else change around you," marveled Robbie.

"Well, we didn't change. I don't know that this has ever happened to anybody else. And it is a phenomenon. And that's why I feel bold enough to refer to it as a musical revolution. Because the world came around. We didn't. We didn't do anything that much different," he laughed. "We just went out there and hit it between the eyes. And now people have a completely different reaction to it. And I thought, 'That's kind of incredible that the world actually came to this place,' you know. And I don't know who else has been through that."

54 THE STORY OF THE BAND

Bob Dylan's *Eat the Document* is a documentary filmed by D. A. Pennebaker that chronicled Dylan and the Hawks' 1966 tour of Europe. Footage includes the infamous Manchester Free Trade Hall concert of May 17, complete with an audience member shouting "Judas!" during the electric portion of Dylan's performance backed by the Hawks.

The movie was originally commissioned and filmed for network television and scheduled for broadcast for *ABC Stage 67*. Dylan edited the film with Howard Alk and Gordon Quinn, but it was subsequently rejected by ABC programmers who decided it didn't fit the demographic of a mainstream audience.

Portions of Pennebaker's footage for *Eat the Document* were incorporated into director Martin Scorsese's 2005 documentary film *No Direction Home: Bob Dylan*.

D.A. PENNEBAKER

"After *Dont Look Back,* Dylan said, 'I want you to shoot a film and I'm going to direct it and it will be my film. You have your film and this will be mine.'

"That was the kind of handshake arrangement. We didn't have anything signed or [any] papers about it. We went off. I only knew how to film one way. I didn't change the way I filmed. And Dylan really didn't know how to direct and nor did I. It kind of stumbled along. We were moving around a lot. Sweden, France, England. It just wasn't a tour of English music halls.

"And I think that Dylan got really intrigued by the kind of locales he was in. And how they responded to him. Dylan was playing onstage with four or five musicians and having a great time doing it. I mean, it was so much more interesting than what he had been doing all by himself. And he kind of took to it. And I could see by shooting [that] the stage performances were really an important part of it.

"At one point I actually got out onstage with the band and he didn't know I was gonna be there, and when he saw me he really cracked up. Because it was such a funny idea that I was just like the band.

"I felt that he was really writing music sort of with Robbie Robertson and for Robbie. . . . There was something going on that drove him so that he would stay up all night. I filmed him endlessly where he'd write many songs during the night and Robbie would play along. Robbie made him somehow do this."

JAMES CUSHING

"During *Eat the Document* and now the Scorsese-assembled *No Direction Home: Bob Dylan* DVD, we first see the wild-haired 1966 Bob laughing uncontrollably with his face on a table. 'Ever heard of me?' he asks. Dylan sits at the hotel's piano and plays. Then we see train footage, with Bob and various (shockingly young) Hawks walking up and down the aisles as in *A Hard Day's Night,* but no comic scene develops.

"Instead, we get momentary fragments filmed by a camera that keeps cutting to and away from Bob as though ambivalent about his charisma. But we get memorable isolated bits, some bluesy solo Telecaster from Robbie, 'I Still Miss Someone' by Bob with Johnny Cash, 'Ballad of a Thin Man' with the red stage light exploding around Bob's curls, making him look *ignited*."

OPPOSITE PAGE: Scenes from the 1966 Dylan and the Hawks tour; from directional to directional: Richard Manuel; Rick Danko; Robbie Robertson; Garth Hudson; and Dylan and Robertson.

LEAVING THE NEST AND PREPARING TO FLY 55

CHAPTER 4
THE BASEMENT TAPES

Dylan and the Hawks' exhaustive tour had concluded in May 1966; or, a more apt way of putting it, the soldiers had returned from the war, bloodied but unbowed. Like other revolutionary moments—think James Joyce's *Ulysses*, Pablo Picasso's *Les Demoiselles d'Avignon*—unintended consequences carried the day. The brash, mercurial folkie turned unrepentant rock 'n' roller quickly adapted to the perquisites of pop stardom, the now-ubiquitous shades hiding the rush of being too easily indulged. It was time for a time-out.

On July 29, 1966, Dylan unexpectedly received his exit strategy on the sylvan backroads of Woodstock, the rustic artist community two hours north of Manhattan, albeit in an unfortunate manner. Tooling along on his motorcycle, the brakes, it is believed, suddenly locked up, catapulting him into months of enforced recuperation while further fueling the intrigue that surrounded his every endeavor.

Was this a smokescreen for detoxing from the road, or maybe a publicity stunt concocted by the ever-canny Albert Grossman to heighten his star's profile by placing him on the down low? While his broken neck healed (the likeliest scenario), Dylan was considering his next play; the psychedelic journey was over, to be followed by an equally vexing, equally profound undertaking. And it was going to take a bunch of Hawks to help him get there.

During his convalescence, Dylan fully acquainted himself with his new setting, as far removed from the Village and Fourth Street as anyone could imagine. Woodstock provided a cool, cleansing air, as restorative as bed rest and clean living. It facilitated Dylan's move to recast himself as the proverbial family man, changing nappies, chopping wood.

OPPOSITE: Bob Dylan and the Hawks onstage kicking off the last month of their 1966 tour, on May 1, at the K.B. Hallen in Copenhagen.

Domestic bliss, though, was no substitute for the rush of writing and playing.

Dylan wasn't the only casualty of the '66 campaign. The Hawks were also in need of some serious down time to consider their next move. Robertson followed Bob to Woodstock, periodically visiting the other members, who were bivouacked in New York City. There were even some desultory attempts to record there, exploring new musical avenues while remaining on retainer from Dylan. With their paymaster out of commission—plans for more touring put on permanent hold—the future seemed uncertain.

In the winter of '67, Grossman encouraged Hudson, Manuel, and Danko to relocate to Woodstock as well. They assembled first at Dylan's home, playing with some ideas, and then moving to a nondescript pink clapboard house at the end of a long gravel driveway deep in the local woods of West Saugerties. Manuel, Hudson, and Danko called this musty abode their home, where any itch—musical, sexual, pharmaceutical—could be scratched without the fear of prying eyes. For months, they gathered round at the house, which they nicknamed "Big Pink," and pick and chewed over any lick, phrase, old standard, sea shanty, or semblance of threadbare Americana that could coalesce into something resembling a song. Big Pink became a hothouse of inspired reinvention, where the Hawks slowly, inexorably blossomed into a band—The Band.

Hudson had converted the basement into a makeshift studio, a two-track reel-to-reel machine the sole concession to professionalism—that, and his artisanal skills with a tool kit and a soldering gun. Beneath Garth's stoic veneer there lurked a Tesla-like command of electrical wiring that complemented his facility with a Bach partita.

"With his huge, crackling beard, high forehead, and tweedy jacket, Garth looked like a cross between

ROBBIE ROBERTSON

"We did have the experience with Bob Dylan and in doing *The Basement Tapes* with the songs that were supposed to be shared with other artists to record. It was because so many people recorded Bob's songs and we were hooked up together, you thought, 'Oh. That's part of it.' . . . I didn't think about it in [terms of] writing the songs or making the records that other people would do. This was a very interior thing. This was a thing between the five of us in the band. Something that we had collected over ages and pulled it together and made this gumbo.

"But Bob already had such a track record that you thought people are going to be drawn to this. If he put something out there for people to record, people are going to be drawn to it. . . .

"You know, we would record a song like 'You Ain't Goin' Nowhere.' And Bob would say, 'Whatta you think? Ferlin Husky? Right?' And it was half kidding around and half meaning somebody is going, too.

"But with the way that he is and the way that he thinks, Bob could insist on sending that song to [country music singer] Ferlin Husky first. You know what I mean? Just because he would do something like that. . . . We said, 'OK. We've got to pull some of these things.'

"We were recording a lot of stuff. We were covering songs and just having fun. And then every once in a while there would be an original one . . . . And when we were doing this not with Bob, that was the germ and the idea and the beginning of *Music from Big Pink*. That was happening kind of in the back room too. So when we chose those songs to send out, we were choosing what we liked. . . . Manfred Mann could do a really great job on 'The Mighty Quinn.' I didn't know that. But we were saying that 'The Mighty Quinn' thing had something to it. It really was what felt right in putting that collection together."

General Grant and a professor of archeology at some Ivy League university," wrote Scottish author John Niven with a vivid flourish in 2005, in his novella *Music from Big Pink*. In keeping with Hudson's scholarly sensibilities, it was his fastidious preservation of the recordings that would allow hungry listeners to finally feast, decades later, on the legendary performances known simply, immortally, as *The Basement Tapes*.

Grossman made the first move, slyly underplaying his hand. Anxious for Dylan to generate some much-needed revenue—concertizing was out, let alone returning to the studio—Grossman beckoned his reluctant star to record some rough demos for their publishing company, Dwarf Music, and send 'em out like chum, hoping to get some nibbles from artists keen to affiliate themselves with Dylan. It was a low-energy attempt to get the creative juices flowing. And, besides, charting with a cover was good business, keeping the brand fresh.

Dylan and his playing partners recorded over a hundred songs. The teaming yielded traditional covers, wry and humorous ditties, off-the-cuff performances, and, most important, dozens of newly written Bob Dylan songs, including future classics "I Shall Be Released," "Quinn the Eskimo" (also known as "The Mighty Quinn"), "This Wheel's on Fire," and "You Ain't Goin' Nowhere."

Originally circulating on a fourteen-song acetate, the Bob Dylan and The Band sessions were finally released by Sony Music's Columbia/Legacy record label in 2014 as *The Bootleg Series, Vol. 11: The Basement Tapes Complete*, a six-disc box set, featuring 138 tracks!

OPPOSITE PAGE INSET: The British rock band Manfred Mann in 1968; their recording of the Dylan song "Quinn the Eskimo (The Mighty Quinn)"—released as "The Mighty Quinn" in January 1968—hit No. 1 in the UK and peaked at No. 10 on the *Billboard* chart in the United States.

BELOW: The Band outside of Big Pink in West Saugerties, April 1968. Standing, from left to right: Garth Hudson, Richard Manuel, Robbie Robertson, Rick Danko; Levon Helm kneeling at left. Photograph by Elliott Landy.

A formal compilation of songs was assembled by impromptu producer Garth Hudson in October 1967.

"When I first was given a cassette tape of *The Basement Tapes* by Garth Hudson in the fall of 1967, I felt like it was the American version of the Soviet *samizdat*—a handmade piece of art secretly passed from hand to hand," ventured Jonathan Taplin when we corresponded via e-mail in 2014. Taplin, a former road manager of The Band and director emeritus of the University of Southern California Annenberg Innovation Lab, said: "I think credit needs to go to Garth for recording these songs in the Big Pink basement with a rather amazing fidelity. In a sense he was following in the 'field recording' tradition of Alan Lomax. For both Dylan and The Band it was a way to let friends know about their new work, with none of the commercial pressures of putting out a record. And in that sense, much like the development of bebop during World War II when there were no recordings, a new kind of 'Americana' was birthed outside of any market pressures."

The Byrds recorded two Dylan songs on their 1968 *Sweetheart of the Rodeo* LP: "You Ain't Goin' Nowhere" and "Nothing Was Delivered."

"Chris [Hillman] got the demos of the two Dylan songs in the mail," the Byrds' Roger McGuinn recalled in a 2010 interview for *Goldmine* magazine. "Dylan as a songwriter was so much better than everyone. We had been out of touch for a few years and it was interesting to notice that at this same period he was going in the same musical direction we were in."

"I have no idea why I got the two Bob Dylan *Basement Tapes* songs in my mail," Hillman added in a 2011 phone interview. "I sensed something was good there and I took them to McGuinn."

BELOW LEFT: The Byrds' Chris Hillman at the KFRC Fantasy Fair and Magic Music Festival on Mount Tamalpais, Marin County, California, June 10, 1967.

BELOW RIGHT: Peter, Paul & Mary—Peter Yarrow (center), Mary Travers, and Paul Stookey—recorded numerous Dylan songs, including "Blowin' in the Wind" (a No. 2 *Billboard* hit in 1964), "Too Much of Nothing," and "I Shall Be Released" (the latter two on the 1968 album *Late Again*).

KIRK SILSBEE
music journalist

"After the motorcycle accident, Dylan was off the public radar for what seemed like a couple of years. We didn't know it but he was holed up in Woodstock, which most of us had never heard of before the festival. That absence gave way to all kinds of speculation on his whereabouts and well-being. Though he wasn't speaking for himself, Dylan had several interlocutors in the form of his songs, performed by others on the emerging FM rock radio. Peter, Paul & Mary introduced 'Too Much of Nothing,' the Byrds gave us 'You Ain't Goin' Nowhere,' 'This Wheel's on Fire' was done by Julie Driscoll with Brian Auger & the Trinity, and Manfred Mann did 'Mighty Quinn.'

"The songs were all introduced to us by those artists, and it was a form of mental sport to try to divine some kind of secret code being sent to us from Dylan through them. I imagined him in the same kind of cloistered bunker that Thelonious Monk stared out from on the cover of his classic *Underground* album of 1967, furtively sending cryptic messages to the front any way that he could."

JAMES CUSHING

"Peter, Paul & Mary had first dibs on the tunes. The tape recorder was from Peter Yarrow. Tin Pan Alley marketing concepts were involved simply by getting Dylan and Hawks tunes out on acetate done for other people to cover.

"At the time, when I heard early bootlegs of these songs and a few of the early cover versions, the offerings from *The Basement Tapes* were like little secret packages that came from somewhere. The one that I remember most was Peter, Paul & Mary's 'Too Much of Nothing' . . . even though they did change the words. What Dylan wrote had the names of Valerie and Vivienne, which is key to the song because Valerie was T. S. Eliot's first wife's name and Vivienne was his second wife's name. And 'Too Much of Nothing' is an answer to The Waste Land. . . . He left this big glowing clue. [Peter, Paul & Mary] had it saying 'hello to Marion' [instead of 'to Vivienne'] because they misheard it on the recording."

> **"Bob Dylan would come over [to Big Pink] for a year, seven days a week, and we would spend four or five hours together playing. We must have come up with 150 to 200 songs in that time."**
> —Rick Danko, to Dennis Loren, *RPM* magazine, 1985

"This Wheel's on Fire"

Of all the privileges of youth, none is more intoxicating than the sense of being in the right place at the right time. And nothing personifies that fleeting, mesmeric moment more than a captivating song. In the riotous summer of '65, it was the Stones' '(I Can't Get No) Satisfaction'; the lysergic palpitations of '67 were made manifest in Procol Harum's lambent dirge 'A Whiter Shade of Pale.' And in 1968, as the soft focus of idealism gave way to darker, less enchanting meditations, Julie Driscoll with Brian Auger & the Trinity delivered their moody, bluish, dimly sinister pas de deux with Bob Dylan and Rick Danko's "This Wheel's on Fire."

One of the legendary *Basement Tapes* acetates circulating among music publishers on London's Denmark Street, the song achieved an unlikely success underscored by its orphan status; it was among the last of the fourteen or so tunes that had been earmarked by Grossman for others to cover. Its spare, ghostly sound, just Dylan's voice, an occasional strum, and a lonely, loping bass line by Danko provided little evidence that a hit was lurking within.

Driscoll and Auger were equally ill suited as wannabe pop stars; they were jazz and R&B enthusiasts who recognized that their peers—as well as their audience—were hungering for big ideas, reveling in the shock of the new. It was a seismic leap from Dylan's rhombic musings to chart-topping acclaim, earning the bewitchingly photogenic Ms. Driscoll the moniker "The Face of '68" from a gobsmacked media. And dig the organ solo at the fade!

BRIAN AUGER

"I'd just come out of my previous band, Steampacket [featuring a very young Rod Stewart], looking to put together something with a James Jamerson–style bassist, a Bernard Purdie feel on drums with balls-out organ solos on top. Easier said than done! My manager, Giorgio Gomelsky, told me that Julie Driscoll was keen to join us, and that worked for me. She brought in a different feel; she was really into Nina Simone and Aretha Franklin, and that sounded good to me as well. We were doing mostly covers—I was just beginning to write some stuff for the band and we were always open to new material. Gomelsky called us into his office and played us the acetate of 'This Wheel's on Fire.'

"Now, we knew other bands had been after Bob's songs; Manfred Mann had just done 'The Mighty Quinn,' and it was a big hit. But to be honest, I didn't know what to make of this song. It was so minimal, almost nothing but a certain kind of atmosphere. Julie latched on to it immediately and I said, 'All right, I'll take it home and see what I can do.'

OPPOSITE: Julie Driscoll and Brian Auger, whose version of "This Wheel's on Fire" stormed the UK charts in 1968, at a Byrds concert at the Boston Tea Party club in late February 1969.

At most, maybe, we can make it work as an album track . . . at most.

"Nothing came, man, nothing I did made it happen. But we're in the studio and it all comes together. As a 'jazz man,' I'm thinking, let's get a straight-ahead groove going with a kind of walking bass line with a march feel, like something out of New Orleans. So we laid down a basic track—piano, bass, and drums. I overdubbed the organ and then spotted a mellotron just lounging in the corner. The mellotron is a strange instrument, difficult to manage. It generates a spooky, orchestral sound from prerecorded tapes of strings . . . a floating quality very much of the period—very psychedelic. Julie's been there the whole time and has a strong sense of how to deliver her vocal—a real soulful reading. And then our engineer, Eddy Offord, pulls out this shoebox-like device with a big dial on the front. 'Hey, Brian, check this out!' It's a prototype phasing device and we use it on the strings and organ. And wow, I'm hearing something else, man. . . . This is a single. Giorgio and Julie agree and a few weeks later it's blowing up the charts. Unbelievable, man.

"The key to the song, the hinge, is the walking bass line. It's a jazz move in a pop song and it sounded completely different from anything else on the radio. We didn't think about marketing or pleasing the label; our only concern was whether it was a good piece of music and did it represent us properly or not. In one day we went from 'can't make it happen' to having a career moment. Right after, we're playing at the Montreux Jazz Festival (sharing a bill with Aretha Franklin), the Berlin Jazz Festival, developing a really wild cult following which carries over to this day. Thank you, Bob. . . .

"I was such a jazz snob. I came to appreciate Dylan as an incredible poet who used music to bring life to his words. The songs were conundrums, a real challenge to work out, and that really appealed to me. And the same is true about The Band—they were always putting the song first. I got into their albums straight away. [The 1969 song] 'Look Out Cleveland' was a particular favorite. No flashy moves, no empty notes, just taste and elegance. They played as a band, with discipline, and you could hear it. That was a real lesson for me early in my career, always wanting to solo, an ego thing. 'Settle down, Brian, and play the groove,' be it a Chicago blues or Motown, all these different feels. That's what Dylan and The Band were all about: feel."

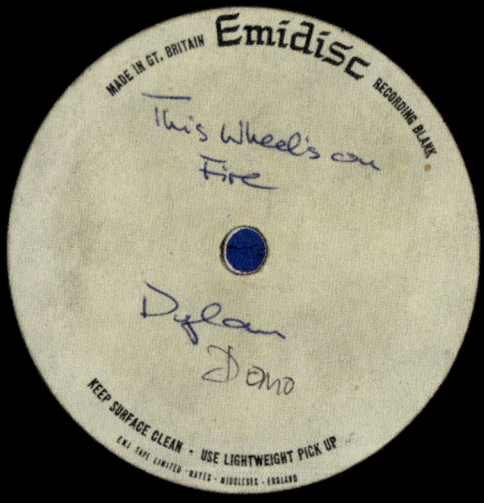

Basement Tapes demo acetate of "This Wheel's on Fire."

Back in the fall of 1967, a Hawk named Levon Helm was still voluntarily grounded in Los Angeles, California. The Hawks were riding high on a creative surge and needed their long-absent compadre to complete the journey they'd started all those years back in Canada. They were now ready to put their name on some music they could claim as uniquely their own. Helm had been living a roustabout life; at one time he was working on an oil rig in the Gulf of Mexico.

In the 2001 documentary *The Band: The Authorized Video Biography*, Levon recalls that he was "certainly lonesome for the band. I guess I believed at some point we would get back together. I didn't figure that they would give up their dreams just to be Bob's backup band. Nor did I have any false ideas about becoming a troubadour and thumbing my way through life with a set of drums strapped to my back."

He was in Memphis when the others reached out to him. In October '67 the prodigal son returned to the fold.

From left to right: John London, John Ware, Jeff Hanna, and Chris Darrow of the Corvettes, Linda Ronstadt's backing band, c. 1969.

JOHN WARE

"Jesse Ed Davis had moved to L.A. in 1967. . . and was staying in the Okie youth hostel known as Leon Russell's house. Eddie called me (I was in college in Southern California) and asked if I wanted to be in a band with Levon Helm. *Really*?

"Levon had arrived in L.A. with a girlfriend, a poodle, and a desire to play without being booed. This band idea gathered in a house in Santa Monica, and the prospect of two drummers morphed into three drummers when Sandy Konikoff arrived. I was shifted to bass guitar. Odd. The few weeks that ensued were educational, to be blunt. I had to withdraw because I was, after all, a full-time student, and Levon heard the siren calls of his former bandmates, but I learned more about actually playing drums than I imagined.

"There was a young girl living in that house in Santa Monica too. Just a couple of years later I heard she was looking for players for her first backing band. . . . I tried successfully to get that job and was aided by the fact that we realized we knew each other from our mutual association with Levon. I became Linda Ronstadt's drummer [with her backing group the Corvettes, 1969–71]. Jesse Ed became Taj Mahal's guitarist. The Band changed music forever. We all went on the rock 'n' roll highway.

"By 1975 I was playing drums for Emmylou Harris and the Hot Band—perhaps the best country rock band ever assembled. . . . I met Emmy while on the road with Linda. We toured in several packages before we were ready to headline. One of those packages was James Taylor, The Band, and Emmy.

"There I was, on the bill with Levon, and he was watching *me*. It was a bizarre sensation. By then I'd become a *far* different player than the high school kid who worshiped Levon, but I certainly owed all that was good about my playing to meeting and knowing Levon some fifteen years earlier."

Woody Guthrie was a true American original, cussed and compassionate as befitting his storied, hardscrabble life. Guthrie exerted an enormous influence over Dylan, who practically impersonated him in style and substance early in his career.

On October 3, 1967, Guthrie, who suffered from Huntington's disease, died. Bob Dylan immediately contacted Guthrie's manager, Harold Leventhal, to stage a benefit concert. It took place at Carnegie Hall in New York on January 20, 1968. This was Dylan's first public appearance since the motorcycle accident eighteen months earlier. He was backed by the "Crackers" (as they were introduced that evening); in a matter of months, everyone would know them as "The Band."

During the first part of the show, Dylan, Jack Elliott, Richie Havens, Odetta, Pete Seeger, Tom Paxton, and Arlo Guthrie shared the stage in a production written and directed by screenwriter Millard Lampell, who was a member of the Almanac Singers. Actors Will Geer and Robert Ryan served as narrators, reading from Guthrie's works. Proceeds from a live LP recording of the event were earmarked to the Guthrie Library and the Huntington's disease fund.

Then Dylan and the boys hit the stage. Performing three songs—"I Ain't Got No Home," "Dear Mrs. Roosevelt," and "Grand Coulee Dam"—they barreled their way through what had been, up to that point, a staid if reverential salute by Guthrie's distinguished cohorts.

There was no booing; Dylan now occupied a rarefied ground commensurate with his exalted status, above and beyond reproach. Like a lightning strike, Dylan's mere presence conferred an elemental grandeur, his fans quivering at a "Bob sighting." It was almost comical, the veneration, but there was no escaping his centripetal pull. As for the Crackers, they spun off into their own trajectory, free to finally paint their own masterpieces.

Bob Dylan performs with The Band at the Woody Guthrie Memorial Concert at Carnegie Hall in New York, January 20, 1968.

Carnegie Hall Blues

HARRY E. NORTHUP

"Every morning I would sit in my rockin' chair and read the *New York Times*. I saw a paragraph advertising the Woody Guthrie benefit with Bob Dylan and others. Immediately I got dressed, took the bus down Central Park West, and got two tickets for myself and my (then) wife Rita Solomon at Carnegie Hall. Fourth row.

"Woody Guthrie had always fascinated me because my people were working-class people. I was born in Amarillo, Texas, and grew up in Sidney, a small town in western Nebraska. . . .

"Dylan socked home the notion of compassion and righteousness and justice. That concert is one of the top two concerts I ever attended, and I will always remember seeing Bob Dylan and his group on stage together.

"The thing I remember most about the show was that each folk performer would do a tune, like Judy Collins would be on stage right, she would sing, and Pete Seeger would be on the opposite side of the stage and he would sing. And they would alternate.

"In the back of the stage I saw these guys who all had beards, sitting. 'Who are they?' Toward the end of the first half of the show all of a sudden Bob Dylan came on and these guys got up and played with him. Instead of doing one tune in a folk way, Dylan did like twelve or thirteen minutes of Woody Guthrie material and really socked it to you.

"It was like a rock concert. It was rockabilly with Dylan's voice on top of it. I remember Dylan looked at me and I looked at him and I felt he was looking right at me. It was one of the two best concerts I ever went to. I went to the Elvis Presley show in 1961 at the Pearl Harbor Auditorium in Hawaii. I was in the Navy. I was sitting in the balcony. And I remember looking at a guy walking around with an attaché case and it was Colonel Parker. Elvis would make a little move with his finger and the whole crowd would go nuts. He was the king.

"Bob Dylan was just beautiful and electrifying when he came on. He transcended the folk genre, lifted it up and really hit me square between the eyes with a force of nature. . . . I was in the fourth row and I thought he was talking directly to me. You know what I mean? God bless him. What a great artist."

Actor and poet Harry E. Northup, c. 1967.

CHAPTER 5

WHICH ONE IS BIG PINK?

Life at Big Pink was crackling with energy, a spirit of camaraderie and playfulness redolent of a Boy Scout jamboree. There were footballs flying, arts and crafts (Dylan developed a yen for painting at this time), and creative writing (everyone took a turn at tapping out a lyric or two at the communal typewriter). It was almost wholesome, if you overlooked the wholesale consumption of fermented spirits, smoke, and other "enhancements" courtesy of well-wishing entrepreneurs who slinked around the overgrowth.

Calling themselves "The Crackers," a derisive term for Southern working-class white boys, or "The Honkies," when Levon was feeling particularly prickly, they threw in their lot with Mr. Grossman. After a brief dalliance with Warner Bros. Records—Albert's idea of tuning up—he closed with Capitol Records, negotiating an unprecedented ten-album contract.

Rock music was becoming very big business, and this high-profile signing with the Beatles' American label meant that, at a minimum, a group of burly backwoodsmen, far removed from the paisley pop of contemporary music, was going to cause a stir, if not a complete ruckus. Grossman was a fervent advocate for his artists; he genuinely loved the music and the gifted souls who made it. If he came off as combative, imperious, so be it.

OPPOSITE: The Band poses with Rick Danko's vintage car outside of his house in Woodstock, 1969. Photograph by Elliott Landy.

Sequestered in their playhouse in West Saugerties, a world removed from the antic fripperies of "the love generation," the band worked on a clutch of songs born out of the *Basement Tapes* sessions. For every throwaway like "Orange Juice Blues," something inspired would emerge, like pulling an ivory netsuke out of a box of cereal. Robbie, for one, was honing his songwriting skills with a master carpenter's aplomb, anything extraneous left on the floor like plane shavings. Robertson had long established his credentials as a blazing lead guitarist, but even virtuosity could turn to verbosity.

JOHN SIMON
record producer, composer, arranger

"Back when I was breaking in as a producer at Columbia, in 1965 I co-produced an album by tenor sax player Charles Lloyd, *Of Course, Of Course*, along with veteran jazz producer George Avakian, featuring Tony Williams, Ron Carter, Albert Stinson, Pete LaRoca, and Hungarian guitarist Gábor Szabó.

"Charles and Robbie knew each other slightly, and Charles invited Robbie to join his band in the studio for the song 'Sun Dance.' That's when we first met.

"In the fall of 1967, after the residence in Woodstock working on *You Are What You Eat*, I returned to New York City and soon heard from Robbie Robertson."

For the liner notes for the Capitol Records 2005 box set *The Band: A Musical History*, Robbie told writer Rob Bowman that "the song is becoming the thing, the mood is becoming the thing. . . . I'm not gonna play a guitar solo on the whole record. I'm only going to play riffs, Curtis Mayfield kind of riffs.

"I didn't want screaming vocals," he explained. "I wanted sensitive vocals where you can hear the breathing and the voices coming in. . . . I like voices coming in one at a time, in a chain reaction kind of thing, like the Staple Singers did. . . . This is emotional and this is storytelling."

The final element in this ambitious enterprise came in the form of producer John Simon, an accomplished musician in his own right.

Simon was born in 1941 in Norwalk, Connecticut. In his early twenties he joined Columbia Records as a junior producer and worked on various studio projects under the aegis of label head Goddard Lieberson, including Broadway cast albums, audio documentary albums, and an audio production of Marshall McLuhan's 1967 book *The Medium Is the Message*. Simon subsequently worked with Peter Yarrow on the soundtrack to the 1968 music documentary *You Are What You Eat*, edited by filmmaker Howard Alk, a friend of Grossman, who introduced Simon to The Band.

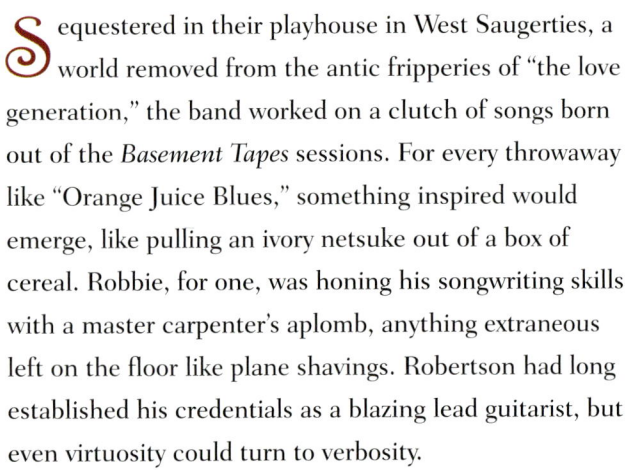

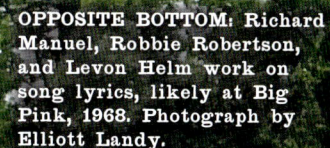

OPPOSITE BOTTOM: Richard Manuel, Robbie Robertson, and Levon Helm work on song lyrics, likely at Big Pink, 1968. Photograph by Elliott Landy.

BELOW: Contemporary photograph of Big Pink.

"WE'D BEEN AROUND SO LONG THAT WE COULDN'T TAKE A NAME SERIOUSLY. SO WE MADE THE FIRST ALBUM AND WE CALLED OURSELVES THE BAND. IT'S LIKE NO NAME AT ALL, BUT PEOPLE NOW HAD A WAY OF REFERRING TO US."
—ROBBIE ROBERTSON

The Band and Simon rehearsed material and felt comfortable enough to record a demo tape for Albert Grossman to peddle to record labels. Simon steered them into a studio that felt very familiar to him—Columbia's old Studio A.

RICHARD BOSWORTH
record producer, engineer

"By the fall of 1966, Columbia Records had built new facilities at East 52nd Street in Midtown Manhattan. The label closed one of the world's great recording studios, their Westside 799 Seventh Avenue complex, which had been Columbia's premier studios since the 1930s.

"Phil Ramone, a top New York recording engineer, was looking to expand his successful 48th Street studio, A&R Recording, and negotiated a deal with Columbia to acquire the rooms, which he took over in the fall of 1967.

"Studio A had been utilized for all of Bob Dylan's records through the initial tracks for *Blonde on Blonde.* Simon & Garfunkel had recorded all albums and singles to that point in time in Studio A as well. The Lovin' Spoonful recorded 'Summer in the City' in Studio A.

"John Simon had worked in the room as a Columbia staff producer, and Robertson had been with Dylan at the same facility."

FRED CATERO
record producer, engineer

"Columbia studios had Altec Lansing A7 speakers. The 'Voice of the Theater.' . . . [They] had great natural echo, reverb, and leakage.* And you wanted that. In fact, it added to the drama."

*"Leakage" refers to the sound of musical instruments or vocals bleeding into the microphone of another musical instrument from a distance, adding depth to the overall sound.

LEVON HELM

"Watching Bob and helping Bob construct some songs helped everybody get a better idea of how to put a song together and learning that there wasn't any set formula. It could happen from a groove, from an idea, from a title, from a song.

"We would get a song going and all sing it. Rick would sing it, then Richard, then me, and we'd start to figure out whose song it was. At the same time there were lines that Rick sounded good on or maybe my voice would fit on and it was more fun for us as performers [to mix it up]."

Bob Dylan and his manager, Albert Grossman (seated, with round glasses, on Dylan's right), and producer Tom Wilson (seated at table, left) listen to tracks from *Highway 61 Revisited* (released August 1965), with engineers and other industry professionals in the booth of Columbia's Studio A in New York, summer 1965.

THE STORY OF THE BAND

WHICH ONE IS BIG PINK? 73

The Band's debut long-player with Simon at the helm, *Music from Big Pink*, was released by Capitol Records in July 1968. Simon's sessions for the album, engineered by Tony May, Don Hahn, and Shelly Yakus, began in New York at Phil Ramone's A&R Studio in the fall of 1967. Upon its release, *Music from Big Pink* didn't so much "drop" as detonate, yet another catalytic disruption in a year fraught with change.

Regarding the album's masterpiece, "The Weight," Robertson told Kevin Ransom in the May 1995 issue of *Guitar Player* magazine, "Our attitude was, 'Well, just in case something else isn't working, we've got this song to fall back on. . . . Someone suggested that maybe Garth should play piano and Richard should play organ, because it seemed like there was room for some fills that would sound more natural coming from the piano than the guitar. It wasn't until we listened back to it that we realized, 'Holy shit, this song's really got something.'"

AL KOOPER
multi-instrumentalist, founder Blood, Sweat & Tears

"John Simon went from doing the first Blood, Sweat & Tears album to doing *Music from Big Pink*. . . . I put him right up there with George Martin, Jerry Ragovoy, and Phil Spector. John had an understanding of the singer-songwriter. He was an erudite musician. And that was the important thing."

OPPOSITE: Rick Danko (far left), producer John Simon (center, with guitar), Robbie Robertson (at mixing desk in back), Levon Helm (far right), in the studio at Sammy Davis Jr.'s pool house recording *The Band* album, 1969 (see Chapter 7). Photograph by Elliott Landy.

JOHN SIMON

"There seemed to be some magic on the first session with The Band. 'Chest Fever,' 'Tears of Rage,' 'Lonesome Suzie,' and 'We Can Talk' were all cut in one afternoon! We were very well rehearsed. Fate had brought the six of us together back in 1967 and we worked very closely together for about three years. There they were and there I was. In the right place at the right time.

"What was my role in the process of making records with them? They brought their talents into the studio and I, like each of them, brought mine. We drew from all of our resources to record those songs. So after they played me what they'd come up with in the basement of Big Pink, we started further polishing the songs and the arrangements.

"There was 'I Shall Be Released,' a Dylan original; 'This Wheel's on Fire,' which Bob had cowritten with Rick; 'Tears of Rage,' which he'd cowritten with Richard; and 'Lonesome Suzie,' which was all Richard. He wrote it. He sang it.

"The very first sound on 'Tears of Rage' was a sort of fanfare declaration on the guitar through an amp with a Leslie sound. That amp was a weathered box that had a Leslie speaker inside that we simply called 'the black box.'

"With the exception of a cover of a country song, the other four songs on *Music from Big Pink* were written by Robbie. He had obviously learned a lot from being in such close proximity to Bob, particularly in the story songs and the freewheeling imagery. He had been quite a student as well of many different types of music, so that the chords and structure of the new songs he was writing tended to be more adventurous than Bob's folk music sources."

In February 1968, The Band did some additional recording and mixing in Hollywood on Vine Street at Capitol Records' hallowed Studio B (where Frank Sinatra, the Beach Boys, Bob Dylan, and many other top artists had recorded), which had an eight-track machine; Ramone's A&R facility only had four-track capabilities. Simon was able to employ the coveted Capitol echo chambers, as well as their custom-made EMT plate reverbs and the fabled isolation vocal booth.

In 2000, an expanded and remastered *Music from Big Pink* was issued with nine new "bonus" tracks, including several that were recorded by The Band February 20–21, 1968, at the landmark Gold Star Studio B in Hollywood with engineers Doc Siegel, Larry Levine, and co-owner Stan Ross. Countless hits had been created at Dave Gold and Stan Ross's sonic temple on the corner of Santa Monica Boulevard and Vine, including chart-toppers from Phil Spector, Darlene Love, the Beach Boys, and the Monkees.

In an interview with Harvey in 2000, Stan Ross explained, "Gold Star was built for the songwriters Jimmy Van Heusen, Sammy Fain, Sonny Burke, Johnny Mercer, Jimmy McHugh, Frank Loesser, and Dimitri Tiomkin. We didn't use pop filters and wind screens, we got mouth noises. Isn't that life? Our studio echo chamber gave it the wall of sound feel. Dave Gold built the equipment, echo chamber, and custom-designed board." Songwriter, composer, and record producer Jack Nitzsche recalled to Harvey in 1998 that "I remember Stan Ross telling us many times that the echo chambers were acoustically and geometrically designed to get the right amount of balance and reverb. I loved the echo. It's like garlic. You can't get too much."

In 1968, the standard record-business LP configuration traditionally incorporated twelve tracks, six on each side of the disk. The 2000 CD reissue of *Music from Big Pink* includes some demos and outtakes for their historical value, including the Gold Star session of "Orange Juice Blues (Blues for Breakfast)" and an abridged rendition of Bob Dylan's "Long Distance Operator," initially cut at A&R in New York (the full version of "Long Distance Operator" recorded at Gold Star appears on disk two of *The Band: A Musical History* box set). The tune was first performed by Dylan and the Hawks in December 1965 at the Berkeley Community Center, and Dylan sang it in 1967 at a Woodstock *Basement Tapes* session.

Recording engineer Larry Levine, the Beach Boys' Brian Wilson, and Danny Hutton (future Three Dog Night vocalist) at the famed Gold Star studios in Hollywood, November 1966.

Capitol Records recording artist Brian Wilson of the Beach Boys, labelmates of The Band, also did sessions at Capitol Records and Gold Star studios. During a 2007 interview with Brian, I asked about their facilities. "I liked the Capitol rooms, and I liked the instrumental sound, but I didn't like the vocal sound," he said. "I didn't like that kind of echo chamber. . . . So we switched over to Western, and Gold Star. Western had a big room, and Phil Spector was over at Gold Star. I went to Gold Star and asked Larry Levine, the engineer, 'What is the secret of the Phil Spector echo trip?'

"'Well, we have two echo chambers under the parking lot. Phil uses both the chambers at the same time.'

"So I tried that myself and it worked."

Levine explained that "because the rooms were small, with low ceilings . . . unlike other studios with isolation, your drums sounded the way you wanted them to sound. They would change accordingly to whatever leakage was involved."

In Rob Bowman's 2005 liner notes for Capitol Records' *The Band: A Musical History,* Robbie Robertson stressed the importance of specific studio locations. "There's a vibe to certain records, whether it's a Motown thing or a Sun Records thing or a Phil Spector thing."

ROBBIE ROBERTSON

"We were doing some recording at the studio at Capitol Records in Hollywood and it was one thing, but there was such talk about just 'the vibe' and 'the sound' at this other place, Gold Star. We were kind of off the clock, and we were going to record some things that weren't necessarily going to be on the record, so we thought, 'Let's just go and check it out.' I think we were only there one day or two days.

"I thought the sound was really important to me, too. It still is. My first attraction to rock 'n' roll was just as much [about] the sound. . . . So when I heard these early Sun and Chess records, I thought, 'What is going on here?'"

The iconic Capitol Records building in L.A., c. 1960.

WHICH ONE IS BIG PINK?

Just before *Music from Big Pink* was completed, some executives at Capitol Records balked at releasing an album by "the Crackers," the name on the contractual agreement. A group decision was made to simply call themselves "The Band." Friends and neighbors routinely referred to them as The Band, evoking that potent sense of community that defined their musical identity. Strategically, it was good for business; the LP could be easily filed in bins domestically and internationally.

All that remained was the cover art, which, in keeping with their contrarian sensibilities, was absent a title, the artist's name, and an identifying photograph. Not exactly Marketing 101 for a debut recording, but less turned out to be a whole lot more. Bob Dylan painted the now-iconic cover, an evocative composition of musicians at work and play. The gatefold sleeve from photographer Elliott Landy opened to reveal a touching portrait of the group and their families, hardy, plainspoken folk who looked like they'd stepped out of a Willa Cather novel.

In the August 10, 1968 edition of *Rolling Stone*, Al Kooper suggested, "I hear the Beach Boys, the Coasters, Hank Williams, the Association, the Swan Silvertones as well as obviously Dylan and the Beatles. . . . The singing is so honest and unaffected." When I spoke to Kooper in 2017, he recalled, "I heard *Music from Big Pink* when it was finished at Albert Grossman's office. I went, 'Holy shit! This is ridiculous.' I didn't think it was gonna be like that. I had no idea what that was gonna be like. . . . I kicked myself for not going to the sessions since I was invited."

> **"Well, really we were on our own, and long away from Bob at that point, but thanks to Bob and his vehicle, I'm sure it helped us land a contract with Capitol Records as the Crackers. We even wanted to call the band the Honkies but . . . Capitol kind of came up with [the name The Band], or Richard Manuel—I'm not sure."**
> —Rick Danko to Dennis Loren, *RPM* magazine, July/August 1985

JOHN SIMON

"We went back to New York in springtime to mix the album. The mixing engineer was a fine, musical gentleman named Tony May who taught me a lot about mixing and with whom I had the pleasure of working many times over the years. The place we mixed [it was] the old Columbia mixing rooms now owned by A&R.

"Tony maintained a nonflusterable, gentlemanly equilibrium in the studio, which was often a subtle anchor for the loose-cannon personalities who were sometimes in the room. We tried to do as much live as possible. . . .

"Of course I loved the material. The songs drew from so many different traditions. The guys had a deep respect, bordering on reverence, for the roots of American music, stretching back from the music of their generation, through rockabilly and early rock 'n' roll, to the bluegrass of Appalachia, the blues of the Mississippi Delta, and even Stephen Foster and popular music of the nineteenth century. And it seemed to me that they had a sort of unspoken commitment to be as good as they could in order to earn their place as part of that tradition."

OPPOSITE: The cover artwork to the Band's groundbreaking July 1968 album *Music from Big Pink*, painted by Bob Dylan.

Bob, The Band, and Albert

ROBBIE ROBERTSON

"When we hooked up with Bob Dylan it was made clear to Bob and to Albert 'this is a whistle stop for us.' We are on our own path. We'll do this in the meantime but we're going to do our own thing. . . .

"After we did the thing with Bob [he] wanted to do more. But he had this accident and . . . Albert had no idea what we were or what we could do. No idea. He liked us. He thought it was really interesting what we did with Bob. But he said, 'I think I can get you a deal for doing an album of instrumentals of Bob Dylan songs.' So I said, 'All right. Let me talk to the guys about that.' And I thought, 'Albert has no idea.'

"When we recorded *Music from Big Pink*, Albert was astonished by the results of that record. And he so embraced it and made it his own and all that other stuff vanished. He was like, 'I knew it all along.' It fit so perfectly into his scenario.

"Bob and The Band were so close to Albert. We had been through everything together. Like I say in the book [*Testimony*], we were like war buddies. And we had gone to the edge together. And because we had done all that stuff and *The Basement Tapes*, and through all of this, [we] still had no idea of what this was going to be when we did it. That was thrilling.

In *Testimony*, Robertson recalls: "We had a little listening session at Albert's house in Bearsville. Bob came over with [his then-wife] Sara, and Al Aronowitz joined too. After some gourmet snacks, Albert put the acetate on for Bob, who was hearing it for the first time; we had all been busy and had wanted to finish the album before we shared it with him. 'Tears of Rage' started the record, and as it played Bob looked at me like he barely recognized me. At the end of the song, he yelled out, 'That was *incredible*, Richard!' Richard acted a little shy but thrilled. After each song, Bob looked at 'his' band with proud eyes. When 'The Weight' came on, he said, 'This is fantastic. Who wrote that song?'

"'Me,' I answered.

"He shook his head, slapped me on the arm, and said, 'Damn! You wrote that song.' What a joy it was to push Bob's button. At the end of 'I Shall Be Released' . . . he stood up and said, 'That was *so* good. You did it, man, you did it.'"

OPPOSITE: Albert Grossman, 1974.

" That was like an apprenticeship really. That was like boot camp. We were with [Bob Dylan] for three years.

"In America it worked pretty well, we played over here in England with Bob in 1965/66 and we got booed just about everywhere we went.

"Being with Dylan probably did help us, it would be silly to say it didn't, but I'd hate to say that we wouldn't have made it otherwise. It would have probably just taken us *longer*."

—Richard Manuel to Caroline Boucher, *Disc and Music Echo*, May 29, 1971

CHAPTER 6
SOMETHING WAS DELIVERED

On July 1, 1968, *Music from Big Pink* was shipped from distributors of the Hollywood-based Capitol Records to reviewers, radio stations, retailers, and rack jobbers, including Sam Goody, White Front, Discount Records, Musicland, the Wherehouse, Wallichs Music City, and Korvettes.

Playboy magazine published a rather interesting review of *Music from Big Pink* in their November 1968 issue: "While nobody in this untitled group really sings well, it doesn't matter; their instrumental conceptions and their togetherness are a gas on the likes of Robbie Robertson's 'To Kingdom Come' and Richard Manuel's 'We Can Talk.' All in all, it's one of the best folk-rock sets we've heard."

The release of *Music from Big Pink* in the summer of 1968, a little over a year after the Beatles' *Sgt. Pepper*, radically altered the music landscape, underscoring the myriad ways thoughtful musicians were seizing the moment, heedless of commercial considerations.

The music "business," for all its crass acquisitiveness, was, briefly, equally open to creative challenges. There was room for both Andy Williams and the Fugs. The suits didn't have to understand the music—just look at some of the advertising campaigns from the period. It was enough that they wanted proximity to the "next big thing," whatever it might be.

OPPOSITE: This iconic image of The Band was taken by noted photographer Elliott Landy in spring 1968, in the Woodstock hamlet of Bearsville, New York, and appears on the sleeve gatefold of *Music from Big Pink*.

Music from Big Pink arrived on the scene during a year of great turmoil in America. It was released on July 1, 1968, less than a month after Robert F. Kennedy was assassinated on June 5. Here, a memorial in the window of Lucy's El Adobe restaurant in Los Angeles in July 1968; the famed eatery was across the street from RFK's California headquarters.

ANDREW LOOG OLDHAM

"I loved the debut LP and felt they were changing the size and depth of the pitch we played on; they did what the first Paul McCartney album and subsequent *Ram* [1971] were supposed to be.

"Not that *Ram* was bad. It was a British breath of fresh air, the way that Paul McCartney stripped it all down. That's one thing. But here we are in the early summer of 1968 when the first Band album arrives. After what America had been through: Robert F. Kennedy getting killed in Los Angeles in early June 1968, and previously the murder of Martin Luther King Jr. in April 1968; recovery from the music of England from 1967 and '68, and us, the Rolling Stones in '67; and all the psychedelic bullshit, then this LP appears.

"It was the real *Heaven's Gate*. Michael Cimino should have filmed The Band's songs."

CHRIS DARROW
multi-instrumentalist, record producer

"In the summer of 1968, when *Music from Big Pink* was released, I had left the Kaleidoscope and was a member of the Nitty Gritty Dirt Band. B. Mitchel Reed, a disc jockey on KMET-FM in Los Angeles, spun the record for a week on his radio show. That's when I first heard the album and I loved it.

"I earlier became aware of the personnel of *The Band* through a drummer friend of mine, John Ware. He had grown up in Oklahoma and had taken drum lessons from Levon Helm. The songs on the album were great, the playing was organic, and the church-like, mystical sound of Garth Hudson's Lowrey organ sealed the deal. My favorite song is the classic, 'The Weight.'"

"*Music from Big Pink* arrived here in the late-'60s, a time when many native Americans were choosing self-imposed exile from their roots and realities. The Band, however, were five spiritually hungry young men who had left Canada, 'The Land of Snow,' committed to a respectful wandering. Their first album, *Music from Big Pink*, was simultaneously a celebration of and a rededication to the traditional values which many Americans were in various stages of discarding."
—Harvey Kubernik, *Crawdaddy* magazine cover story on Robbie Robertson, March 1976

Solomon Feldthouse, Chris Darrow, and Chester Crill of Kaleidoscope, performing at a be-in California, 1967.

SOMETHING WAS DELIVERED   85

Hudson Valley

JAMES CUSHING

The first Band LP and the earlier *Basement Tapes* evidence an environment where confinement and freedom are linked together. There is a sense of community, but not everyone is on top of everyone. Both Dylan and The Band had left traditional recording facilities in New York City and Nashville and were now working in a place where human agency and not record labels determined the product.

"I remember that, in 1968, we all had a sense of expectation for this album, since it was the closest thing to 'a new Bob Dylan album' since *John Wesley Harding*. But one of the marvelous things we all quickly discovered devouring *Big Pink* was Jaime Robbie Robertson, who not only played great guitar but had studied songwriting craft with Dylan.

"In hearing the debut Band LP and seeing the album graphics, one gets a sense of the rustic world that informs these recordings. But it's important to remember that the actual environment played a big part in the reality (not the myth!) of *Big Pink*. When you actually visit the Hudson Valley, you notice the large number of churches and bars in the area—places to sin, places to gain forgiveness. And between November and March, it's covered in snow. It's a world that's been going for two hundred years.

"West Saugerties and the surrounding vicinity gives context to the hymn-like aspect of 'I Shall Be Released' and 'This Wheel's on Fire,' two Dylan tunes that he gave to the newly christened Band to record. Also, *Big Pink* can be seen as a return to a place of cold weather, the promise of lots of snow. In other words, it's a place not unlike the Mesabi Range in northern Minnesota, where Dylan grew up.

"Bob Dylan's shadow does not loom or lurk around the album. It's a light. And the light shines at the very beginning and the very end. And the light shines on all the songs in the middle. . . . Curtis Mayfield's influence on the high-pitched vocal on 'I Shall Be Released' is obvious. Robbie Robertson had seen Mayfield with the Impressions in the early sixties and loved Curtis's guitar work and vocals.

"The more you listen, the more mysterious it becomes and the less you can explain what is going on. The visuals on the album and the rustic vibe were new as well."

View of Woodstock woods in the winter. As James Cushing notes, "that the actual environment played a big part in the reality. . . of *Big Pink*."

DENNY BRUCE
artist manager, record producer

"Sometime in the summer of 1968, Jack Nitzsche, Neil Young, and I heard The Band's *Big Pink* LP on Jack's home-stereo sound system in Hollywood, designed by engineer John Judnich—a longtime associate of Lenny Bruce, who also built the Whisky a Go Go house sound unit. Jack was producing Neil's debut solo LP at the Sunset Sound studio. Neil knew the group from Toronto and he said to me, 'If I would ever want to be in a band again, it would be with these guys.'"

GENE AGUILERA
author, music historian, record producer

"The first time I heard 'The Weight' was on the *Obscene Steven Clean* show, over the airwaves of KPPC-FM, the short-lived underground radio station out of Pasadena. It was *Big Pink* music. It was mountain music by The Band. American roots music brought to you by Canadians. After shaking down East L.A. to find the 45 (on the familiar Capitol Records orange-and-yellow swirl label) I *was* had—hook, line, and sinker. 1968 was a formidable year that saw album releases by the Beatles, Van Morrison, Hendrix, Cream, the Stones, and the Doors; yet the auspicious debut of *Music from Big Pink* was like a breath of fresh country air. Yes, they were Dylan's backup band—but Mr. Jones repaid his debts—by inking three chestnuts and painting the front cover."

DON WAS
multi-instrumentalist, record producer

"I heard about The Band's *Music from Big Pink* record, and anything associated with Bob Dylan was gonna get my attention. It appealed to me on a deep emotional level. And it transcended fashion. And fashion is the thing that keeps life cycles brief in popular music.

"In 1967, in Detroit, I was back at school and talking to Doug Fieger [later founder of the Knack]. I pulled Doug aside and he put me on headphones and it was the first time I heard *Are You Experienced* and *Fresh Cream*. I was on headphones from the Beatles' *Sgt. Pepper* going forward. And then, in 1968, *Music from Big Pink* on headphones!

"Detroit in the summer of 1968. I never heard anything like it in my life. Even though all the elements were familiar, no one put it together like those guys. They tapped into something. We call it Americana now. Like it evokes something from Stephen Foster. But I always felt The Band tapped into something really primordial. I can't quite explain it, but something that was a thousand years old. The music addresses the DNA. It was speaking to me in a special way."

RIGHT: Portrait of multi-instrumentalist and record producer (and current president of jazz label Blue Note) Don Was, 1989.

Although the album only reached No. 30 on the *Billboard* 200 chart when it was issued, it has become recognized over time as one of the most important albums in the history of rock, and its lead single, "The Weight," remains enshrined in various radio format programming. *Music from Big Pink* had such an outsize critical and musical influence that it is now considered one of the ur-texts in rock history.

Although well respected and hailed by nascent music press and trade magazines in their native homeland, it took a while for *Music from Big Pink* to attain pivotal radio rotation airplay and reach a high position on the charts in Canada.

JOHN DONABIE

"One morning back in the late '60s before CHUM-FM, I was coming in to do a Saturday shift at radio station CKFH. It was a Top 40 station, with one free-form show late in the evening. Anyway, as I pass the switchboard, I see an album laid out on the reception desk. Must have been delivered after hours. There was a note attached, addressed to Glenn "Big G" Walters, who was my mentor and a force within Toronto radio when Levon and the Hawks were on the scene.

"On that slip of paper was written: 'Glenn? Robbie Robertson here. Well we finally did it. I hope you like it Glenn.'

"It was *Music from Big Pink*. First time I ever saw it in person. Had to figure the boys were in town and Robbie dropped it off.

"I had seen the Hawks with Dylan at Massey Hall, but this would be the first time I would hear *MFBP*. When it came out we were in what was called a psychedelic era. Groups with wacky names and weird outfits. Suddenly here are these five guys who kind of resemble Quakers playing a mixture of rock 'n' roll, alternative country rock, mixing a dose of R&B as well."

PETER LEWIS
singer/songwriter, cofounder of Moby Grape

"When I heard those songs I was hooked. In my opinion they were the last voice from the subculture of the '60s. To me, their sound matched up exactly with their group-of-itinerant-preachers' look from the 1800s. This made them all the more hep to me since it proved to me that they could dig what people thought was cool about them."

LARRY LEBLANC

"Nobody in Canada . . . was waiting for *Music from Big Pink* because nobody knew for sure it was coming. Also nobody thought The Band—and we didn't even know they had a name at that point—had enough material to be an album group.

"Don't forget Levon and the Hawks had a handful of singles—'Stones That I Throw' reached No. 22 on CHUM chart in 1965—but nothing that you'd think of them being an album group. Plus when they left Toronto and were working on the album they were off the radar. . . .

"CHUM-AM in Toronto chose [to play] Jackie DeShannon's version of 'The Weight' and it might have reached No. 10 on the national *RPM Weekly* chart."

> "Levon drove The Band with his voice as much as his drums, and 'The Weight' found its perfect home in the tracks of *Big Pink*."
> —David N. Pepperell

JOHN BROWER
concert promoter

"*Music from Big Pink* was so good: The playing. The singing. The harmonies. All that stuff was transcendent. The Beatles' harmonies were amazing, but these were like a half-tone up and a quarter-tone over. Whatever you wanna call it, they were different. It was my kind of music. I was a Canadian who went to America in 1966 and came back in '68. So I could relate to where they had traveled."

DAVID N. PEPPERELL

"Like everyone else in Australia, I first heard of The Band with the single 'The Weight.' A Faulknerian fantasy with echoes of *Gunsmoke* and *Wyatt Earp*. With Dylan, the Hawks had all been gangsters, replete with black shirts and white ties, but now they had segued into the Jesse James Outlaw Gang sporting mustaches, beards, cowboy hats, jeans, and high-heeled boots. The times had changed again. . . .

"What a massive shockwave that album caused! Full of mystery songs, even a few by Dylan himself from the famous *Basement Tapes*, plus a plethora of musical gems from Robbie and Richard's pens. Despite having a few morbid ballads, as all country records do, the overall mood of *Big Pink* is of joy and discovery.

"Having so many great singers made The Band seem more like a medicine show than a rock band and there seemed no end to the different sounds they could get out of themselves. I loved Richard's mournful wail on 'I Shall Be Released' and 'In a Station' the most, I guess, but that is just cherry-picking the greatest from the marvelous."

ABOVE: Australian music journalist David N. Pepperell, 1966.

LEFT: "The Weight" (incorrectly attributed to artist Big Pink) ranked No. 29 on WKYC Cleveland's "Power Poll" of August 14, 1968. The classic single, which peaked at No. 63 on *Billboard*'s Hot 100 in September 1968, is still a staple on the radio today.

survey

#	Song (last week)	Artist
1	People Got To Be Free (1)	Rascals
2	Light My Fire (2)	Jose Feliciano
3	Magic Bus (5)	The Who
4	Born To Be Wild (4)	Steppenwolf
5	You Keep Me Hangin' On (3)	Vanilla Fudge
6	Dream A Little Dream Of Me (7)	Mama Cass
7	Eyes Of A New York Woman (10)	B. J. Thomas
8	Montage (8)	Love Generation
9	I've Gotta Get A Message To You (18)	Bee Gees
10	You're All I Need To Get By (13)	Gaye & Terrell
11	Fool On The Hill (21)	Sergio Mendes
12	Sealed With A Kiss (9)	Gary Lewis
13	Midnight Confessions (29)	Grassroots
14	Hush (25)	Deep Purple
15	Classical Gas (6)	Mason Williams
16	Do It Again (16)	Beach Boys
17	Stay In My Corner (12)	Dells
18	Sky Pilot (11)	Animals
19	On The Road Again (30)	Canned Heat
20	Love Is Like A Baseball Game (19)	Intruders
21	I Can't Stop Dancing (22)	Archie Bell
22	In-A-Gadda-Da-Vida (—)	Iron Butterfly
23	Tuesday Afternoon (23)	Moody Blues
24	Give A Damn (27)	Spanky & Our Gang
25	House That Jack Built (26)	Aretha Franklin
26	Don't Give Up (28)	Petula Clark
27	Six-Man Band (—)	Association
28	Harper Valley P.T.A. (—)	Jeannie C. Riley
29	The Weight (—)	Big Pink
30	Time Has Come Today (—)	Chambers Bros.

The WKYC Radio "Power Poll" represents the judgement of WKYC's record selection committee as to relative popularity of current recordings in the Cleveland area and is conditioned by such factors as industry tabulations and local record sales.

POWER PREMIERED AUGUST 14, 1968

The Band's maiden-voyage vinyl certainly made a big impression in the United Kingdom. The weekly music British periodical *Disc and Music Echo* bannered Dylan's Band as a cool rave LP of the month in its November 9, 1968 issue: "Piano and organ together—shades of Procol Harum—give a fine and rich sound. Bass and drums are unbelievably tight and exciting. And the guitarist is something of a genius. In fact the feel of the whole album is one of controlled magnificence." Ringo Starr, George Harrison, and Eric Clapton all hailed the platter.

During a May 29, 1971 interview that London-based reporter Richard Williams of *Melody Maker* conducted with Robbie Robertson, Williams asked Robertson about the origins of the band's piano-and-organ-group instrumentation.

"We were into gospel music . . . not particularly spiritual gospel music, black gospel music, but white gospel music," Robertson said. "It was easier to play. And it came more natural to us. We were trying to get a bigger sound going on—we had like piano, guitar, bass, and drums for a long time, and we tried horns and all kinds of things but there were too many people."

Robertson added, "So we realized that the only instrument that could make that fullness, and take the place of horns or anything like that, was an organ. We met Garth at that time, who was a hundred times superior musician to any of us. . . . I mean he was, to us, just a phenomenon. He could play rings around all of us put together, and he joined the group and his job was to play organ and horn and to teach us music . . . and the organ was incorporated and we thought, 'great,' we loved it."

In the March 1976 interview with Robbie Robertson for *Crawdaddy* magazine, I [Harvey] asked Robbie about the double-keyboard combination of piano and organ. I wondered if as a guitarist he ever felt suffocated by this format.

"No. I play as much as I want to play. No one is telling me 'Listen, you're playing too much.' That's my own decision. That's how much I prefer to do. When I hear other people play a lot more than required, I find it really drivel and there's nothing in this fuckin' wide world that's going to do anything for the song; I don't care. I like a good guitar part where it adds something, has a nice place and is a nice solo. Not too much, not too little. But I think as time goes on, it just takes different proportions, and too much is unnecessary."

Robertson's guitar theory seems to simply extend his basic life philosophy of unhurried discipline.

Or, as Bob Dylan said when he called to talk about Robbie for my *Crawdaddy* article, "Listen to his guitar playing. That's all you have to know about him."

"LISTEN TO HIS GUITAR PLAYING. THAT'S ALL YOU HAVE TO KNOW ABOUT HIM."
— BOB DYLAN

Robbie Robertson on guitar at the Woodstock Festival, August 17, 1969.

CHAPTER 7
FAITHFUL SERVANTS

Jonathan Taplin had the brains to land a coveted spot at Princeton University, but his rambunctious heart was committed to rock 'n' roll. It was 1965, a momentous year, when the bells of freedom not only chimed, they roared. Taplin, like so many of his baby-boom cohort, was infatuated with how pop music was becoming a defining aspect of one's life. It wasn't enough to say you could dance to it; you listened with a voraciousness that left no lyric or riff unexplored.

Taplin, all of eighteen and dying to be where the action was, attended the Newport Folk Festival, agog at Dylan's electrifying performance. It was a line in the sand, and Taplin reported for duty, come what may. He hustled a gig at Grossman's New York office, a gopher among the foxes and wolves. It helped pay the tuition; it also earned him a PhD in the bare-knuckle school of artist management and promotion.

Shortly before completing his degree in May 1969, Taplin had been reassigned to scout locations for The Band. In time he would become their tour manager (which no Ivy League education could prepare you for); his job that January was to locate a studio in Los Angeles for the group to record their second album.

Inspired by the harmonious setting of Big Pink, Taplin alighted upon a singular dwelling high in the Hollywood Hills off of Sunset Plaza Drive. It had the right admixture of attitude and architectural dignity. It was also Sammy Davis Jr.'s digs—how cool was that! (He allegedly bought it from Wally Cox, TV's *Mister Peepers*, and Marlon Brando's closest confidant, so there was definitely some mojo in the walls.) The pool house was repurposed as the studio, the recording equipment on loan from Capitol Records. And John Simon was brought back on board.

OPPOSITE: The vintage sign at the intersection of Hollywood Boulevard and Vine Street. The Band decamped for the Hollywood Hills in February 1969 to make their second album.

For all their rapscallion tendencies, the group remained disciplined throughout the low-fi recording process; the siren allure of L.A. remained tantalizingly at a distance while John and Levon labored to find the right drum sounds, Robbie fussed over guitars and vintage amps, and Garth unspooled a tangle of wiring that connected him—like Franklin's kite—to electromagnetism itself. It was, by everyone's reckoning, a kinetic experience.

"[We] found a big upright with a nice full sound and easy action. Garth and Levon found a vintage set of wooden drums in a pawnshop and we were off and running. We had heard a particular 'moaning' tom-tom sound that Ringo got on the Beatles records, and we worked to duplicate it." —John Simon

LEVON HELM

"Boy, [the drums] they sounded good on tape; the mics could really hear the difference between those wooden rims—more skins, more stick.

"We started playing with time, halving the beat, like 'Up on Cripple Creek.' The kickoff is kinda a hook, sets up the song and keeps repeating. Then there's a break and Garth does that 'jaw-harp' thing—a Clavinet through a wah-wah pedal—pulls your ear right in. And then we'd roll back through that kickoff again."

BELOW: Recording *The Band* in the Sammy Davis Jr. pool-house studio in the Hollywood Hills, 1968. From left to right: Rick Danko on the violin, John Simon and Garth Hudson sorting out wiring; Robbie Robertson on guitar; Levon Helm on mandolin. Engineer John Simon made the unconventional decision to work inside the room with the musicians instead of outside in a control booth. Photograph by Elliott Landy.

ROBBIE ROBERTSON

"Before *Big Pink*, I had had this dream of having a workshop. A place. A sanctuary where we could go into the privacy of our own world and do something and not be on somebody else's lawn, to really be in our own environment, let alone away from studio union breaks. . . . We go into a studio and the guy is like 'Well, it's almost 4:00 P.M. . . .' So all of these things are playing into it a little. Although the experience in the studio of recording *Music from Big Pink* was fabulous. . . . When I said 'we want to do this thing that started in the basement of Big Pink. We want to bring the equipment to us in our own atmosphere. And we want to record at whatever time we feel the spirit. We don't want to be on somebody's clock,' John was like, 'Okay.' 'We just need the equipment to come to us.' . . .

"We came to do it in Hollywood because it was too cold in Woodstock. And we were from Canada. So we knew cold and we knew when to get out of the way. So we thought 'Wouldn't it be wonderful to go and do this thing and go outside, where it feels beautiful and sunny and everywhere else it's stormy.' It was a good feeling inside and we felt we were getting away with something.

"I went to Dublin, Ireland, to do some experimenting with U2. . . . They were recording in the living room of Adam [Clayton]'s house, and when I walked in, the producer Daniel Lanois, Edge, and Bono said 'Does this feel familiar?' And I didn't quite understand what they meant. What they were saying was: 'You are the guys who started this whole thing.' When we [later] did *Stage Fright* at the Woodstock Playhouse, we brought the equipment into that room. But it's very common today."

JOHN SIMON

"Capitol Records had agreed to set us up with our own studio in a house in L.A. . . . complete with instruments, mixing board, eight-track recording machine, speakers, and even a clunky, old, but wonderful EMT reverb plate. They would send a maintenance engineer out every couple of days to make sure the equipment was in great shape. But other than that, there would be no recording engineer. We were on our own.

"By this point I realized that I preferred to be in the room with the musicians rather than behind a glass in the control room . . . being there in the room where the music was actually happening instead of being physically removed from it. It was a new thing to throw out the idea of a control room and set up the mixing console in the room with the musicians, but that's what we did. . . .

"[Sammy's pool house] was a capacious room. Down a short staircase was a bathroom that we sometimes used for additional echo, and up a short staircase was Levon's bedroom, which also became a hangout area for listening, writing, and playing checkers. We tried to do as much live recording as possible. We did do more overdubbing on this album than on the first, which was mostly recorded on four tracks. This time we took advantage of all eight tracks. When we got the speakers installed, we were anxious to try them out.

"Robbie was writing all the songs but didn't have everything done, so we would work on the parts until we had it all [worked out], then cut 'em the next day. I spent a lot of time at those sessions with my elbows on the baffles in front of Levon's drum doing multiple takes, workin' on different drum patterns for different songs."

The Producer's Tour of The Band

JOHN SIMON

"'Across the Great Divide' turned out to be the opening song on the album.

"Once again, these were days when programming the sequence of an album was real important. So, just as *Big Pink* had started with a slow mournful 'Tears of Rage,' this one started off, not in rhythm, but out of tempo ('rubato' in music lingo), Richard standing by the window in pain. After the song got going, those Band horns came in again. As a onetime horn player, I can't help but think that the horn sound Garth and I came up with was a big part of The Band's identification. Other horn parts that I heard on other recordings were clean, well-executed. Ours were rough—lots of 'personality.'

"On the next song, 'Rag Mama Rag,' the horn challenge was even greater. Rick came up with a fiddle part and there was no one to play the bass, so the guys said to me, 'Hey, you play the tuba, right?'

"Wrong. . . . I had played that baritone horn in high school, but that's a much smaller instrument. I had never played a tuba before. But that didn't stop us. We rented a tuba and I huffed and puffed into it. It took so much wind, I got dizzy a couple of times and started to see stars. But the show must go on.

"Garth played rollicking piano, Levon sang the lead and played mandolin, and Richard was the drummer. This is a good example of what I've called his 'galumphy' approach to the drums. But he kicks ass! What energy in this track.

"So the album began with the suicidal portrait of 'Across the Great Divide' and followed that with 'Rag Mama Rag,' which is a lot of fun. And so the pattern was set for an album whose pendulum swings back and forth between light-hearted joy and gravitas.

"'The Night They Drove Old Dixie Down' has a dead-serious lyric, intoned in Levon's authentic Delta drawl. At this point, one realizes that there's more to this album than just fun. Garth gets a harmonica sound out of his rig and plays a bona fide trumpet over the fade at the end.

"'Up on Cripple Creek' is pure fun again. Garth gets his Clavinet to sound like a Jew's harp. . . .

After he wrote the words to Richard's melody for 'Whispering Pines,' Robbie told me he'd never written a song like that before, and I suppose what he meant was a forlorn lyric about lost love. It was more like a lyric that Richard might have written, and it suits Richard's vocal perfectly. Levon and Richard play vocal ping-pong, sharing the last verse.

"'Look Out Cleveland,' though it was a rocker, had a doomsday lyric of foreboding. The organ in it reminds one of 'Chest Fever' from *Big Pink*. There's a tease of that organ solo at the end, but then it's cut off.

"'Jawbone' was intentionally tricky, rhythmically. We were always particular about what the drum patterns were. So, once again, I was a living music chart for Levon, leaning on one of the gobos in front of the drums and pointing at a particular drum or cymbal as we entered each new section of the song and it would be time to change the rhythm pattern. The song is another portrait, this one of a thief. And the person portrayed in the song that follows also did something wrong, though 'Unfaithful Servant' is sympathetic to its subject.

"Rick sings the lead but, instead of any harmony vocals, those moaning horns give him some support and there's a wonderful guitar solo that starts with tremolos worthy of a Neapolitan mandolin serenade.

"'King Harvest' is as serious as 'The Night They Drove Old Dixie Down,' but this time the subject is unionization. There's nice contrast in the lyrics. Levon sings an intro to each verse—a beautiful bucolic landscape sketch over almost no rhythm at all. No bones about it—Robbie Robertson can write a real good lyric. Then the rhythm picks up as Richard sings about the hardships of the hardscrabble working man. I got to play piano on this tune.

"'Rockin' Chair' is a touching portrait. A beautiful, wistful lyric. Here's Robbie, barely thirty, writing about being seventy-three. Nice imagery, nice stuff. Richard sings the lead until the choruses when the three voices stack up, Levon on the bottom, Rick in the middle, Richard singing falsetto on top."

The Band album evocatively portrayed southern, rural Americana, with songs like "Across the Great Divide," "King Harvest (Has Surely Come)," and "Up on Cripple Creek." Here, *Harvest Moon*, a Currier & Ives print of c. 1865.

In the spring of 1969, drummer Jim Keltner was the first musician in Hollywood to get a sneak peek of what The Band was concocting up at Sammy Davis Jr.'s place, when he was invited to a few sessions.

I [Harvey] spoke with him at length about this momentous occasion, first asking him to set up his introduction to The Band. "I was playing with the Charlie Smalls Trio," he told me. "Wilton Felder was the bass player. Charlie sang and played piano. We had two great girl singers. Charlie later wrote the big Broadway hit, *The Wiz*, which they later made into a movie. . . .

"I met The Band through my dear friend and the amazing bassist, Carl Radle. . . . Carl took me up to Sammy Davis Jr.'s house high up in the Hollywood Hills where The Band were doing their second album for Capitol. . . . Carl knew Levon and the guys, and he was the one who turned me on to the *Music from Big Pink* album. That album blew my mind. I listened to it all the time. I thought they were all Southern guys. And it was kind of a shock when I met them—Levon was the only guy from the South."

When Keltner recalled the experience of hearing the album and then attending the sessions, it was an emotional memory: "So to hear that *Big Pink* LP and then go to a couple of tracking sessions in Hollywood for their next album and to hear Levon singing and playing with one of the greatest singing bass players, Rick Danko, who always made me wanna cry," he said. "Such a sweet soulful voice. And Richard Manuel was the voice that sounded like it was coming straight from heaven. Garth Hudson creating a totally unique sound for The Band. His keyboards seemed to have a voice just as soulful and timeless as Rick and Richard's. And, of course, those epic songs and perfectly formed guitar parts and solos of Robbie Robertson."

RIGHT: Drummer Jim Keltner, who attended several of *The Band* 1968 album sessions in Hollywood, is shown here in July 1989.

In the summer of 1969, Keltner also encountered The Band in New York and attended a recording session. "I was in New York in July 1969 with Delaney and Bonnie," he remembered. "One night I ended up at the Hit Factory, I think, could have been A&R studios. John Simon and Robbie and the guys were mixing 'The Night They Drove Old Dixie Down.' They had recorded the track a few weeks earlier in Hollywood.

"I can't even begin to describe what that scene was like. I was sitting in the back on a couch watching this happen. There were four or five pairs of hands all over the studio console. The song seeped into my soul so much that later when I would hear it on the radio and remember that evening with those guys as they mixed, I would just cry. It still gets to me when I hear it. Levon makes you believe this guy Virgil Kane and his deep Southern pride. I am so glad I met Levon as early on as I did. His goodhearted soulfulness helped change my outlook on music and people. I will never tire of hearing The Band play and sing those great songs."

Keltner later toured with both Levon Helm and Rick Danko. "In 1989, Levon, Rick Danko, and I all played together in the first Ringo Starr & His All-Starr Band," he said. "We had Billy Preston and Dr. John on keys, Joe Walsh and Nils Lofgren on guitars, and Clarence Clemons on tenor sax. Every night was such a treat to hear all those guys doing their solo spots."

"If you are a singing drummer, you have a great advantage. I've always played to the vocal, and I found out that Ringo and countless other drummers, I'm sure, do as well. Levon was able to push or pull the groove any way he felt it by singing and playing at the same time. The way he felt space was magnificent. His biggest influences were the blues bands he heard as a young man, the geniuses from the Delta and around where he was from."
—Jim Keltner

Keltner toured with Levon Helm and Rick Danko and members of the first Ringo Starr & His All-Starr Band, shown here in c. 1989. Left to right: top row—Clarence Clemons, Billy Preston, Rick Danko; middle row—Dr. John, Ringo Starr, Joe Walsh; bottom row—Jim Keltner, Levon Helm, Nils Lofgren.

FAITHFUL SERVANTS

The Band declined to tour until late spring 1969. In the early summer of 1968, Bill Graham had actually driven up to Woodstock to meet the group and their manager Grossman to pitch a debut at one of his Fillmore venues. At first, Grossman and The Band didn't jump on the initial proposal; they didn't have fond memories of their 1966 tour with Bob Dylan, they preferred to remain in Woodstock, and the figures suggested didn't sway a firm commitment. Besides, their reputation and album reviews were doing the roadwork for them. But Graham's offer was seriously considered, and a late 1968 booking was put in motion.

Then Rick Danko suffered an automobile accident, breaking his neck and back and placing him in traction for many months in the fall and winter of '68, delaying their projected concertizing.

Meanwhile, Robbie stockpiled songs earmarked for Band recordings. Others in the group liked to party and enjoy indoor fireworks. But the aloofness and limited media accessibility around the music-making clan all seemed to create a growing mystique, first taught to them at a music business college operated by professors Dylan and Grossman.

Mystique can only take you so far though; it was time for The Band to perform in concert. Their reluctance was understandable, given their formative years living and breathing the toxic fumes of life on the road. With Rick having sufficiently recovered from his accident, no other excuses availed themselves. Finally, in early 1969, Bill Graham met with Robbie, employing that snake-charmer's guile to coax them to the stage. The Band agreed to play three nights at the Winterland Ballroom in San Francisco—April 17, 18, 19—to be followed by two nights in May at Graham's newly opened Fillmore East.

Before the first show, Robertson came down with a debilitating condition—physical or psychological, no one could say for certain. It was perhaps the flu or a case of the nerves. Medical professionals were notified, but his condition didn't improve.

John Simon knew a brain surgeon in the area who suggested Dr. Pierre Clement, a hypnotist, who then made a house call to the Seal Rock Inn Motel. He cast a spell that would allow the guitarist to rise, phoenix-like, and rock an increasingly perturbed crowd, primed to welcome their new heroes.

What they got was just over thirty minutes of a group barely there, Robertson clinging to his Telecaster as if it were a life jacket. The fans were as crestfallen as the band. Fortunately, the next two nights went without a hitch.

> "It just went on and on, into the second set Friday night and through both performances on Saturday. Richard Manuel's vocal on 'Tears of Rage' was probably the finest singing that has ever been heard at Winterland; so dramatic that one could almost see the song's story taking place on stage."
>
> —Greil Marcus,
>   *Good Times,* April 23, 1969

OPPOSITE: The Band onstage during their virtuoso performance at Fillmore East, New York, May 9, 1969. Photograph by Elliott Landy.

GREIL MARCUS

author of *Mystery Train*; *Good Times* newspaper review of the Winterland shows, April 23, 1969

"They are an amazing group of musicians. Not one of them stands out as a star, and yet they're each of them as distinctly different as the Beatles. . . . They went through their repertoire, each song more exciting and colorful than the last, and then Hudson began to play the organ solo that leads into 'Chest Fever,' perhaps their best composition, certainly their most effective performance in person. When the whole band took over, the music seemed to expand, filling the hall to all of its corners, not blasting away the emptiness but simply making it impossible for anything else to occupy the same bit of space and time. Robertson heightened the drama of the song by hitting tough notes at the end of every line, and a tension grew up around the room, out of a realization that something monumental was happening and we were there to hear and see it."

The Band at Fillmore East

ANDREW SOLT

"I graduated from college the day I turned twenty-one in December 1968. I was looking forward to starting UCLA journalism school six months later, and now I had a serious chunk of free time.

"With my best friend, Jack Egan, we sailed off in my VW bug in May and headed out from L.A. to New York via anywhere in between. We set out in search of great music, awe-inspiring national parks, and never-seen cities we would discover across America. It was my first cross-country adventure.

"Rock music blasted from our windows and through the sunroof. *Nashville Skyline* was on the radio and in the foreground. The Band, Dylan, the Beatles, the Stones, and the sound of rock and R&B's finest were accompanying us as the heartland spring of '69 embraced us.

"When we were in New York City, we heard The Band would be appearing that weekend at the Fillmore East. I loved everything about *Music from Big Pink* (from the cover to the delights on the vinyl) and I couldn't believe I might actually be able to see them live. I had seen them in December 1965 when they were Dylan's touring band, but they had come a long way in the intervening few years.

"This was an opportunity that could not be missed. It was one of the best of all the gifts that came my way on that eye- and mind-opening trip. To see The Band performing songs from *Big Pink* and their follow-up album, *The Band*, seemed way too good to be true. We made sure we arrived at the Fillmore East in time to buy tickets at the box office. And then the curtain went up.

"Their magical sound—that unique, perfected blend of American roots music mixed with soul-stirring R&B, was on display before us. Robbie, Levon, Rick, Garth, and Richard were spinning their beautiful musical web. It was entrancing.

"I can't recall the specifics of their set, but I do remember one thing. It was beyond perfection. I think it included 'Tears of Rage,' 'Chest Fever,' 'The Night They Drove Old Dixie Down,' 'I Shall Be Released,' and undoubtedly one of the greatest songs of the twentieth century—'The Weight'—and many more. The Band was as tight and pure as it gets. It remains way up there as one of the greatest musical nights of my life."

Although the majority of *The Band* album was done inside Sammy Davis Jr.'s pool house-turned-recording studio, "Up on Cripple Creek," "Whispering Pines," and "Jemima Surrender" were cut in New York at the Hit Factory. On the weekend of May 9–10, 1969, they performed two successful shows at Bill Graham's Fillmore East in New York; *New York Times* reviewer Mike Jahn noted that they breathed "fresh country air" into the venue, "and worked into a rocking fever of an intensity seen only occasionally."

Then, on the weekend of June 21–22, 1969, the Toronto Pop Festival was held. It would be the first time the Hawks returned to Toronto as The Band. Ken Walker and John Brower were the promoters.

JOHN BROWER

"The Band were friends of mine. When they played with Ronnie Hawkins, I was a young musician playing bass and singing in a band in 1963 called the Diplomats, in Toronto. Ronnie was truly amazing in his heyday. And the Hawks were the high-water mark. I had the Rockpile club in Toronto during the late sixties on Yonge Street. I knew Albert Grossman through Robbie Robertson, because his best friend Jerry Hebscher was my aide-de-camp.... Albert was the guru. It was like being in the presence of John Lennon.

"The Band had a problem playing for me at their first outdoor date in June 1969 at Varsity Stadium at the Toronto Pop Festival. Thirty thousand people a day for two days. A milestone. Steppenwolf... coming home to Canada for the first time.... The Band couldn't get the right sound check. It was not happening.... Bill Hanley, considered 'the father of festival sound,' brought a great system and they couldn't get their sound right before we let people in. Robbie was not happy with that but still played a great set. Everybody had a good time."

Toronto radio station 1050 CHUM-AM's *CHUM Chart* ad for the Toronto Pop Festival of June 21–22, 1969, featuring The Band along with Sly & the Family Stone, Steppenwolf, Chuck Berry, and others.

In the summer of 1969, the new Los Angeles–based TMQ (Trademark of Quality) label released an underground album clothed in an unassuming plain white cover. Eventually titled *Great White Wonder*, this was the first real rock bootleg recording—a Bob Dylan two-LP set of multiple-source demos and room recordings that housed seven tracks culled from summer 1967 Dylan/Band sessions in West Saugerties, coupled with 1961 recordings done in a Minnesota hotel room; studio outtakes from an assortment of Dylan albums; and audio performances from Dylan's June 7, 1969 appearance on the ABC-TV *Johnny Cash Show*.

KPPC-FM in Pasadena, California, would spin Bob Dylan's version of "This Wheel's on Fire," which differed from the same Dylan/Rick Danko composition on *Music from Big Pink*. Record collectors and Dylan freaks, as well as a whole generation of music sleuths, further discovered The Band away from the bosom of Bob.

The album was initially stocked and sold behind the counter by vendors in Southern California independent underground record stores. The popularity of the coveted item heard on regional radio stations including KMET-FM and KRLA initiated a national demand for this illegal audio pleasure, which by September of that year had generated press coverage in *Rolling Stone*, the *Wall Street Journal*, and the *Los Angeles Herald-Examiner*.

DAVID N. PEPPERELL

"*Great White Wonder* was very hard to find in Melbourne, Australia. Record shops wouldn't stock it for fear of reprisals from CBS Records, and mail order has never been a big thing in Australia. I finally found it in a flea market in a small lane in the city.

"[The songs] seemed to be a whole new direction in songwriting for Bob Dylan—not so much the prophesying or pamphleteering of his previous work but more an attempt to write simple, mysterious songs about strange people and places. The tracks collectively known as *The Basement Tapes* were remarkable—I knew some of them as they had been hits for other bands, but most of them were quite new.

"A reviewer over here titled his review of *GWW* 'Dylan's Isolation,' and I echo that. He was so far ahead of anyone else in his chosen sphere at that time, and nothing illustrates that more than the *Basement Tapes* tracks on this amazing double LP."

JAMES CUSHING

"It was selling for $10, which was more than my teenaged allowance would allow. The friend's copy I heard had both the Dylan/Cash songs from the 1969 TV broadcast, no more than two or three outtakes from *Freewheelin'*, a side from *The Basement Tapes*, and the rest from the December 1961 *Minnesota Hotel Tape* recorded at Bonnie Beecher's apartment in Minneapolis (she hosted so many out-of-town travelers that her pad came to be known as Bonnie Beecher's Hotel)."

LEFT: The mysterious spare album cover of 1969's *Great White Wonder*, the first real rock bootleg recording, which featured a range of Dylan recordings and outtakes as well as Bob Dylan/The Band recordings from 1967.

"THE *MINNESOTA* SIDES HAD AN EDGY URGENCY THE FIRST COLUMBIA LP LACKED. THE BASEMENT TAPES SIDE WAS OF SUCH LOW FIDELITY THAT I FELT AS THOUGH I WERE LISTENING TO MUSIC RECORDED IN THE EARLY NINETEENTH CENTURY ON WOOD OR SOMETHING."
—JAMES CUSHING

Max Yasgur's dairy farm in Bethel, New York, could never be confused with the pine-scented glens and glades or the swooping mountaintops that define the Elysian allure of mythic Woodstock. But in an early example of branding winning out over geography, Sullivan County's gentle fields played host to the now-storied Woodstock Festival: 3 Days of Peace & Music on August 15–17, 1969.

The Band were the only musicians scheduled to perform who actually lived in Woodstock, approximately sixty miles northeast from the festival site.

Concert promoter Michael Lang convinced Albert Grossman that this was a golden opportunity, gilding the lily by booking The Band to close the festival on Sunday, August 17. After Jefferson Airplane finished their set Sunday morning at 9:40 A.M., there was a break of several hours, followed by sets that began at 2:00 P.M. and went until 11:10 A.M. on Monday the eighteenth. The lineup, in order of appearance, was: Joe Cocker and the Grease Band; Country Joe and the Fish; Ten Years After; The Band; Johnny Winter; Blood, Sweat & Tears; Crosby, Stills & Nash (and Young); the Paul Butterfield Blues Band; Sha Na Na; and Jimi Hendrix.

ROBBIE ROBERTSON

"I'll tell you something. It doesn't matter if there's thirty or three hundred thousand—once you get in front of people, you have to do something. The festivals are for people to get together. Who is playing is secondary.

"Anytime we've done those things, we've never really felt natural about doing it. We played the large dates because some terrific people were involved or we admired the other acts and they asked us to. We're a puppet show in the distance, and the music is an excuse."

BELOW: Henry Diltz's portrait of the soaked, bedraggled crowd at the Woodstock Festival (August 15-17, 1969), during one of the weekend's several rainstorms. As Levon Helm noted in his memoir, by the festival's third day, Sunday, when The Band was set to appear, "The crowd was real tired and a little unhealthy."

The maddening logistics, foul weather, and residual mayhem (courtesy of the ubiquitous "brown acid") led to a litany of delays and foul-ups. Helicoptering into this hippie-dreamscape-turned-sodden-quagmire, The Band acceded to Jimi Hendrix's earnest request that he be the last one standing (which he did on a debilitated Monday morning).

And so, around 10:00 P.M., The Band took the stage, much like the Rough Riders taking San Juan Hill. Indifferent to cries of "Boogie!" and "Rock 'n' roll!" they performed songs mostly plaintive and mindful in tone, more akin to a front-porch reverie than a hell-raisin' bacchanal. Closing with the Ivy Jo Hunter/Stevie Wonder composition and Motown standard "Loving You Is Sweeter Than Ever," The Band confirmed their rising status as uncompromising artists (enhanced by playing under the darkest operational lighting).

Levon Helm, in his memoir *This Wheel's on Fire*, co-written with Stephen Davis, recalled "There weren't any dressing rooms because they'd been turned into emergency clinics. . . . The crowd was real tired and a little unhealthy."

Woodstock Journal Entry
August 16-17, 1969 Henry Diltz

8/15 Fri. Walked down the hill shooting crowd pics and performers. Onstage pics of Richie Havens, Canned Heat, Joan Baez. All the time defending my shooting space & right to be there against over-efficient security boys & pushy movie co.

8/16 Sat. Left house at 9. Went back roads & arr at 11 in caravan of J. Airplane station wagons. Walked around taking pics, trailer, hog farm (dancers) perf. John Sebastian onstage. Jefferson Airplane at Dawn. Went to sleep on mattress in a sta. wagon.

8/17 Sun. Pics of Joe Cocker. Lens broke. I fixed it in Mike Hanley's trailer. Then camera was fogged & in fixing it some 'helpful' *Crawdaddy!* Photog tried to switch Nikon bodies & prisms & make off. Telling me someone had stolen my body. I called Ins in LA to get several #'s & he feigned discovery of my camera. Pics all nite. Band, J Winter, CSN&Y.

Photographer Henry Diltz at the Monterey International Pop Festival, Monterey, California, 1967.

FAITHFUL SERVANTS

The Grateful Dead's Jerry Garcia, January 1971.

JERRY GARCIA

"Woodstock. The ultimate calamity. It was raining and it got dark and we went on. There was maximum confusion going on about sound logistics. Really weird. . . . The stage had sheet metal on it. It's wet, and I'm getting incredible shocks from my guitar.

"It's dark, and you don't see any audience, but four hundred thousand people are out there. Then, somebody says the stage is about to collapse. I'm standing there in the middle of this, trying to play music. Then they turn on the lights, and they're a mile away. Monster supertroopers. Totally blinding, and you can't see anything at all.

"Here's this energy and everything is horribly out of tune. 'Cause it's all wet, damp, and humid. It was humbling. That was a total disaster from our point of view. We played probably the worst set of our career. I'd like that one erased from the books."

RICHARD BOSWORTH

"When The Band took the stage . . . in addition to the dampness it got very cold. Musical instruments and musicians' hands can be challenged by that kind of weather. Guitars go out of tune and bodies stiffen up, and that's how The Band came off at Woodstock. Stiff and wooden. Of course the audience was under the effects of the weather as well, and we were pretty uncomfortable at that point. . . .

"One noticeable element was the unique way the group set up. Garth Hudson was in the center on a high riser, normally the place the drums would be, and Levon was far right facing stage right, not facing the crowd. Richard Manuel was far left facing stage left, and Rick and Robbie were in the center below Garth.

"I had been very excited about seeing them. *Music from Big Pink* was such a world-changing record in 1968. . . . Their second album wouldn't be released until the following month, and they didn't play anything from that. I had high expectations but was slightly disappointed by The Band's perfunctory performance. I've since seen video where they play with great feeling and fire, but at Woodstock that was not the case."

GRAHAM NASH

"Woodstock. The getting together of half a million people that thought the same way that we did. Hanging out backstage in John Sebastian's tent . . . and then realizing that nobody there has ever seen our band. And this is the Grateful Dead, The Band, Richie Havens, John Sebastian, and Santana. None of them had ever seen us. They loved the record and they were all going 'Well, you know, fuckin' show us. Shit or get off.'"

OPPOSITE PAGE, TOP ROW: From left to right: Rick Danko, Richard Manuel, Garth Hudson, Robbie Robertson. BOTTOM: Levon Helm and Robbie Robertson, during The Band's evening performance at Woodstock on August 17, 1969.

"I'll tell you something. It doesn't matter if there's thirty or three hundred thousand—once you get in front of people, you have to do something." —Robbie Robertson

FAITHFUL SERVANTS 109

"For rock 'n' roll . . . these people are not opera singers, okay? It's not the business of how fine and pristine your voice is. They came to see you perform . . . It's about the entertainer enjoying himself. Not the audience. Hopefully the audience will. If the entertainer is enjoying himself and feels at home on a stage, that's 50 percent of it." – Grace Slick

Jefferson Airplane performing at Woodstock, August 16, 1969.

The Band didn't appear in Warner Bros.' 1970 Oscar-winning *Woodstock* documentary or the multiplatinum-selling triple-album soundtrack on Atlantic Records' Cotillion label, also released in 1970.

Looking back, it only added to their mystique. Sometimes less is truly more. But there were reasons you didn't see the group onscreen or hear them on your turntable.

"Somebody from the movie approached us with the proposition that if you want to be in the movie, you have to give back half of what you get from the concert in return for a percentage of the profits from the movie," Robertson told *Rolling Stone* journalist Phil Levy in the magazine's July 9, 1970 issue. "We turned them down. He still wanted to film us, and we said okay, but no fooling around on the stage and don't interfere with our performance. So, they filmed and taped it."

In the May 29, 1971 issue of *Melody Maker*, Rick Danko explained to interviewer Richard Williams: "I just didn't feel that their sound was too together, and I didn't believe that it would be the sort of film that I'd want to look at myself in twenty years from now because I'm sure all that comes back, at one time or another. To me it was terrible. It was not our PA system; we were using other people's facilities, which means that we didn't have any control over it, and if you can't control it then I don't consider the people are getting their money's worth."

The Band onstage at Woodstock, August 17, 1969.

The Isle of Wight sits in the English Channel, a windswept landscape worthy of J.M.W. Turner's brush, once home to the poet Alfred, Lord Tennyson. Twelve days after the Woodstock Festival, three British producers and organizers, Ray, Ronnie, and Bill Foulk, staged their own multiday music extravaganza highlighted by Bob Dylan's August 31 return to the concert stage, accompanied by The Band.

The Who, Joe Cocker, and Richie Havens were fellow sojourners from Woodstock, helping to facilitate a tempest of rock music gatherings throughout England and the Continent over the next couple of years.

The rock aristocracy turned out in full force: Keith Richards and Charlie Watts represented the Stones; John, George, and Ringo for the Fabs.

A press conference in Britain ahead of the Isle of Wight Festival of August 30–31, 1969; from left to right: Rick Danko, Robbie Robertson, Bob Dylan, and festival cofounder Ray Foulk.

" I worked with [engineer/producer] Glyn Johns to record Bob Dylan and The Band at Isle of Wight… then Albert Grossman called me a little later and asked what I wanted. Expenses and a fee. Albert was in love with The Band. He thought they were the Holy Grail."
–Elliot Mazer
 audio engineer, producer

Bob Dylan "resplendent in a tailored white suit" at the Isle of Wight.

FAITHFUL SERVANTS

But there was room for only one star turn here, and he was no longer the pixilated dandy wearing a polka-dotted shirt. Strolling onstage after a three-year absence (and a two-and-a-half-hour delay to clear some disruptive members from the bedraggled throng—two hundred thousand, according to some press reports), Dylan was resplendent in a tailored white suit, short-cropped curly hair, and a cabbage-patch beard. He busked his way through an hour's worth of material, some new—"Lay Lady Lay"—some old—"It Ain't Me Babe"—and some having gathered dust in a certain hallowed basement—"The Mighty Quinn (Quinn the Eskimo)."

The Band had preceded Dylan with a set of their own, having quickly found the groove that defined their halcyon '66 tours. In a September 2, 1969, review in the *Guardian*, music journalist Geoffrey Cannon commented: "Robbie Robertson and Levon Helm, especially, know each other so well that as they sing and play together, interchanging instruments, their music becomes love's body, which they create, but which does not belong to them. They celebrate their own music, rather than invent it."

A bootleg of the concert quickly made the rounds; it took Sony Music and its Columbia/Legacy imprint another forty-four years to release the master tape. It was worth the wait.

Isle of Wight Festival headliners Bob Dylan and The Band, August 31, 1969.

FAITHFUL SERVANTS 115

CHAPTER 8

RIGHT CREEK, RIGHT PADDLE

Second albums were real make-or-break affairs for groups trying to establish themselves as more than a flash look and maybe a catchy hook that got them some media attention. The Band were bucking all the musical trends of the time, dismissing the paisley prissiness of pop and the inertial drag of whacked-out jam bands.

They drew their sound from music deeply rooted in the loamy soil of the South, the slap echo of the Midwest high plains, of New York's Jazz Age, of the Anglican church, and of the European baroque. They could not have been less attuned to what was commercially trending, what other "hip" bands were getting into. They carved their own path—like water, like wind—and when the novelty of *Music from Big Pink* was over, what did their contrariness deliver? For many, perhaps the best album of all time. They called it simply, most eloquently, *The Band*.

On September 22, 1969, *The Band* was released by Capitol Records. Critics raved.

Mike Jahn, in a *Pop Scene Service* syndicated review of October 11, 1969, proclaimed "The album, simply called *The Band*, is less complicated than *Big Pink*. Approaching this album, the question is how can they possibly top *Music from Big Pink*? Apparently, they have succeeded by not even trying.

"This new album is not cataclysmic, poetic, and intellectually wiry in the same way *Big Pink* was. It is just a collection of tunes; melodies and songs to be appreciated leisurely and without intense analysis. *The Band* is such a record. It is pleasant, relaxed and funky in the group's unique mountain way."

OPPOSITE: An outtake by Elliott Landy from the 1969 photo shoot for *The Band* album cover; the image was taken on a rural road in Zena, a hamlet of Woodstock.

The album's most enduring track, "The Night They Drove Old Dixie Down," powerfully evokes this sense of time and place. Like a Stephen Crane short story, Robertson places the listener in the midst of fraught conflict, the martial cadences of Levon's drum fills rising and falling like soldiers facing their fate, the scent of death wafting through the chorus with poignant urgency. Within the song's three-plus minutes, The Band reaches a kind of apotheosis, the torment of North versus South made manifest in the very life stories of the musicians themselves, bridging the greatest of divides.

"Rockin' Chair" is another example of The Band's protean ability to shape-shift their personalities to suit the song. Richard moved to the drums, and he lays down a warm, amber groove; Rick paws at the fiddle and Levon picks leads on the mandolin, its stately, higher-pitched gleam offset by the campfire-heartiness of Garth's accordion. John Simon holds the bass part down on the tuba. All together, they sound like timeless mariners, giving voice to a truth only something barrel-aged can bestow. Indeed, throughout the album, there is

JAMES CUSHING

"It's an album with a William Faulkner vibe and it's filled with beautifully familiar hymn tunes to an America that may have actually existed in history.

"On some level, both Rick Danko and Levon Helm have said Richard Manuel was The Band's true lead singer. All you have to do is listen to 'King Harvest (Has Surely Come).' It's an absolutely convincing vocal performance. You get the sense that this person has found a way to bring a true emotional presence into play in such a way that doesn't overwhelm or flood him or anyone else. That the mind and the heart and the body are somehow in perfect balance in this."

BELOW: A rare image of soldiers at a Confederate camp—in garb reminiscent of the Band's nineteenth-century-inspired attire—at the Warrington Navy Yard in Pensacola, Florida, c. 1861. "The Night They Drove Old Dixie Down" powerfully evokes the sense of the time and place of the Civil War era.

> "I'm Canadian and I wrote the song about the Civil War ['The Night They Drove Old Dixie Down']. I didn't know the story and it fascinated me. Everyone else took it for granted—they read about it in history class. When it's strictly about yourself you're 'not allowed to deal with fiction.' So it's something that opens the gates a little bit."
>
> —Robbie Robertson to Harvey Kubernik, *Crawdaddy*, March 1976

a palpable sense of battles won and lost, of spirit taking flight, and bodies sundered. As in a Mathew Brady photograph, many of the songs evoked an antebellum world on the brink, tradition at the precipice.

Songwriter Robbie Robertson has done his share of writerly introspection, grasping at any glimmer of a word or phrase that opened a lyrical door, and then honing it down to its essential core. In the March 1976 *Crawdaddy* interview [with Harvey] the tunesmith explained his process:

"I just think it's part of storytelling," Robertson reinforced. "It isn't anything to put the songs in the third person. Sometimes when you get that little detachment you can write about more."

Regarding Robertson's guitar solo in the track, Robbie outlined the methodology to Kevin Ransom of *Guitar Player Magazine* in May 1995.

"I was sitting with my amp literally beside me, because we recorded it live, in a small room, and I didn't want my guitar to leak into the other mikes. . . . I was plugged into this old Gibson amp with a very dry, low-fi sound with no top and no bottom. Typically, you really had to crank these things up to get them to speak, but 'Harvest' didn't call for that. I wanted a dry sound so that the basic drums and guitar all seemed like they were coming out of the same speaker."

MICHAEL MACDONALD
Australian writer

"In early March 1970, I was quite enamored with Ronnie Hawkins's Atlantic 45 'Down in the Alley.' . . . . One of my then–high school classmates had an older brother, very much a serious music head, who had gotten wind of this and decided to give me a potted history on Hawkins himself. It was also suggested that if I were serious about good music I should investigate The Band's first two albums . . . and understand their uniqueness.

"What I first heard on both albums was almost alien—their music owed nothing to psychedelia and it was as if the British Invasion never happened. [It] sounded a hundred years old, played by five men who looked as if they'd walked off the set of *McCabe & Mrs. Miller*. Lyrically it owed more to William Faulkner and Mark Twain than it did to Dylan, who had donated three songs and the cover art to their debut album. Their own offerings seemed to have come from riverboats, gambling houses, and tobacco fields, and were instantly memorable on so many levels.

"There were other anomalies—a five-piece combo that housed both piano and organ, a guitarist who played with remarkable economy and three distinctive vocalists. . . . Pianist and sometimes-drummer Richard Manuel sang like a tortured Ray Charles; bassist Rick Danko was something of a hillbilly soul man; and drummer Levon Helm, a youngish man, could yowl like a rural bluesman twenty years his senior. No surprise that I was captivated.

"The Band never really had a big hit record in Australia but they gained enough airplay . . . and their influence was certainly demonstrative. There was a time when nearly every Aussie band aimed to sound like the Beatles, but, as the '60s leaked into the '70s, many local combos wanted to be just like The Band. That, in itself, says it all."

On November 2, 1969, The Band performed "Up on Cripple Creek" on CBS's *The Ed Sullivan Show*. As much a right of passage as the run of a gauntlet, appearing on Sullivan's nationwide broadcast had enormous impact as a promotional tool for new as well as established artists. Grossman jumped at the prospect; the group, having passed on *The Glen Campbell Show*, was not about to skip out on America's favorite Sunday-night pastime.

Arriving in New York a few days earlier to rehearse—Levon was particularly nervous—they shared the stage with singer Pearl Bailey, country & western stalwart Buck Owens, and comedian Rodney Dangerfield, who, the story goes, hit the boys up for some "reefer."

Performing live (a major inducement), the group found itself positioned among stacks of hay; all that was missing from this cornpone tableaux was Rick chewin' some straw and Arnold the pig skittering across the set. The show's director, who seemed to have taken the "drunkard's dream" lyric a little too literally, insisted on tight shots throughout, creating a peculiar tension that stripped the musicians of their vaunted interplay—five bewhiskered heads in search of a body.

Surprisingly, Sullivan called them over for that priceless moment where the stolid host parries with the "something for the kids." He stumbled over the pronunciation of Levon's name ("What is that? *Leh-von* or *La-von*? "*Lee-von*," said Richard) but seemed genuinely charmed by their hearty, rusticated appearance.

Audiences were equally enthusiastic, pushing *The Band* into the rarefied air of the Top 10. Their *Ed Sullivan* appearance was a coronation of sorts, a bunch of hirsute tumbleweeds, as far-removed from the pageantry of pop in ways the old crowd from Yonge Street could scarcely imagine.

Stills from The Band's performance of "Up on Cripple Creek" on *The Ed Sullivan Show*, November 2, 1969.

RIGHT CREEK, RIGHT PADDLE 121

Time for The Band

ELI ATTIE

The Band's second album was hailed as a touchstone event in the burgeoning world of rock music as a fine art. There was a December 1969 photo shoot for a *TIME* magazine cover by acclaimed photographer David Attie. His son, writer and producer Eli Attie, recounted the story behind the photos, shown here:

Pages 122-125: Acclaimed photographer David Attie took these striking images—perhaps the only studio photographs of The Band at this time—in December 1969 for a January 12, 1970 *TIME* magazine cover. In the end an illustration was used instead, and the photographs remained unseen until they were unearthed in 2014.

"In very late 1969, TIME magazine decided to do a cover story on The Band, a nod to how important they'd already become—influencing the Beatles, Eric Clapton, and many others with their rootsy, back-to-basics sound. It may be hard to appreciate what a singular honor this was for a rock band forty-four years ago. TIME was in every way the voice of the establishment. Few rock acts had ever been featured on its cover, and not a single one from America or Canada. (The Beatles had only made the cut in late '67, after Sgt. Pepper had become a global phenomenon; the Stones wouldn't grace a TIME cover until 1989.)

"David Attie was asked to shoot the cover, and took studio portraits, which were extremely rare for The Band—these may be the only such photos from their peak period. They were taken in Saugerties, New York, although the exact location is not known. You can almost feel the weight of the moment in Attie's images.

"The Band were certainly trying to look their best, from the careful crease pressed into Levon Helm's jeans, to the shiny new shoes and boots that all but Robbie Robertson appear to be wearing. Attie's intention was to blend these individual portraits together to make a photo-collage, using instruments and sheet music as well, which he photographed separately.

"Ultimately, TIME decided not to use photographs at all, opting for a Bob Peak drawing of The Band on its January 12, 1970 cover. The Band's appearance on a TIME cover is still mentioned as a career highpoint. Yet these images were never published or seen until their rediscovery by Attie's estate last year."

Jay Cock's cover story in the January 12, 1970, issue of TIME magazine dubbed them the progenitors of "country rock," a style imbued with a respect for regional musical traditions being lost in the welter of a madcap culture quaking under social and political strains.

"IT MAY BE HARD TO APPRECIATE WHAT A SINGULAR HONOR THIS WAS FOR A ROCK BAND FORTY-FOUR YEARS AGO. . . . YOU CAN ALMOST FEEL THE WEIGHT OF THE MOMENT IN [DAVID] ATTIE'S IMAGES."
—ELI ATTIE

In December 1969, "Up on Cripple Creek" landed in the Top 30 (as No. 25) on radio station KHJ, an important outlet in the Southern California market. A month later, The Band entered the new decade riding the back of that fearsome goddess, Success. Their second album was hailed as a touchstone event in the burgeoning world of rock music as a fine art.

Now a full-fledged rock phenomenon, they were primed to perform in prestigious concert halls before rapt listeners and expanding rock music media.

> **"The entire industry got right back to songwriting, and Robbie Robertson, one of the great songwriters of all time, had effectuated that change by his own sensibility, and The Band's sensibility."**
> —Steven Van Zandt, from the 2016 documentary *Rumble: The Indians Who Rocked the World*

PREVIEWED DECEMBER 24, 1969

Last Week	This Week	Title	Artist	Weeks on Boss 30
(2)	1.	RAINDROPS KEEP FALLIN' ON MY HEAD	B. J. Thomas	6
(3)	2.	JAM UP JELLY TIGHT	Tommy Roe	8
(1)	3.	SOMEDAY WE'LL BE TOGETHER	Diana Ross & The Supremes	9
(11)	4.	WHOLE LOTTA LOVE	Led Zeppelin	5
(7)	5.	ELI'S COMING	Three Dog Night	7
(10)	6.	VENUS	The Shocking Blue	5
(9)	7.	MIDNIGHT COWBOY	Ferrante & Teicher	5
(8)	8.	CHERRY HILL PARK	Billy Joe Royal	7
(6)	9.	NA NA HEY HEY KISS HIM GOODBYE	Steam	9
(5)	10.	BABY, I'M FOR REAL	The Originals	8
(4)	11.	LEAVING ON A JET PLANE	Peter, Paul & Mary	9
(15)	12.	LA LA LA (IF I HAD YOU)	Bobby Sherman	5
(16)	13.	WONDERFUL WORLD, BEAUTIFUL PEOPLE	Jimmy Cliff	6
(19)	14.	MIND, BODY, AND SOUL	The Flaming Ember	4
(17)	15.	SHE BELONGS TO ME	Rick Nelson	4
(14)	16.	FRIENDSHIP TRAIN	Gladys Knight & The Pips	6
(20)	17.	SHE LETS HER HAIR DOWN (EARLY IN THE MORNING)	Gene Pitney	6
(12)	18.	DOWN ON THE CORNER	Creedence Clearwater Revival	11
(26)	19.	I WANT YOU BACK	The Jackson 5	2
(22)	20.	CUPID	Johnny Nash	3
(21)	21.	BABY TAKE ME IN YOUR ARMS	Jefferson	4
(24)	22.	WALKIN' IN THE RAIN	Jay & The Americans	3
(23)	23.	JINGLE JANGLE	The Archies	4
(25)	24.	ARIZONA	Mark Lindsay	3
(18)	25.	UP ON CRIPPLE CREEK	The Band	7
(27)	26.	WITHOUT LOVE (THERE IS NOTHING)	Tom Jones	2
(28)	27.	I'LL NEVER FALL IN LOVE AGAIN	Dionne Warwick	2
(29)	28.	EVERYBODY IS A STAR	Sly & The Family Stone	2
(30)	29.	WALK A MILE IN MY SHOES	Joe South	2
(HB)	30.	WINTER WORLD OF LOVE	Engelbert Humperdinck	1

PAUL BODY

"In January 1970, The Band was coming to town. I had seen them five years earlier at the same Pasadena Civic Auditorium when they were the Hawks and they were backing Dylan. They looked like extras in *Night of the Hunter* then, all dressed in black preacher suits. A lot had happened since then—music had gotten louder and the world had gone a little crazier since 1965. . . .

"Word got around that they were coming to the Civic, so I bought two tickets for both shows. . . . I ended up taking a friend of a friend. It was a Saturday night. The crowd was mostly hippies, the last few survivors of the Woodstock age—things were about to change in 1970.

"Paul Siebel opened the show. I just remember that he was real pale. All the while I was wondering how The Band was going to be accepted here—the last time in the Civic, people were walking out. After a short intermission, there they were. They kicked it off with 'This Wheel's on Fire'—literally *kicked it off* because each song was counted off by the stomping of feet. They jumped right into both albums. They were tight, quite the opposite of the Stones, who I had seen a few months before; the Stones were ragged but right, as usual. The Band sounded like their records, only louder. No yak-yak between songs, just the songs: 'Up on Cripple Creek,' 'The Night They Drove Old Dixie Down,' 'I Shall Be Released,' 'The Weight,' and others.

"The three singers sang as one; matter of fact, they played as one. I heard that they usually encored with 'Slippin' and Slidin','; but on this night they did 'Don't Do It' and 'Loving You Is Sweeter Than Ever.' Motown. No one walked out that night. The second show was just as good."

> "At the Woodstock Playhouse, we were able to set up The Band onstage without the traditional solo booths of a typical recording studio. They preferred a circular setup, to be able to see and play off of each other. It was a very visual method, sometimes prompted by a wink or a grin. I loved that. I began to see how they all interacted throughout their creative process."
>
> —William Scheele, equipment manager for The Band

In June 1970, The Band returned to Woodstock to record their third album, *Stage Fright*. The manifold changes taking place within the group found expression in Robbie's latest compositions.

John Scheele, noted photographer of The Band and the brother of the group's equipment manager, William Scheele, recalled that "there was a plan for a live recording at the Woodstock Playhouse the year before, but now they were playing much tighter—really hitting their marks." But the local constabulary, in cahoots with the town elders, put the kibosh on that, fearful of the hippie hordes in search of their next music festival fix. The *Stage Fright* album itself was recorded under somewhat chastened circumstances. Instead of going live, The Band buckled down for an intense private two-week session at the Playhouse, accompanied only by engineer Todd Rundgren (whom Robbie had met earlier while collaborating on a Jesse Winchester recording) and their longtime associate John Simon.

Talking to journalist Phil Levy in 1970, for a July 9 *Rolling Stone* article titled "A Recent Encounter with Robbie Robertson," Simon laid out the mechanics of their much-anticipated new album. "It was the same arrangement we had before—Capitol Records provided the equipment. The control room was down in the prop room and the recording room was on the stage. "In the past, we've mixed the albums ourselves.... This time we decided to go two paths. We decided to let [English engineer] Glyn Johns, who we all respect for his ears, mix it with completely fresh ears. We sent him sort of a rough mix of what we thought the album should sound like.... [Todd] went over to London with the tapes, and he's going to mix it there in a completely different studio.... Neither of them cares which mix we use, it's not any kind of competition thing at all."

OPPOSITE TOP RIGHT: The December 24, 1969 chart (from Southern California's KHJ Boss 30 radio—"Up on Cripple Creek" is at No. 25.

TOP LEFT: John Scheele, noted photographer of The Band and the brother of the group's equipment manager, William Scheele, 1976.

LEFT: The Woodstock Playhouse during the *Stage Fright* recording sessions, June 1970.

RIGHT CREEK, RIGHT PADDLE

Setting the Stage
WILLIAM SCHEELE

"I saw Dylan and the Hawks play Cleveland in 1966. Whatever Ronnie Hawkins did to hone them worked because they showed great confidence and held nothing back. They just let it rip and left nothing on the ground. It was all out there.

"I knew [writer and producer] Jonathan Taplin growing up in Cleveland, Ohio. In the summer of '68, Taplin called me to help him with equipment for Judy Collins and Arlo Guthrie, who were playing at Blossom Music Center, just south of Cleveland. He mentioned that The Band wanted to start touring in the spring of 1969 and if I was interested, to stay tuned. . . . He called in early April and arranged to fly me from Cleveland to L.A.— and the adventure began!

"I met them when they were working on the second album. Jon Taplin picked me up at LAX and we drove to the Sammy Davis Jr. house in the Hollywood Hills. I was introduced to all of the members of The Band, along with John Simon, and all of their wives, girlfriends, and even Robbie's mother. Everyone was warm and welcoming and the vibe was good. My brother John was set to be The Band's road manager and I was to be equipment manager and truck driver.

"As a young man—only twenty years old—in my position I had to quickly develop professional responsibility for taking care of musical instruments and sound equipment. First, I had to learn each musician's instruments, set up the stage to their liking, and then tear down all the equipment and pack the truck after each show, efficiently and carefully.

"Garth suggested that I get a notebook and write everything down, as there was much to remember. Initially, I had to drive and navigate my way across the country and be on time for concerts . . . all alone in pre-GPS and pre-cellphone years. I took great pride in being the best I could be for these musicians I had admired since my first exposure to *Music from Big Pink*.

"After the first concerts in San Francisco, we all returned to Woodstock to establish our home base.

William Scheele, his wife, Nina, and Garth Hudson, working at the Scheele's house in Maine, 1969.

Early on, Garth confided to me, 'Well, you know that guy with the guitar has the hottest instrument onstage. Now I've got to compete with that.' Garth went from one Leslie speaker out of his organ to three with the help of electronics wizard Ed Anderson. And his keyboards grew from just the organ and Clavinet to other electric keyboards. Later on, he worked with the Lowrey Organ Company to develop a new polyphonic synthesizer. His musical knowledge was vast and he was the maestro of The Band.

"I liked Albert Grossman very much and learned a great deal from him. I appreciated his making Jon Taplin and me full-time management for The Band, both on and off the road. This was unique for the music business at the time. He wanted to develop a feeling of family closeness for everyone. We spent time together, personally and professionally, on a daily basis. Albert was a father figure to all of us."

William Scheele, The Band's equipment manager, 1975.

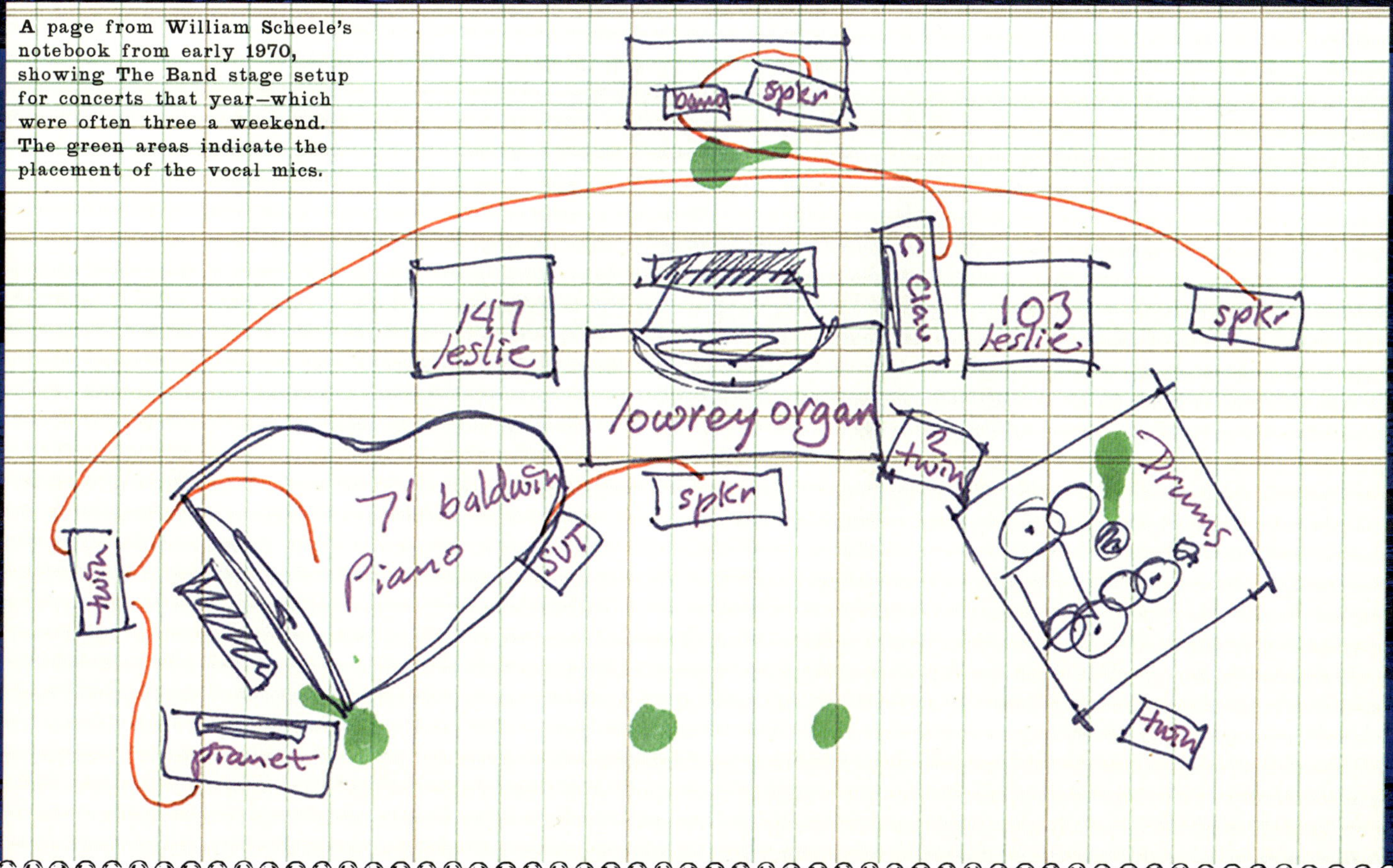

A page from William Scheele's notebook from early 1970, showing The Band stage setup for concerts that year—which were often three a weekend. The green areas indicate the placement of the vocal mics.

Richard Manuel and Robbie Robertson working on vocals, Woodstock Playhouse, June 1970.

OPPOSITE LEFT: Tour manager Jonathan Taplin, Robbie Robertson, Todd Rundgren, and John Simon in the control room at the Woodstock Playhouse, June 1970.

OPPOSITE RIGHT: John Simon, Robbie Robertson, Rick Danko, and Albert Grossman listening back to recordings for *Stage Fright* at the Woodstock Playhouse, June 1970.

On the new album, The Band's cloak of kinship—tight vocal harmonies, vivid instrumental interplay, lyrical density—now seemed frayed at the edges. Instead, the songs explored a leaner, more introspective tone—"confessional," in the words of many critics. Was Robertson retreating into a defensive, observational mode, as if clinging to the wreckage of this once indestructible brotherhood? Inquiring minds were keen to know.

"When *Stage Fright* came about," Robbie told Band historian Rob Bowman years later in 2001, "all I was doing was feeling my way along. But where everybody was in the huddle on both *Big Pink* and *The Band,* with *Stage Fright* it didn't feel like we were all connected in the same kind of way. In this period of experimentation in life, in music, in drugs, people kept wanting to stretch and reach and go somewhere and try things, and in the course of that, some real alienation can take place as well."

Stage Fright ushered The Band into the '70s. Danko sang the title track, a reflection on the stardom they had achieved, and "The Shape I'm In" showcased Manuel's vocals, both FM radio favorites as album rock burgeoned into a radio rotation format.

In late June–early July 1970, Canadian music promoters Eaton-Walker Associates (Thor Eaton, George Eaton and Ken Walker) decided to stage a series of "mini-festivals" in Toronto, Winnipeg, and Calgary, the performers traveling across the great heartland in a private train—an Orient Express of sorts.

They assembled a collection of rowdies, hippies, folkies, blues hounds, and a star or two. Janis Joplin, The Band, the Grateful Dead, Buddy Guy, the Flying Burrito Brothers, New Riders of the Purple Sage, and Delaney & Bonnie and Friends were among the artists involved. The musicians traveled in fourteen Canadian National Railway train cars.

It quickly morphed into a rowdy hootenanny, the ribaldry and the wreckage captured for all time in a 2003 documentary titled *Festival Express*. Robbie quickly soured on the whole thing and bailed out before the last show in Calgary. Rick found camaraderie in the ever-changing scrum of voices and vices. It was a glorious mess, as impertinent as 1970 itself.

DAVID DALTON
Author

Author David Dalton, shown here in 1970, covered the Festival Express for *Rolling Stone*.

"I was writing for *Rolling Stone* and covering [the Festival Train] with Jonathan Cott. Nothing sensational happened. There weren't any groupies. It was basically musicians playing. We took all the chairs out of two of the carriages. One group sort of played folk and country and the other played kind of blues and rock. It was an unbelievable thing.

"It was a brilliant kind of idea. It didn't quite succeed in the way they thought it was going to. The train was just absolute heaven. In those days, especially those bands, there weren't any roadies or, God forbid, bodyguards or anybody. Everybody was extremely friendly. And the musicians on the train, none of them had a big front like many rock stars do.

"I think the whole mood of the thing was so benign and so optimistic. And they just ended up, like, singing old cowboy songs. For the Grateful Dead and Janis, after 1967, they all became, you know, rock stars . . . so they didn't hang out the way they earlier did in 1965 and '66 in the Haight. And they were all on tour and doing all kinds of other things. And so it was a recreation of the Haight on this train.

"It might have been the first time I saw The Band live. It seemed like fun. I don't know if you can call The Band hippies, but they were certainly a kind of faction. Let's face it, there were a lot of shared values. It was predominantly kind of a hippie crew on that train."

OPPOSITE: Rick Danko and Janis Joplin (center row, left) jam on the Festival Express train, summer 1970, along with Eric Anderson and Sylvia Tyson (front row), Jerry Garcia (third from right), and Ian Tyson (far right) on guitar, with Buddy Cage to his left. Festival Promoter Ken Walker is standing toward the back left.

JOHN SCHEELE

"By the end of the ride, I was somehow judged the most sober of the crew, by a small margin—and got to drive Janis in her limo through the Calgary Stampede crowd to the stage. She cackled and grinned as they parted slowly, like the proverbial Red Sea—people near the car turning their heads to gaze at the cosmic Janis Joplin, drifting by in her chariot."

"We sailed over the Canadian prairie and got high with a truly heavenly band to entertain. Rick Danko and Janis Joplin were literally falling in love as they exchanged looks and sang together—but then everyone was in love that day." —John Scheele

On July 10, 1970, The Band headlined the Hollywood Bowl. Riding the crest of newfound acclaim—the *Time* magazine cover of January had conferred a mainstream media seal of approval—the group was granted carte blanche to pick their opening act. They choose jazz icon Miles Davis, who was, at that moment, performing at his princely darkest with his so-called "Fillmore" band, a whirlwind of musical mystery and magic.

Jack DeJohnette was Miles's drummer. A powerhouse with exquisite instincts, he'd previously held the drum seat with saxophonist Charles Lloyd and pianist Bill Evans, personal favorites of Robbie's and Garth's. DeJohnette had recently moved to Woodstock, drawn by the promise of a bucolic artist's retreat. For all his jazz credentials, Jack was equally taken with Dylan, The Band, and all the rootsy rock and blues flowing out of the Hudson Valley.

Forty-seven years later, DeJohnette himself headlined the Hollywood Bowl as part of the 2017 Playboy Jazz Festival, his set highlighted by an eight-ball, corner-pocket rendition of "Up on Cripple Creek."

"A great feeling," said DeJohnette recently [to Kenneth], "to bring it full circle."

JACK DEJOHNETTE

"I had a couple of musician friends of mine from Chicago who played with the Paul Butterfield Blues Band. They were up in Woodstock, so I came to check it out. I knew it was a haven for artists like Hendrix, Dylan. I knew The Band—*Music from Big Pink*—and thought they were terrific, not flashy but real soulful, with great lyrics and great singing. Real Americana. . . .

"That gig at the Hollywood Bowl—the band with Keith, Chick, Gary, Airto, Dave, Steve—that was really memorable. We got to jam briefly with The Band—nothing formal, without Miles—and really dug their musicianship. Garth had a really light, natural touch on the organ, producing all those amazing experimental sounds. He could play anything—the saxophone, and that funky Clavinet. They all did. Levon could really handle the mandolin.

"I loved their grooves. Levon tuned those wooden drums real low; he had a sound and a touch. Because he was a singer, it only enhanced his drum fills, where to place an accent. And he really locked in with Danko's bass."

134 THE STORY OF THE BAND

ROBERT MARCHESE
record producer/manager

"I went to see Miles Davis and The Band at the Hollywood Bowl. I knew Miles's agent Benny Shapiro and met Albert Grossman with Janis Joplin at the '67 Monterey International Pop Festival.

"The day of the show I was coming out of a men's clothes store, Zeidler & Zeidler, on Sunset Boulevard and Crescent Heights. . . . [and] literally bumped into Miles in the little alley.

'Hey man, what ya doin'?' he said.

'Tonight I'm gonna be at the Hollywood Bowl to see you, brother,' I said. And he asked, 'How good are these cats on the bill with me?' And I replied, 'They're the best white motherfuckers in the business right now.' And he glared, 'I'm gonna smoke 'em.' And I split and said, 'I'm sure you will.'

"It was an important show for Miles on a large stage. Miles was still playing clubs at the time and had recently played the Fillmore West in San Francisco. The electric *Bitches Brew* stuff had just kicked in. So, Miles and The Band together was a major event in town at the Hollywood Bowl with eighteen thousand people.

"I've always put Levon Helm and Charlie Watts as the two best drummers ever. And here comes Miles with his group, which has Jack DeJohnette, Dave Holland, Steve Grossman, Keith Jarrett, Chick Corea, and Airto. Jack and Levon on the skins for the entire evening!

"Jack and Miles aren't down the street at Shelly's Manne-Hole on a jazz club booking. They're at the Hollywood Bowl, adjacent to Laurel Canyon, which had some sort of rustic vibe like Woodstock. Plus, The Band's record label, Capitol, is a mile from the Hollywood Bowl, and Miles's record company, Columbia, is on Sunset Boulevard. They were promoting this big gig with support from FM radio stations.

"Don't forget, in the summer of 1970, after the November 1969 US tour of the Rolling Stones, The Band were the shit. The Beatles had retired. And in jazz, Miles was the king."

OPPOSITE: Levon Helm with Jack DeJohnette, who performed in the 1970 Hollywood Bowl show as the drummer for Miles Davis, seen here c. 2008.

ABOVE INSET: A newspaper ad for The Band/Miles Davis show at the Hollywood Bowl on July 10, 1970.

ABOVE: Record producer and manager Robert Marchese, photographed at the Renaissance Faire in Southern California, May 1967.

CHAPTER 9
LIFE IS A SIDESHOW

The Band was built on a paradox; celebrated leaders in the escalating rock music movement, they were by temperament and artistic sensibility the very essence of soulful sidemen. When it sounded like every other group was striving for excess—extravagance in lieu of substance—The Band doubled down on their three-minute epiphanies, content to let concision speak louder than endless noodling over a minor blues chord progression. Their very restraint had the inverse effect of rousing their most vocal fans to plead for more virtuosic displays—more Robbie solos, more phantasmagoria from Garth!

Once on tour, expectations to "open up" onstage only reinforced their commitment to sticking to the script. Various bootlegs from the early 1970s showcase the fragile alchemy required to deliver a momentous reading or mere recitation—Levon or Richard being a little too lubricated could slack the pinpoint rhythms; Robbie losing interest mid-gig would strip the sting from his Fender-bending punch.

In June 1971, the Band returned to Woodstock to record their fourth album, *Cahoots*. In the aftermath of Albert Grossman's own worldly travails—Dylan's serpentine departure from his fold, Janis Joplin's tragic exit—the über manager directed his energies to building a state-of-the-art recording facility adjacent to his Bearsville estate.

OPPOSITE: Setting up the stage for one of The Band's shows at the Academy of Music, New York City, held from December 28 to 31, 1971.

The ultimate romper room for musicians keen on following their muse down any and all rabbit holes, this studio served not only as a creative incubator but as a safe harbor from all the destructive temptations that harassed them on the road.

But rather than liberating the Band, their shiny new space was a palpable reminder of what a miserable rut they had fallen into.

Robbie had assumed de facto leadership of the group if for no other reason than authorship of most of their material. But even he was tilting at windmills, bereft of lyrical or melodic inspiration.

Rick Danko onstage at the De Doelen concert center in Rotterdam, June 6, 1971.

Unlike the narrative cohesion of their first three albums, *Cahoots* languished under the dissolute haze of a brotherhood at odds with itself. Richard had semi-retired, drink and drugs taking their psychic toll; Rick and Levon were also indulging.

Garth was always present, a whispering pine content to follow his own whimsical preoccupations. Robbie surmised that "Every once in a while we could come to the surface and be who we really were, just because there was a bunch of talent there, but we were fighting the demons the entire time."

The highlight of *Cahoots*, released in September 1971, was "Life Is a Carnival," an increasingly rare collaboration between Rick, Levon, and Robbie. With its Crescent City backbeat, Hudson's sweeping keyboard perorations, and those delicious vocal harmonies, rueful and revelatory in turn, the song was a valiant return to form. It was further enhanced by the exquisite pen of arranger/orchestrator extraordinaire Allen Toussaint.

It was Robbie's inspired idea to contact Toussaint, who readily agreed to the commission. His deft use of brass instrumentation pointed a way forward for the group, struggling with creative drift. It was the beginning of a fruitful association soon to yield a most bountiful harvest.

In his review of *Cahoots*, Jon Tiven, writing for the *Phonograph Record* in December 1971, declared:

> Yes, The Band is still good, doncha fret none. They are a lot more studio-ish (their simplicity is quickly disappearing), less apt to solo extensively, and prone to a bit of gimmickry (check out the intro to 'Chinatown'). However, The Band have not gotten bad/lazy/contrived or any of the other adjectives you might find people applying nowadays.
>
> Warning Do Not Attempt to Listen to This Album As Background Music. Please. This is one album that you have to listen to intensely quite a few times before you even **begin** to appreciate it. This album is guaranteed to last a lifetime, supplying an infinite number of surprises with each new listening.

SARAH KRAMER
multi-instrumentalist

"Part of 'Life Is a Carnival' is really straight and part of it very much with melody rhythm and accents. And then they added those horns, especially the arrangement of Allen Toussaint and his ears, and his background, that brass band music from New Orleans.

"The second-line stuff has so much melody within the rhythm. This goes back to slavery, and also the New Orleans flavor. The African rhythms and the kind of melodic second-line approach to drums and just the gathering of the parade, is kind of like the rising beyond the struggle of things. And you listen to 'Life Is a Carnival' and realize life is a struggle but life is [also] a joy."

"As a horn player, and hearing The Band's music with the horns—specifically a song like 'Life Is a Carnival'—I really loved the influence of New Orleans and the carnival aspect of the Mardi Gras."
—Sarah Kramer

Multi-instrumentalist Sarah Kramer.

In May 1971, before heading to Bearsville, the Band had resumed touring, embarking on their first dates in Europe. Grossman had them traipsing from Stockholm to Vienna, from Hamburg to Paris's fabled Olympia, the setting for their infamous 1966 performance with Dylan before a mob of seething malcontents. Their final show was at London's Royal Albert Hall. Richard Williams, reviewing their June 2 show for *Melody Maker*, called it "the best rock 'n' roll concert I ever saw in my life."

Like many other commentators, Williams was moved by their discipline; they rocked but they weren't loud, they were virtuosic without being verbose. They were aesthetic outliers who were leading the pack, rock 'n' roll lone wolves with portfolio.

Four concerts were booked to close the year at New York's Academy of Music three-thousand-seat concert hall on December 28–31. Robbie wanted to make it something truly memorable and proposed that they recruit Allen Toussaint to add his special sauce to their now much-celebrated catalogue. Aided and abetted by such first-call jazz players as Howard Johnson, Snooky Young, and Earl McIntyre on brass and Joe Farrell and J. D. Parron on reeds and woodwinds, songs like "Don't Do It," "Rag Mama Rag," and "Across the Great Divide" were rechristened with an insouciant vigor, fresh drama drawn from familiar stories. "The Night They Drove Old Dixie Down," already rife with solemn pageantry, was graced with a totemic sweep, a Lincolnesque reverie drawn from blood and soil.

All the performances were recorded under the attentive eyes (and ears) of ace engineer Phil Ramone with Mark Harman, for a live album that would be released in August 1972 as *Rock of Ages*. Fortunately, there were no major technical glitches, a tribute to the care taken to document the proceedings.

"My fondest memory of those nights at the Academy of Music start with trepidation," volunteered The Band's former road manager Jonathan Taplin. "We had been touring for two years, but the addition of a horn section and charts by Allen Toussaint was a wild card. Because the horn players were playing from written music, the somewhat looser feel that the Band had developed onstage could have gotten lost. But the first time the horns came in, all my worries dissolved. It was such a big sound and so funky that it just added to the joy of the music," underlined Taplin.

WILLIAM SCHEELE

"The Academy of Music was a beautiful, ornate theater with great sound and everyone enjoyed being there . . . for several concerts no less. It felt great to play in one place for more than one night. All of the Band members were in great shape and were very tight. The horn section was an intriguing addition to their songs and integrated beautifully.

"New Year's Eve was highlighted by Garth's masterful, meandering 'Chest Fever' and Bob Dylan's lively appearance for the encores. . . . The crowd went out of their minds!"

JOHN SCHEELE

"The Band really came together for this show—and the horn section took the music to a new level. . . .

"Richard's voice as he kicks off 'Across the Great Divide' was so strong. It was awesome for me to shoot alongside the great Ernst Haas—and documentary filmmaker Murray Lerner even captured some of the rehearsals on 16mm. . . .

"I had been waiting to see Bob Dylan perform live for years—he'd been off the road since his 1966 motorcycle accident. The whole Academy audience was in for the same thrill—the jungle beat cadence of 'Down in the Flood' announcing that Bob and The Band were back again! I rushed out on the stage apron to get a few shots just as they got started—it was a rush to hear that music live."

"It was the final night; there was a thrill in the air. We were excited about New Year's Eve, and then Dylan joined us for the encore. When he came out, we thought we could wing it, and wing it we did. We thought, 'We're not gonna fall off this wire.' That whole night had a bit of magic to it."
—Robbie Robertson

Levon Helm, Bob Dylan, and Robbie Robertson at the Academy of Music, New York City, onstage during one of The Band's engagements there (December 28–31, 1971).

"I had tix for that New Year's Eve show—knowing in my bones that Bob was gonna pull a surprise appearance," reveals writer and musician Michael Simmons. "Three weeks before, my father announces we're going to Miami for the holidays. 'You're going to Miami,' said I. 'I'm going to see The Band at the Academy of Music.'

I was sixteen and overruled and spent a miserable week in Yourami. . . . The minute we got home, I called my friend Larry. 'He showed!' said he. I told my ninety-one-year-old father a couple of weeks ago that I still haven't forgiven him forty-six years later."

"Dylan and The Band's intuitive onstage musical chemistry had developed since 1966, and you can hear it shift in their *Rock of Ages* encore set," observed James Cushing, longtime deejay on radio station KEBF-FM in Morro Bay, California.

> The music's overall roughness (they were winging it, after all) recalls their Isle of Wight concert from two years previously, even down to the inclusion of a rare Basement Tape tune and a missing-verse reading of "Like a Rolling Stone." However, Dylan's voice here anticipates his harshly declamatory 1974 performances captured on *Before the Flood*. The Band, Helm and Robertson especially, provide him with a backup so strong that he sounds ready to reconquer the culture, not withdraw from it as *Self-Portrait* and *New Morning* suggested. The *Rock of Ages* set adds to the mystery of Dylan by representing his public voice at an otherwise private time."

What emerged from this valorous last stand—Robbie had intimated that these shows were both a summation of their career, providing a well-deserved break from the ruthless grind of album/tour that left them all feeling creatively and physically spent—was the justly acclaimed two-disc set *Rock of Ages*.

Although it didn't demonstrate any radical departures from their finely honed strengths—a recherché greatest hits—it was, nonetheless, a powerful statement, taking pride of place alongside a slew of distinguished live albums from their contemporaries like Derek & the Dominoes' *In Concert* and the Who's *Live at Leeds*.

Rock of Ages spent twenty-eight weeks on the charts, peaking at No. 6. Other, less mercurial performers might have seen this as a potent renewal; instead, and in keeping with their ornery nature, The Band walked away, disappearing into the dark Catskill woods and their ever-darkening predispositions. The year 1972, and beyond, were a complete unknown, no direction shown.

"**The first time the horns came in, all my worries dissolved. It was such a big sound and so funky that it just added to the joy of the music....**"
—Jonathan Taplin, on the Academy of Music shows

The Band with jazz tuba virtuoso Howard Johnson at one of the Academy of Music shows.

"We didn't compete with the originals; we complemented and expanded on them. We did most of these songs in clubs and our claim to fame at the time was that we played them really well. I felt on most of the tunes we pulled it off, and that's very hard to do." —Robbie Robertson

The Band performing in June during their 1971 tour, at the Concertgebouw in Amsterdam.

In a 1994 issue of *MOJO* magazine, singer/songwriter Elvis Costello commented about The Band to music journalist and author Barney Hoskyns:

> They're a kind of cul-de-sac in rock 'n' roll history. [The early Band albums] were like letters from the other side of the world. . . . If they left a legacy, unfortunately it was a kind of *muso* mentality, people who wanted to be like them but didn't really understand that what was great about them was this mysterious quality the music had, a quality you can't buy off-the-peg. They were more like jazz musicians in that respect, like one of Miles's really great lineups. Five incredible players and three great singers. How many other bands can boast that?

In 1974 Elvis Costello, then named Declan Patrick MacManus, saw Jesse Colin Young, The Band, Joni Mitchell, and Crosby, Stills, Nash & Young in England at Wembley Stadium. The Band was his favorite group at the time, and he was hoping they'd play "Unfaithful Servant."

This century Elvis shared a UCLA Royce Hall stage with Garth Hudson, and performed with Levon Helm on his *Spectacle: Elvis Costello with . . .*TV series, appeared at a Helm Midnight Ramble in Woodstock, and collaborated with Allen Toussaint on their *The River in Reverse* in 2006.

In fall 1998, I [Harvey] interviewed Costello in Hollywood at Ocean Way studio for *Musician* magazine (his album with Burt Bacharach, *Painted from Memory*, had just been released), where we talked about The Band's 1968–1972 LP catalog. Elvis touted the vocals of Rick Danko, whom he met at the Lone Star Café in New York. He also spoke in general about rock music compositions and recordings with horns:

> I think the 'vocals' come from the compositions. Just the way the tunes lay and the amount of space there is in them. 'Cause it's naturally the way they're paced, and rhythmically the movements that they make, particularly the short phrases followed by longer phrases. There's a vocal quality to all of the solo playing. All of the figures are played on instruments that can continue the emotional content of the song.

ABOVE: Levon Helm, Allen Toussaint, and Elvis Costello, 2006.

RIGHT: The work of Sam Cooke, seen here in the recording studio in the early 1960s, was one of the inspirations for The Band's music on *Moondog Matinee*, their fifth studio album, released in October 1973.

Calibrated to the rush and whoosh of performance—that quaking surge when the curtain lifts—many musicians succumb to a deadening inertial state when the touring stops, the drip, drip, drip of waiting for something/anything to happen.

No group was more prone to this enervating posture than The Band. Lying dormant under the icy blue stasis of their winter retreat in Woodstock, each member suffocated under a melange of rock 'n' roll clichés. Richard pushed his liver to its limit, as if his body was as well conditioned as the sports cars he raced recklessly around Route 87. Rick's marriage was breaking up. Robbie joined his wife in her hometown of Montreal, finding solace in the cosmopolitan French Canadian city. Levon completely stopped an illegal bad habit and enrolled in school (?!), pursuing drum studies at Boston's prestigious Berklee College of Music.

For all intents and purposes, The Band was on life support. "I felt," Levon wrote in his autobiography, *This Wheel's on Fire*, "like we musicians were just waiting around for the reading of the will."

A year into their "sabbatical," drifting aimlessly to sea, Robbie roused them into action. He had been messing around with some formal classical structures, reflecting his growing interest in such avant-garde modernists as Krzysztof Penderecki. But this remained a private pursuit; there were no roles for the others to contribute to. Instead, he proposed that they record an album of their favorite songs—a mix of R&B, soul, gospel, and Brill Building pop standards—which spoke to the very marrow of their collective identity. It would be a tribute as well as a rekindling of their commitment to making music again. And it worked.

In March 1973, they regrouped at Bearsville Studio (with some tracks cut later at Capitol Records in Hollywood) and plowed through an impromptu set that would link them to their storied past on Yonge Street. Chuck Berry, Fats Domino, Bobby "Blue" Bland, Sam Cooke were all acknowledged. But if the songs were familiar fare (particularly to rock 'n' roll purists), their treatments were anything but.

These weren't interpretations so much as transmutations, a conjuring that took, for example, the hillbilly gallop of "Mystery Train" and ramped it up into breathless locomotion. And, while no one questions the nobility in Sam Cooke's original reading of "A Change Is Gonna Come," Danko served up an equally moving rendition—less Baptist, more ecumenical, an anthem rising above racial, national, and religious divides.

"When you played clubs, people didn't want to hear the songs you wrote," Robertson told me in a 1975 *Crawdaddy* magazine interview in Malibu.

"We always strongly objected to the hit parade. We thought of ourselves as beyond the things that were hits at the time. 'I'm Ready' is total jukebox music. 'The Great Pretender' is one of the greatest songs of that era. 'Saved' is a Leiber/Stoller song that really wasn't that popular and few people heard it. We wanted to include a Buddy Holly tune, but the ones we wanted to do had been covered so many times. Listen to Richard's vocal on 'The Great Pretender.' It's really convincing.

"We did *Moondog Matinee* for ourselves. We were in the mood and it was our own personal shot at nostalgia—what we usually do for everybody else. Beyond that, we had no control whether anyone liked it or not. . . . The album was an exercise in our own past and we really enjoyed doing it."

Released in October 1973, *Moondog Matinee*—the album's title a play on deejay Alan Freed's popular radio broadcast and their halcyon days playing afternoon shows during their Canadian apprenticeship—featured cover art by a fellow Canuck, Edward Kasper. It pictured rock 'n' roll's dusky DNA in all its shambolic glory.

Moondog Matinee barely broke into the Top 30. But it served its greater purpose.

The Band was ready to work again.

On July 28, 1973, The Band mounted the stage at Watkins Glen in Upstate New York, their first time performing live in eighteen months. Promoter Bill Graham had coaxed them out with a pinch of guilt and a pitcher of money.

A crowd of 150,000 was anticipated for this festival-like event—an all-day affair also featuring the Allman Brothers and the Grateful Dead. Instead, nearly 600,000 delirious fans endured the heat (and during The Band's set, a cloudburst), as the music played on and on and on.

The Band followed this gig with two shows at Roosevelt Stadium in New Jersey, on July 31 and August 1.

Come January next, Bob Dylan would set out on his next, quixotic adventure, enlisting his reluctant road warriors to help him tilt at some mighty lucrative windmills.

148 THE STORY OF THE BAND

Rick Danko (below) and Levon Helm (opposite) onstage with The Band during the second night of their two-night show at the racetrack at Watkins Glen, New York, July 28, 1973.

WILLIAM SCHEELE

"The Band delivered at outdoor concerts because their music had an energy that transcended the open spaces. . . . My personal impressions:

"Robbie: quiet, focused, assumed business responsibility, serious/remote/separation for writing, smooth rhythm and frenetic lead guitar. He could go from playing a little bit of rhythm to the most ecstatic, harmonic riffs imaginable.

"Garth: in his own world, shy and measured, formal training with an extensive musical knowledge base, ethereal and magical sounds from his numerous keyboards, emphatic sax solos. It was otherworldly watching and listening to Garth's improvisations.

"Levon: original heart and soul of the group, cool and laidback, a funky drummer, drums tuned to a low thud, striking and expressive Southern-drawl vocals, alternate guitar and mandolin work. He was a real core rhythm driver. Everybody counted on him to kick off the songs with his sharp drumming.

"Richard: warm and friendly, solid rhythm piano, hard pounding solos, very funky, floppy drummer, incredibly soulful vocals, great range. Richard let it all hang out but he was fragile and a very sensitive person. He was also fun loving, with a great sense of humor.

"Rick: always fun, joking, friendly, a bob-and-weave visual bass player, uniquely expressive vocal tone, alternate guitar and fiddle work. His bass playing gave them the groundwork to work from, bottom up!

"None of these guys held anything back and everyone always joked around, keeping it loose and fun."

LIFE IS A SIDESHOW

Scenes from The Band shows at Roosevelt Stadium in Jersey City, New Jersey, July 30, July 31, and August 1, 1973. Clockwise from opposite left: a sound check, Richard Manuel, a backstage pass (The Band shared the ticket with the Grateful Dead), and Levon Helm.

GRATEFUL DEAD THE BAND BACKSTAGE ROOSEVELT STADIUM

CHAPTER 10
OUT IN MALIBU WITH A DIFFERENT VIEW

It was one too many listless Woodstock winters for Rick, Robbie, Richard, Garth, and Levon. It was time to bust a move, and the sun-soaked sirens of Malibu beckoned, the promise of heat and sparkling dust offering the perfect antidote to all that miserable cold.

One by one they resettled by the Pacific, leaving behind their now-mythic past, including their complicated relationship with manager Albert Grossman. New opportunities lay ahead, an invaluable reboot for their weary bodies and addled psyches.

Music industry agent/insider David Geffen approached them with a rainbow curve of a pitch that proved irresistible; owing to a clause in their Capitol Records contract, the Band was free to record with Dylan for any label of their choosing.

Conveniently, Geffen was just now establishing a label of his own, named Asylum. Landing the Bob/Band whale for his incipient enterprise would be a professional and personal coup, further confirmation of his status as the business's premier mover and shaker. A deal was signed.

First, a studio album to prime the pump. Dylan penned the tunes in New York during September and October of 1973. *Planet Waves* was hastily recorded over four marathon sessions November 5–14, 1973, at Village Recorders, a 22,000-square-foot former Masonic temple in West L.A., long championed by such discerning artists as Jim Morrison, the Rolling Stones, Steely Dan, and Jimmy Smith. Geordie Hormel, a musician, composer, equipment dealer, and entrepreneur, founded the facility in 1968.

OPPOSITE: Robbie Robertson, Bob Dylan, and Rick Danko onstage during the Dylan–Band tour of January–February 1974.

RICHARD BOSWORTH

"West L.A.'s Village Recorders Studio A is the fourth in a series of recording studios constructed in Los Angeles that began during the latter 1950s and continued on through the 1960s. Prior to that, most significant studios were large high-ceilinged rooms designed to accommodate thirty to sixty musicians and vocalists performing in concert to achieve a finished recording. Many times smaller music combos found these large rooms unsettling.

"With the advent of multitrack tape recording it eventually became apparent that another kind of smaller space was required. Legendary recording engineer, studio owner, and designer Bill Putnam was the visionary who first realized this and achieved it with his Western Recording Studio 3. When former Western employee Wally Heider decided to build his first music recording studio, he booked three hours of time at Western to take measurements and duplicated the room, naming it Wally Heider Studio 3 so prospective clients knew it was a duplicate. Tutti Camarata did the same with his Sunset Sound Studio 1. Village Recorders followed suit with their Studio A.

"All the studios are shoebox-shaped, with the dimensions being around 40 feet long by 20 feet wide with 12-foot-high ceilings. All control rooms are along the 20-foot-wide studio wall."

ROBBIE ROBERTSON

"I moved out to Malibu and Bob and I were hanging out. We'd been talking about a tour for years. All of a sudden it seemed to really make sense. It was a good idea, a kind of a step into the past. We felt if there's anything that everybody expects us to do, that's what it is. We quickly decided it was a good idea and a new day. The other guys in The Band came out and we went right to work. We started rehearsing anyway, so we thought we'd do the *Planet Waves* album and get back to rehearsing, and that's exactly what we did. . . .

"When I came out from Woodstock and New York to the West Coast and David Geffen convinced me to go to Malibu, there weren't many studios in this side of town.

"Anyway, Village was the only studio on the west side. And tons of people made records in this room. Rob Fraboni was already here. When you came here to record, he was the engineer who came with it. And Rob was terrific."

The recording/mixing console in Studio A at Village Recorders in West L.A., where Bob Dylan and The Band recorded *Planet Waves* in November 1973.

"**Bob usually had a nervous but focused attitude** towards the music; whether new or old, **he was always thinking** about what changes might be made to have it sound right . . . for the moment. Many times, **the key or tempo of a song might change, but with so much history between them, The Band could keep up with his rapid-fire changes.** Everyone needed to see each other to make this happen. **It was remarkable to witness** this incredible interplay between such gifted musicians."

—William Scheele

Detail of Levon Helm and Garth Hudson onstage during Tour '74, (see full image on page 162).

The album *Planet Waves* by Bob Dylan with The Band was released on January 17, 1974, and would go on to reach No. 1 on the US *Billboard* chart.

"Forever Young," Dylan's popular copyright, almost didn't make the final lineup. It was engineer Rob Fraboni who convinced Dylan to include it on the disc. In the 2001 biography *Bob Dylan: Behind the Shades Revisited*, by Clinton Heylin, Fraboni describes the 1973 recording of that song as being 'so riveting, it was so powerful, so immediate, I couldn't get over it.'"

WILLIAM SCHEELE

"We went in under assumed names, not Bob Dylan and The Band. One of the necessities of anonymity, Bob was typically booked under a fictitious name to get into places without calling attention to himself.

"We set up in Studio A on the first floor with each musician facing each other. That's the way Dylan and The Band preferred to play. They did it in the basement at Big Pink and it was always their style.

"Geordie Hormel was a wonderful character who made sure everyone was comfortable. He came from Minnesota, where Bob was from, so there was familiar territory to discuss.

"Bob was very relaxed and sociable with his old friends. They didn't spend all that time touring together in 1965-66 and afterward in 1967 at Big Pink to have anything but a very tight and friendly relationship. They all respected each other."

ROBBIE ROBERTSON

"We've been playing with Bob for years. We know the technique very well. There's no surprises involved. We did it and it was over before we knew it. We managed to get several things off very well for such a short time. But it went by so *quick* and we were preoccupied with the tour and all the other things that go with it. With all the decisions to be made, and all the how, when, and where, that album really took a back seat."

JAMES CUSHING

"*Planet Waves* had a Library of Congress feel to it. I loved the LP from the first chords. These are all love songs."

CELESTE GOYER
writer and poet

"*Planet Waves* was a special album to me; nobody else in my small town in California seemed to know about it. I particularly loved 'Hazel'—it was surprising to hear such a straightforward love song from Bob. I found it very tender."

OPPOSITE: The Band and their crew do a sound check before a show at the Oakland–Alameda County Coliseum in Oakland, California, February 11, 1974. See also page 159.

*D*riven more by contingencies than true commitment, *Planet Waves* remains a placeholder in Dylan's canon. The album did serve as a tantalizing appetizer for the main event driving Geffen's agenda.

The announcement struck with the force of a Category 5 hurricane: beginning on January 3, 1974, in Chicago, and continuing through February 14 (Valentine's Day) in Inglewood, a city next to the Los Angeles airport, Bob Dylan and The Band were reuniting—barnstorming their way across North America in the most hotly anticipated concert tour in rock music history.

It was, for a particularly self-congratulatory generation, a fever dream come true, twin '60s icons bringing their magic act back on the road one more time, performing at a sports arena near them.

Over 5 million ticket requests were mailed in for the approximately 700,000 seats available for the six-week jaunt. Promoted by Bill Graham, it promised to be the most talked-about, written-about event in modern media history. *Newsweek* magazine's January 14, 1974, issue proclaimed on its cover, "Dylan's Back."

Dylan hadn't toured in eight years (one-offs like the Isle of Wight notwithstanding); the Band's status was equally elusive in the public's consciousness.

And so off they went, safely ensconced in their private 707 jet, wallowing in dazed luxury; the tour was a velvet cocoon of limos, lavish spreads, and princely hotel suites

The concerts? They were mostly boxes to be ticked: all the hits and Bob solo acoustic too! There were undeniably many magic moments: Robbie cutting through the inescapable boom box sound mix with his straight razor attack; Garth's nuanced grandeur with the slightest of moves; Levon, pumped by the thrill of it all. And Richard and Rick never missed a lick, no matter how ribald the night before or the morning after.

A decade earlier "Like a Rolling Stone" was heard as an act of betrayal; now, it brought fans to their feet, hands raised, striking an anthemic chord.

WILLIAM SCHEELE

"The rehearsals for Tour '74 were held in a mountain camp north of Malibu. It was a seasonal boys' camp and we set up in a screened-in dining room, a fairly large area.

"The Band and Bob would typically arrive midday and start playing a wide variety of songs, reminiscent of the basement days, not just songs targeted for the tour. It was loose, funky, and very relaxed. Richard Manuel and I set up three conga drums—one was mine and two of them were his—and we actually got percussion into the mix. Bob said at one point, 'Why don't you set that up onstage when we go out?' While it never happened on the tour, just to practice with them was a dream come true. . . .

"Dylan and The Band started with an initial song set list that wound up changing throughout the tour. They knew they would all play together in the beginning and that Bob would open the second set after an intermission just with his acoustic material. His guitar and harmonica really caught the audience's attention, harkening back to the Dylan of the early '60s. . . . By the end of the tour, the song set list began and [often] ended with "Most Likely You Go Your Way and I'll Go Mine."

RIGHT: Equipment manager William Scheele's copy of the tour schedule for the Bob Dylan and The Band Tour '74; the party traveled under the alias "M. Franklin Group" to keep a low profile at hotels.

158 THE STORY OF THE BAND

Roger Steffens, ca. 1974.

BELOW: Concertgoers stream into the Oakland-Alameda County Coliseum for the Bob Dylan–Band show, February 11, 1974.

ROGER STEFFENS
broadcaster, actor, photographer, author

"It had been years since the elusive Bob Dylan had appeared onstage and the bootlegged basement tapes had become gigantic underground hits among the cognoscenti. The importance of Dylan's collaboration with [The Band] . . . became the object of university dissertations and verbose critics' fawning dissections.

"Thus anticipation was at fever pitch in February of 1974 in the Bay Area, when Dylan was booked into the Oakland Coliseum. Most of my friends in Berkeley bought tickets immediately, and planned to go together in a rapt pack. Considering that we weren't that far over the brink of the '60s, the general style of the crowd was definitely not psychedelic.

"The crowd had been primed for Dylan's reemergence by innovative underground radio station KSAN-FM, helmed by the rotund Tom Donahue. Ironically, I don't remember much about the show at all, except we all seemed to enjoy seeing Bob back in the saddle, and to hear The Band with its hero fronting it."

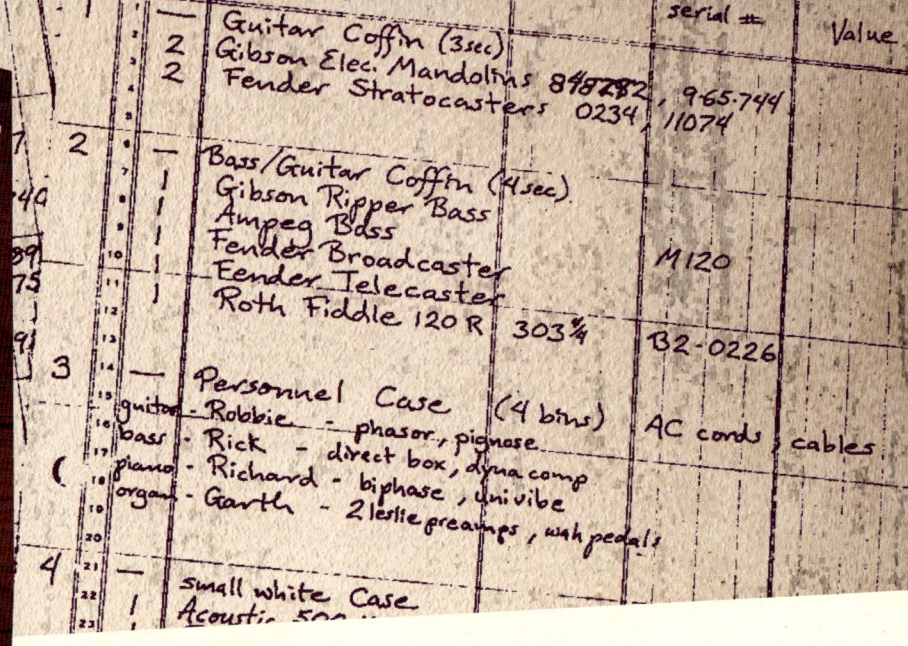

ROBBIE ROBERTSON

It just came natural and we did it. So I feel really good about it. It was done very nicely, very professionally, with nice ads. The way we did the shows was the way we wanted to do the shows. When we played, Bob had a little rest, and when he did his acoustic thing, we had a rest.

"At first we were going to do a few cities, but as we went along, we got stronger and more courage and it ended up pretty large. The whole tour was a high, but I don't enjoy touring that much. With all the time we've done on the road, there's maybe three times that I actually enjoyed it, and [the '74 tour] was one of the times. It was smooth and tasty and a lot of fun to do, and we got through it alive!

"This was a Dylan/Band tour. We enjoyed playing with him. We got accepted very well. Ten years ago we were just some musicians working with Bob Dylan, but this time we were more than a backing band.

"When we did the Dylan and Band tour in '74, where we went and did a lot of the same things we did back in '66 . . . the people's response was 'This is the shit and I knew it all along.' It was like, you weren't really there all along. It's interesting and it's one of the things I talked about in my keynote speech that I had to make at the 2002 SXSW conference."

RIGHT: Set list for Bob Dylan and The Band's performance at the Boston Garden, January 14, 1974.

```
BOSTON - JANUARY 14, 1974

        FIRST SET

      1  - RAINY DAY WOMEN
  A   2  - LAY LADY LAY
  G   3  - TOM THUMB BLUES
  G   4  - I DON'T BELIEVE YOU
      5  - IT AIN'T ME BABE
  BM  6  - MR. JONES
  EM  7  - STAGEFRIGHT
  C   8  - DIXIE
  C   9  - KING HARVEST
     10  - WHEELS ON FIRE
  E  11  - I SHALL BE RELEASED
  A  12  - CRIPPLE CREEK
  AM 13  - ALL ALONG THE WATCHTOWER
     14  - HOLLIS BROWN
  G  15  - KNOCKIN ON HEAVENS DOOR

        SECOND SET

      1  - BOB - ACOUSTIC   times changin
      2  - BOB - ACOUSTIC   don't think twice
      3  - BOB - ACOUSTIC   of war an peace
      4  - BOB - ACOUSTIC   just like a woman
                            its allright ma
      5  - RAG MAMA RAG
      6  - WHEN YOU AWAKE
      7  - SHAPE I'M IN
  A   8  - THE WEIGHT
  G   9  - SOMETHING THERE IS    D  FOREVER YOUNG
  C  10  - LIKE A ROLLING STONE
```

"**There was no booing now, and the fact that most facilities were around twenty thousand seats negated any option for past intimate concerts. As the group reacted to the new, loud, and admiring crowds, the music got louder and the tempo became faster. Everyone was excited.**" —William Scheele

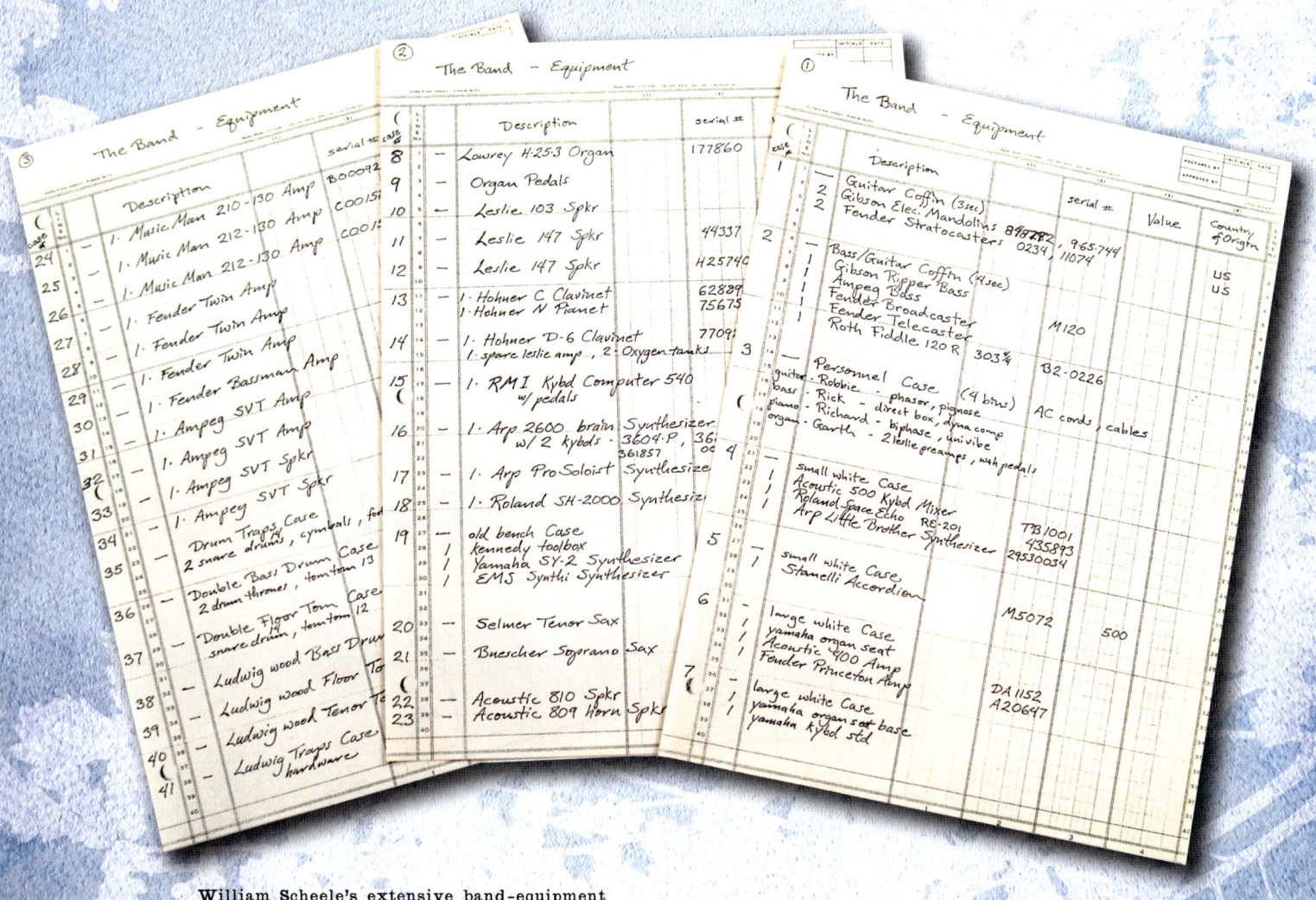

William Scheele's extensive band-equipment inventory lists for Tour '74.

OUT IN MALIBU WITH A DIFFERENT VIEW   161

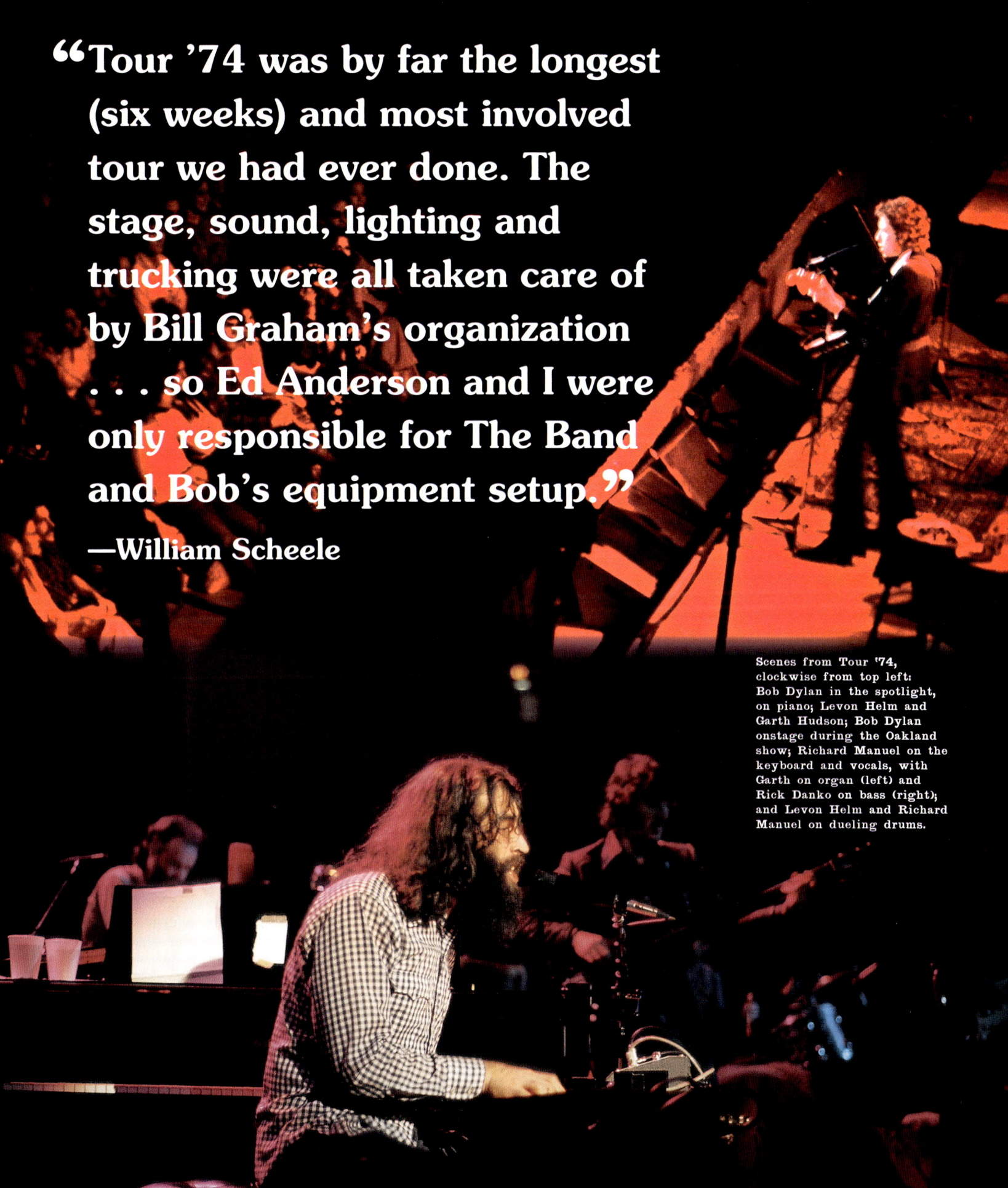

"Tour '74 was by far the longest (six weeks) and most involved tour we had ever done. The stage, sound, lighting and trucking were all taken care of by Bill Graham's organization . . . so Ed Anderson and I were only responsible for The Band and Bob's equipment setup."
—William Scheele

Scenes from Tour '74, clockwise from top left: Bob Dylan in the spotlight, on piano; Levon Helm and Garth Hudson; Bob Dylan onstage during the Oakland show; Richard Manuel on the keyboard and vocals, with Garth on organ (left) and Rick Danko on bass (right); and Levon Helm and Richard Manuel on dueling drums.

"People finally forgot about the possibility of The Band and Bob Dylan playing together again. We decided it was a new day."
–Robbie Robertson

Bob Dylan between songs, during a Tour '74 gig.

Levon Helm in action, Tour '74.

Three shows at the "Fabulous" Forum in Inglewood, California—one on February 13 and two on Valentine's Day—concluded Tour '74.

WILLIAM SCHEELE

"There was a closing party at the Beverly Wilshire Hotel after the last Forum show. Cher arranged the party for David Geffen's birthday and to honor him for arranging the tour with the record companies representing Bob Dylan and The Band. It was held in a large party room, with lots of colored balloons and lights. Many celebrities and friends were there, including Louis Kemp, David Blue, Bobby Neuwirth, Ringo Starr, Jack Nicholson, and Bill Graham. Cher got to sing with Bob and The Band, much to everyone's delight!"

Bob Dylan and The Band setting the stage on fire, Tour '74.

Cher performs with Bob Dylan and The Band at the closing party for Tour '74 at the Beverly Wilshire Hotel.

Hangin' with Richard and Garth

KENNETH KUBERNIK

"My seat was crap, way up in the colonnade, where the Los Angeles Forum isn't so fabulous. It was February 14, the last night of the Dylan/Band tour, and I found some small solace by just bearing witness. I don't recall much about the show—animated figurines viewed through the wrong end of a telescope whose sound and fury took as long to reach me as the light from Orion's Belt.

"Having felt deprived of really experiencing the music, a friend and I decided to pay a visit the next afternoon to Mr. Dylan himself, who was staying at the Beverly Wilshire Hotel, a faux European pile whose elegant interiors and liveried staff demanded a modicum of decorum from a couple of young punks who had no business reaching for the house phone and demanding to speak to Hibbing, Minnesota's favorite blue-eyed son.

"'Mr. Dylan has checked out. Can I direct your call to another party?'

"'Um, yeah, uh, could you call Richard Manuel's room, please?'

"What the hell. We were there, frightfully emboldened, and were holding some killer smoke. It didn't take Wernher Von Braun to know that offering a taste might shake the tree a little. And, lo and behold, he answered the phone with a dazed, 'Yeah, hello.' 'Uh, hey, Richard, we saw the show last night and wondered if you wanted to come down and join us for a drink, uh, just hang. . . ' Incredibly, he couldn't have been more of a sport, beckoning us to 'come on up, but give me 'bout twenty minutes to pull it together.'

"A lovely blonde lady opened the door, and he quickly greeted us with a toothy, disheveled grin, embracing us like long-lost mates from those wild Yonge Street nights.

"'Hey, boys, glad you liked the show. Can I get you a little . . . something?'

"And so it was, for the next hour and change, shooting the breeze with that orphaned voice. Occasionally, a head would pop in to check to see the body was still breathing. And then there was a knock on the door and Garth Hudson entered. He merely nodded, uttering a rumble like the twang of a low E string on a bass fiddle.

"At some point, as a skunky haze settled over the room, Garth said, 'I'd kinda like to go up to that record store up on Sunset.'

"'Oh, you mean Tower Records?'

"'That's the one.'

"'We'd be happy to take you up there.'

"'I'd appreciate it.'

"Twenty minutes later we're pulling into the Tower Records lot on the Sunset Strip. Once inside, Garth browsed without incident; hidden underneath all that facial hair and burnished reticence, he was as unprepossessing a rock god as one could imagine. My own taste in music was gravitating toward that dreaded genre, prog rock, a gateway drug that would lead me to that fatal affliction, jazz.

"Fortunately, Garth was ecumenical in his interests and we ended up in the swing music section, where he enthusiastically flipped through titles by Goodman, James, Glenn Miller. He then pulled out an album, handed it to me.

"'Son, you should listen to this.'

"'Joe . . . Venuti?'

"Long before Google and smartphones, this was how we learned about music, soaking up the wisdom of our elders. Garth thanked us for the ride, insisting on taking a cab back to the hotel, and we parted, leaving him to wander the aisles, a lonesome mariner in search of a lost chord."

Garth Hudson, Richard Manuel, and Rick Danko in Oakland, February 11, 1974.

In June 1974, a live, two-disc recording from the tour, *Before the Flood* appeared—engineered by Phil Ramone and recording and mixing engineer Rob Fraboni with Nat Jeffrey at Village Recorders—a lively keepsake of this one-and-done journey through the past.

One can hear the promise realized, those miraculous songs executed with a heavyweight punch. Given Dylan's Rushmore-like stature, it would have been easy for The Band to slip into backing-band mode, a throwback to their Hawks days. But there is never an instance when they didn't command the stage as anything less than Bob's equals—men to match his mountain.

The balance of the year found them playing the part of a working band; a series of stadium dates in the United States, in London and around Europe had them sharing the stage with the likes of Crosby, Stills, Nash & Young—earning huge paydays but perhaps offering little artistic satisfaction.

Then it was 1975: a new year, another opportunity for The Band to start afresh. There was a beehive of activity back at Zuma Beach, that sparkling stretch at the northern edge of Malibu that housed Shangri-La Studio, a onetime brothel turned bad-boy clubhouse, home to a 24-track recording console, a pool room, a crash pad for Richard, and a place to cast their weary souls.

> "Shangri-La was just a short walk from Zuma Beach in Malibu—quite a change for The Band from basements and rented studio spaces. Light just *poured* in the windows—blindingly bright. So much music happened there but only a fraction was ever released. . . . Robbie was usually in control at the board—directing the process and the mix himself." — John Scheele

The Malibu coast as it looked in 1975, as The Band set up shop there to record their sixth studio album at Shangri-La *Northern Lights–Southern Cross*.

INSET RIGHT: William Scheele's construction notes for The Band's studio at Shangri-La.

WILLIAM SCHEELE

"Shangri-La was a long, extended ranch house complex that ran along a ridge looking down at the Pacific Ocean. It was a pretty cool place, elevated and private. In the beginning, I lived in an old stable on the property and Levon and others lived in the wings off the central studio.

"We converted a large center room that was big enough to hold all of The Band's equipment and move things around as needed. Village Recorder and Ed Anderson put the control-room equipment together, and I was responsible for instruments and amp equipment. In the studio, The Band knew they could do certain things without having to go to the isolation booth concept. Because it was their studio, they could play or sing individually or as a group. We used movable baffles for amplifiers, drums, and general separation of musicians. . . .

"The Band was now in the Hollywood and L.A. area, and this was the kind of thing that turned me off after a while. Way too many hanger-on types started coming around and wasting everybody's time."

At the mixing console at Shangri-La Studio, Malibu, 1975. Seated, from left to right: arranger Larry Fallon, Robbie Robertson, and mixer Rob Fraboni; standing behind them is guitarist-songwriter Hirth Martinez.

June 26, 1975, saw Columbia Records release *The Basement Tapes*, a bowdlerized two-disc compilation from the mythic 1967 performances, remixed at Village Recorders.

Overseen by Robertson (with many indiscreet overdubs and elisions that angered some of the more discerning Dylanologists), it was seen as an attempt to put paid to the many poor-quality bootlegs circulating among hard-core collectors.

"We thought we'd see what we had. I started going through the stuff and sorting it out, trying to make it stand up for a record that wasn't recorded professionally," stressed Robbie in our conversation for the March 1976 *Crawdaddy* article.

"I also tried to include some things that people haven't heard before, if possible. I just wanted to document a period rather than let them rot away on the shelves somewhere. It was an unusual time that caused all those songs to be written. It was better it be out on disc some way than be lost in an attic."

During an interview with journalist and artist Dennis Loren, published in the July/August 1985 issue of *RPM* magazine, Danko discussed *The Basement Tapes*.

"So really, *The Basement Tapes* only reflects a small portion of the songs we wrote. Seems like we did a million of them. In 1973, I moved out to California to do *Planet Waves* and *Before the Flood*. At the time there was a lot of bootlegging going on, and Bob suggested that why don't we put out *The Basement Tapes* as an album. We used the Shangri-La in Malibu and cleaned it up a little bit. We ran it through the new machine and added some tubes and transistors. 'Wheel's on Fire' is one of my songs. I wrote that with Bob Dylan."

OPPOSITE: Levon Helm and Bob Dylan try on costumes for *The Basement Tapes* cover shoot; Dylan's white poncho was eventually swapped out for a colorful striped top.

JOHN SCHEELE

"Reid Miles was the *Basement Tapes* photographer—a true giant in the world of record album design dating back from his Blue Note days. I took documentary stills while everyone got high and tried on different outfits. The guys had gone by Western Costume earlier to get fitted, on the Paramount lot.

"They got dressed upstairs before descending into the boiler room where Reid had been setting up for the shot. Bob tried on a white poncho before settling on a brightly colored Mexican sweater. Then somehow putting on his hat topped it off—and everybody cracked up. Bob was so quick to assume a disguise—that aloof and reclusive personality of his vanished in a flash. They all had great fun acting out character roles for the shoot."

WILLIAM SCHEELE

"Bob Cato arranged the shoot. . . . He had been the graphic designer for The Band going back to *Music from Big Pink*. He incorporated a bunch of Hollywood extras for the project. Bob wanted to have characters from *Basement Tapes* songs, not just he and The Band."

> "Reid created an amazing cover photo down in the Hollywood YMCA basement. . . . Something of the droll and raunchy *Basement* vibe definitely came through . . . even if it was a world away from Big Pink."
> —John Scheele

Also during the spring and summer of 1975, The Band recorded new music for the first time in four years, dipping in and out of the studio at Shangri-La as their inspiration ebbed and flowed. The result, *Northern Lights–Southern Cross*, was released on November 1, 1975, to generally favorable reviews.

For many of the cognoscenti it echoed their early strengths, intertwining vocal lines, deft instrumental coloration (thank you, Garth), and, most important, some of Robbie's finest songcraft. Tunes like "Ophelia" (a tip of the chapeau to legendary Grand Ole Opry comedian Minnie Pearl, whose real name was Sarah Ophelia Colley Cannon) and the rollicking wry nod to "nodding out," "Forbidden Fruit," enjoyed that buoyant cadence that worked well live. The hymn-like "Acadian Driftwood" and Danko's stirring read on "It Makes No Difference" displayed The Band's singular ability to portray epic themes with an elemental grace.

In a January 3, 1976, interview I [Harvey] did with Robbie for *Melody Maker,* we chatted about the LP as he gave me a tour of Shangri-La.

"Our music brings home things that you take for granted. We've been together for fifteen years and it would be unnatural if all of a sudden we were going to be rock symbols or rock stars. That's all meaningless to us.

"I like the way they sing my songs. Rick, Levon, and Richard are just as much a part. Rick wrote one of the songs we had to take off. It's just a particular time when one of the guys has more songs written than other times. It just fell that way.

"The album title," Robbie declared, "came from the air. I was sitting by the water one night, looking up at the sky, and it just popped into my mind. I mentioned it to everybody and they seemed to like it. It fits for some reason. It's a Band album. Not a Band album with 101 strings, horn sections, and a bunch of arrangers."

Robbie then provided some background on "Acadian Driftwood" and "Ophelia." On the former, he explained, "When you grow up in Canada, the weather is very predominant in your upbringing. The summers are very hot and the winters are very cold and these things play a big part in your disposition. Your way of life is probably left over from that. It's not that I'm a nature freak."

Regarding "Ophelia," he said "I was always fascinated by that girl's name. I always like the mystery factor. I may be writing a song and the music may imply a certain lyric, or vice versa. It's not that deliberate, or an intellectual exercise. It just comes out naturally."

Robbie also made time to produce records by Hirth Martinez, an idiosyncratic singer/songwriter from L.A., and Neil Diamond, whose Brill Building backstory chimed with Robertson's deep regard for that storied songwriter's arcadia.

Levon, in his own fashion, manned the helm for an album at Turtle Creek Studio in Bearsville by Clarksdale, Mississippi's own Muddy Waters, paying tribute to the iconic bluesman as well as his own Southern heritage.

CELESTE GOYER

"'Ophelia' has that wonderful contrast between subject and style. The lonely, abandoned man isn't mournful; he's on a full romp with his mates. What a change from the soft solo songwriters who'd been comforting my adolescent confusion. The Band were adults, with a capable, rough, and earthy masculinity. I had the feeling they could walk off the stage and build a cabin from raw timber with just hand tools. . . . They had their edges intact. It wasn't a calculated PR department sexuality, but a complex, fully adult stance of immense appeal."

SARAH KRAMER

"You hear the New Orleans influence again in 'Ophelia.' And Levon's musical feel and vocal delivery on the recording is awesome.

"As a drummer he sounds melodic to me, even though he is doing a rhythm job. And when you are doing both, which Levon did, it's like the full circle. . . .

"I sang and played trumpet on 'Ophelia' in 2017 at the Wild Honey Foundation Band Big Pink Autism Benefit in Glendale. I asked the music director, Rob Laufer, to include it in the show."

The Band at Shangri-La Studio working on *Northern Lights–Southern Cross*, 1975.

CHAPTER 11
THE BAND HAS LEFT THE BUILDING

America's bicentennial year, 1976, found the group back on the road, playing a variety of theaters and outdoor venues better suited to their multilayered, artisanal sound. Momentum was building in their performances; a lightness in their dynamics carried them through to the fall until Manuel brought the carnival to a frightening halt.

A boating accident following a gig in Austin forced the cancellation of ten concerts. Richard's endless dance with death was taking a wearying toll on them; awaiting the dreaded "phone call" never drifted far from anyone's consciousness.

It's often been stated that a band is like a marriage—when it fails, it can get ugly, which is one word to describe the others' response when Robbie announced that he had had enough of life on the road.

In a May 1995 interview with Kevin Ransom in *Guitar Player* Magazine, both Robbie and Rick looked back over the decision to end the journey.

Danko concluded that "Robbie wasn't the only one who wanted to do other things. Before *The Last Waltz*, I signed a production deal with Clive Davis to do my solo show. Sometimes it breaks my heart when I remember that, in '76, Warner [Bros.] offered us a $6 million deal to do an album a year, and we passed. But there's more to life than living off your royalties."

And then there was the elephantine presence of substance abuse, which had a ruinous effect on so many musicians of that era.

"I didn't know anyone who wasn't completely fucked up at the time," Robbie told Ransom. "As a result, making records became very painful. . . It bruises you in your soul. . . . And believe me, I was no angel during that period, but, to put it really bluntly, I was just more scared than they were."

Robbie was now reaching his wit's end; the ceaseless carousing, the exhausting oversight brought him to the edge of exhaustion. He believed that it was time to pull the plug, the road having taken one last bite.

OPPOSITE: Rick Danko, Robbie Robertson, Richard Manuel, and Levon Helm onstage at the Winterland Ballroom during *The Last Waltz*, Thanksgiving Day, November 25, 1976.

Their ten-album deal with Capitol Records was to be fulfilled with a collection of original tracks and cover tunes culled from 1972–77 sessions at Shangri-La and Village Recorders (*Islands*, eventually released in March 1977), a deceptive coda to the more grandiose event hatched by Robertson to send The Band out on an unprecedented high note.

He proposed that they put on a show, an extravaganza, a celebration of all the artists and inspirations that informed their music—the ultimate musical roundup, "The Last Waltz." And he suggested that director Martin Scorsese film it and that Bill Graham provide the facility, the set design, and the food services, and hold it on America's national holiday for giving thanks.

The project began in 1976 when Jonathan Taplin, executive producer of *The Last Waltz*—who had been The Band's road manager for years and had produced Scorsese's breakout film *Mean Streets*—introduced Robertson to Scorsese, who had helped edit *Woodstock* and *Elvis on Tour*.

That this still viable but dysfunctional outfit could still mount the stage one last, epochal time and perform with such fire and fury is one of the most heroic acts in the calamitous history of rock 'n' roll.

Before the final curtain fell on November 25, 1976—Thanksgiving Day—at San Francisco's Winterland Ballroom, the location of their first-ever performance in 1969, The Band, along with a rogues' gallery of fellow musical travelers, reached across their resplendent past to rage one last glorious time.

"The idea came around in probably September," Robertson mentioned to me in a 2002 *Goldmine* magazine interview.

> Then I needed to talk to everybody about it and it had to germinate, the whole thing.
>
> What happened with the idea was—and this is what I have found in my experience, this is the way things often happen—when you come up with something so right it takes on a life of its own. And when I started thinking about originally that we were going to do this and who we were going to invite, we'd only talked about Bob Dylan and Ronnie Hawkins. And then there were other people

who had been so supportive and that we respected so much musically, that we said, 'If we're gonna invite them, we shouldn't forget Eric [Clapton].' Over the years I saw him a lot.

The same thing with Van [Morrison]. And then there's our countrymen from Canada, Joni and Neil, and the whole thing just snowballed in a way and it was almost like your job, a good portion of time was to get out of the way.

Robbie further added in a 2016 interview we did for *Record Collector News* magazine, "And in mixing it up, we ran through a bunch of crazy ideas too. Like, Bob said, 'Should we do a Johnny Cash song?' And he would start singing a Johnny song and we all knew this was never gonna fly. But it would be fun to play it. We'd play through it and say, 'No.' But all of this stuff, it was really like throwing things up in the air and see where they would fall."

"Bob said, 'You know, one song I think we should do is 'Hazel.' We were like, 'Really? OK. Let's do it.' And we ran through it and it felt pretty good. . . . We knew we wanted to do 'Forever Young,' because it connected to the occasion with all the people there and this generation and all of this stuff. Like Dr. John singing 'Such a Night.'"

—Robbie Robertson

MICHAEL HACKER
filmmaker

"The morning Robert Hilburn's column announcing The Band's farewell concert ran in the *Los Angeles Times*, the details seemed unreal. They were going to serve Thanksgiving dinner from 4 to 6 p.m.? At Winterland? There would be chandeliers?

"Of course, the biggest question of all was would Dylan show? All my friends in L.A. and the Bay Area were music freaks, but none of them were willing to shell out the twenty-five bucks for a ticket. So, the day before the show, I drove up to San Francisco by myself in my mom's 1970 Buick Wildcat.

"People started lining up and it wasn't long before Bill Graham came by, checking out the crowd and saying hello.

"And The Band seemed generous, not like they were trying to make some final statement, but rather wanting to thank some of their fellow travelers for accompanying them on the journey."

OPPOSITE: Closeup of *The Last Waltz* marquee at the Winterland Ballroom, November 1976.

In spite of the backbiting and the verbal jousts, The Band were forever tied to the mast by their shared artistic destiny. Like water to wine, they transubstantiated everything they heard, felt, and encountered over those incandescent years into a seamless, bespoke quilt, humbling in its detail, majestic in its scope. And so it was on such a night.

Over the course of four breathless hours, more than five thousand delirious fans—their bellies full of turkey, stuffing, and all the trimmings, courtesy of Mr. Bill Graham—rejoiced to a juke joint jamboree, their ears ringing with the glow of one imperishable magical moment after another, preserved forever under the hot-wired reverie of director Martin Scorsese.

JOHN DONABIE

"My family and I are living on the West Coast, in Vancouver. The phone rings one day and it's Levon. 'John D?'—which is what he called me—'We're calling it quits.'

"After getting over the shock, he invites me to *The Last Waltz* in San Francisco. Each member of The Band would invite particular friends. 'I'll take care of you when you get here.'

"It's important to note that there would be long time frames I would not see him. However, every time you saw Levon, he treated you as if it were yesterday you were together with him.

"We're at a rehearsal one afternoon and Ronnie Hawkins, myself, and Levon are standing on the stage. Everyone's taking a break. They bring out the food. Tons of chicken wings. I was hungry and grabbed a wing. One of Bill Graham's people tells me to keep my hands off the food. It's only for musicians. "Levon looks at him and says, 'If you want this drummer to rehearse you'll give him what he wants.' Levon could look right through you. The guy was definitely intimidated.

"The only rehearsals for *The Last Waltz* I didn't and couldn't see were the rehearsals with Dylan. Everything else, I attended. Best week of my life. I do have to point out during the concert that when the Canadian flag was behind them and they did 'Four Strong Winds' by Ian Tyson, there wasn't a dry eye from the Canadian contingent I was surrounded with at the time."

"The Last Waltz" Welcome

We hope you enjoy spending Thanksgiving with us here at Winterland. We'd like to let you know what arrangements have been made to make sure that everyone is served dinner, comfortably. Here's the order of events.

When you enter the lobby, you have two choices. You may proceed to the main floor, or to the balcony. The same Thanksgiving dinner will be served on both levels.

On the main floor, tables have been set up so you may sit for dinner. After you've finished, please clear your place so that another person may sit down. Upstairs, you may sit in the balcony seats after getting your dinner at the buffet tables on the mezzanine. After your meal, please take care to discard your plates. Ushers will be circulating with trash bags to assist you.

For the vegetarians among you, special meatless dishes have been prepared. They will be served at a table at the end of the right aisle on the main floor.

Beginning at 5:00 p.m., the 38 piece Berkeley Promenade Orchestra will be playing. A formal dance floor has been set up in front of the stage for your dancing pleasure. We welcome you to dance with us until 8:00 p.m. when the dance floor and the tables will be cleared in preparation for the 9:00 p.m. concert. After the concert, you are again invited to enjoy the dance music of the Berkeley Promenade Orchestra. We hope that our visiting artists will join us during these festivities.

We thank you for your courteous cooperation in making this a day to remember. It could only happen in San Francisco, and that's because of you.

Happy Thanksgiving! Happy listening! Happy Waltzing! Enjoy!

Cheers!
Bill & All the other Turkeys

LEFT: Concertgoers line up outside the Winterland Ballroom before the doors open for *The Last Waltz*, November 25, 1976.

TOP: A circular welcome card handed out to attendees of *The Last Waltz* with information about where to sit for Thanksgiving dinner and the order of festivities.

THE BAND HAS LEFT THE BUILDING

"The Band's Last Stand"

HARVEY KUBERNIK

The Last Waltz was the live-music education class curriculum I never took at Fairfax High School, now displayed straight out of my own record collection. The December 11, 1976, issue of *Melody Maker* published my review, excerpted here, of the concert under the headline "The Band's Last Stand":

"'The blues at its most!' Robbie Robertson exclaimed. 'Muddy Waters!' Pinetop Perkins was in on piano, and Bob Margolin on guitar, as Muddy, in a sharp green suit, performed 'Caldonia' and 'Mannish Boy.'

"Robbie continued: 'To play a little guitar, Eric Clapton.' He did two numbers: 'All Our Past Times'

182　THE STORY OF THE BAND

from *No Reason to Cry* and then a barn-burning version of Bobby 'Blue' Bland's 'Further On up the Road.' I hadn't seen Clapton smoke like this since 1970 when I caught Derek and the Dominos at the Pasadena Civic Auditorium.

'"A friend of ours from Canada,' enthused Robbie. 'Neil Young.'

"'Thank you,' spoke Young. 'It's one of the pleasures of my life being on this stage.'

"Neil sang 'Four Strong Winds' and 'Helpless,' joined by Joni Mitchell on harmony who sang 'Coyote' and 'Shadow and Light.'

OPPOSITE: Joni Mitchell and Neil Young harmonize together on "Acadian Driftwood" during *The Last Waltz*.

ABOVE: A view of all of the performers onstage during one of the group jam sessions.

"Van Morrison was then introduced. A riveting 'Caravan' ended Morrison's portion. A few energetic kicks and he split the scene of the rhyme. The Band finished the first half with 'Acadian Driftwood.'

"The intermission was a handful of poets from San Francisco and City Lights Books who all read.

"At midnight, Garth Hudson's Lowrey organ started 'Chest Fever,' and the rest of The Band took their places. 'The Last Waltz Theme' was next—a new song so fresh the lyrics had to be written on huge cue cards for the vocalists to read. The Band was so flexible and flawless in execution yet far from programmed. A musical delight.

"'The Weight' ended their segment before Robbie introduced the last guest. 'We'd like to bring on one last friend of ours, Bob Dylan.'

"They began with 'Baby, Let Me Follow You Down,' followed by 'Hazel' and 'Forever Young' from *Planet Waves*. Then a penetrating 'I Don't Believe You (She Acts Like We Never Have Met).' Helm's drum work hammered the words over the auditorium and The Band propelled Dylan, who responded to the professionals behind him. A short reprise of 'Baby, Let Me Follow You Down' signaled the climax of Dylan's appearance.

"The Band waved for all the previous participants to join them along with Ronnie Wood, Carl Radle, and Ringo Starr sitting in on drums for a lengthy 'I Shall Be Released.'

"Off they went and Robbie returned. 'We're having a party and you're all invited.' Two more

Poet Lawrence Ferlinghetti reads his poem "Loud Prayer" during intermission.

fifteen-minute jams with a late-arriving Stephen Stills showing up, embracing Young, while Governor Jerry Brown, along with Albert Grossman, Bobby Neuwirth, and Ronee Blakley, watched from the sidelines."

John Simon served as concert musical director. The Filmways/Wally Heider team of engineers was led by Elliot Mazer. The soundtrack was produced by Robbie Robertson, with co-production by Rob Fraboni and John Simon.

> "At midnight, Garth Hudson's Lowrey organ started 'Chest Fever,' and the rest of The Band took their places.... The Band was so flexible and flawless in execution yet far from programmed." —Harvey Kubernik, "The Band's Last Stand"
> *Melody Maker, December 11, 1976*

Bob Dylan joined The Band for six songs at the concert, including "I Shall Be Released," which he is shown singing here with Van Morrison and Robbie Robertson.

*T*he *Last Waltz* film was released theatrically on April 26, 1978, and became the first concert documentary to be shot in 35mm and the first to use a 24-track recording system. It has become a sacred totem among connoisseurs of rock music documentaries, the metric by which all other concert films are measured. In 1977, I interviewed Rick Danko for *Bay Area Music* about the show. He recalled,

> The cameras didn't inhibit anyone. We wanted to feed five thousand people a gourmet dinner, and I think we also gave 'em a good show. You were there. You saw the concert. Wasn't it terrific? We had people stashed behind the curtains giving us hand signals. The movie is a labor of love. At the start, The Band had to raise a few hundred thousand bucks so this event could become a reality. We were taking a chance—we almost hocked our houses.
>
> We were the perfect house band. Even the rehearsals were incredible. It was a special night.
>
> Preparing for the gig was a trip in itself. For four days we did nothing but play music. We finished *Islands*, our last album for Capitol, and then nonstop rehearsal for *The Last Waltz*.
>
> The Band really came alive that night. We were cruising the last year and it was obvious. We were onstage for six hours and The Band worked until 5 A.M. that morning. We rehearsed with Bob [Dylan] at the hotel. We played for sixteen hours before the gig.

ROBBIE ROBERTSON

"Thank God this was captured in such a beautiful way, too. And that you can really see this and really go inside it, and really feel a part of the whole thing.

"This is the real thing in a setting of such respectful elegance. This was like an outstanding experience. Sometimes I had to just catch myself not to be standing there with my mouth open.

"Because it's a movie. It isn't just a video of something, where you're looking at it and saying, 'Is this fake?' 'Is this real?' 'Is this being fluffed up like a television commercial?'"

Eric Clapton did two songs: "All Our Past Times" (which Rick Danko cowrote with Clapton) and "Further On up the Road."

THE STORY OF THE BAND

"The Band has always been into precision, like a fine car. We didn't take it easy during preparation. I think that will show in the movie. No split-screen stuff and very little backstage footage. No way was I gonna walk out onstage and wing it next to Joni Mitchell. And Muddy Waters...." —Rick Danko

Muddy Waters (with Robbie Robertson to the left) during his rousing performance of "Mannish Boy."

"OF COURSE I'VE WATCHED *THE LAST WALTZ*. WHAT A GREAT TRIBUTE TO THEIR LEGACY. I JUST KEEP LISTENING AND PLAYING THEIR MUSIC, LIKE JAZZ STANDARDS, YOU HOPE EACH NEW GENERATION DISCOVERS AND REINTERPRETS THEM."
— JACK DEJOHNETTE

BELOW: Another *Last Waltz* jam session, featuring, from left to right: Carl Radle, Neil Young, Levon Helm, Robbie Robertson, Paul Butterfield, Eric Clapton, and Ron Wood

TOP: Rick Danko, Ronnie Hawkins, and Robbie Robertson perform the Bo Diddley classic "Who Do You Love?"

BOTTOM, From left to right: Dr. John, Neil Diamond, Joni Mitchell, Neil Young, Rick Danko, Van Morrison, Bob Dylan, and Robbie Robertson during the performance of Dylan's "I Shall Be Released." Other performers who joined in (but not shown) include Ringo Starr and Ron Wood.

THE BAND HAS LEFT THE BUILDING   189

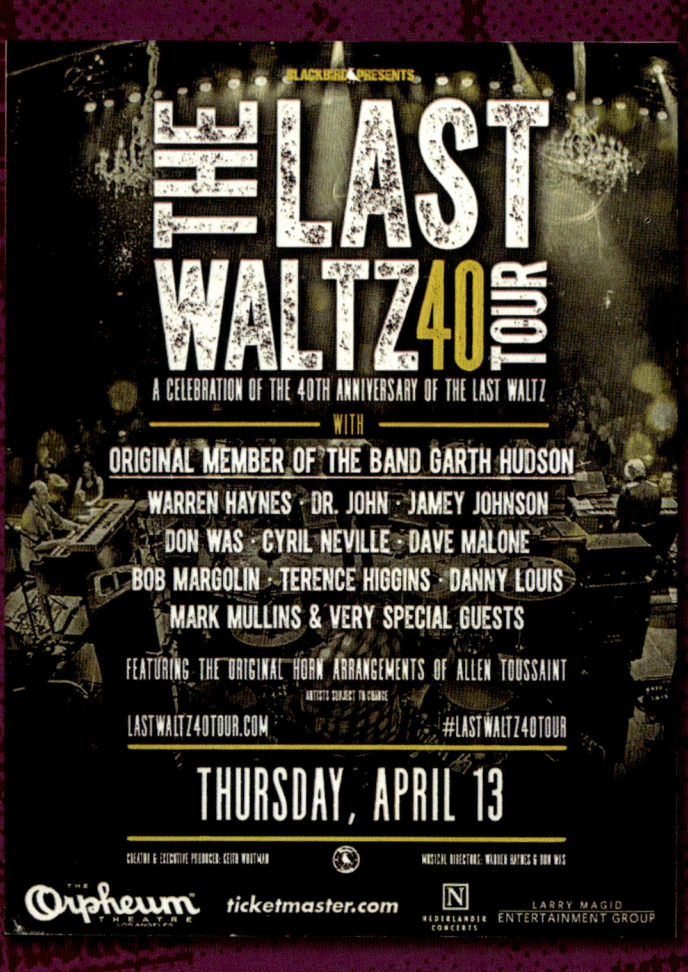

DON WAS

"When I went out in 2017 and did the Blackbird Presents *The Last Waltz 40 Tour: A Celebration of the 40th Anniversary of The Last Waltz*, you see the faces in the audience. They were standing up from the first song and sang every song. They knew everything. And we could see a real hunger to hear this music performed en masse. It had become an integral part of their musical lives."

MIKE STOLLER

"I loved the *Music from Big Pink* album, especially 'The Weight,' one of so many great songs Robbie wrote. I was especially knocked out when The Band recorded a terrific version of our song 'Saved' on *Moondog Matinee*, and very surprised and pleased when Leiber and Stoller were mentioned in the film *The Last Waltz*.

"I've bumped into Robbie occasionally over the years, and it's always been a happy moment. Robbie's such a great guy. And I'm still really impressed by his guitar playing."

WILLIAM SCHEELE

"If you examine the catalog of The Band, their strength and appeal lies in the fact that they tell compelling stories and examine the feelings and emotions of people. There was nothing abstract about it, and they embellished their words with incredibly intricate and strong musical accompaniment.

"The group was a highly precise five-piece band. They were sharp and powerful. Their expression was full and exuded emotion in their performances. And their desire from the start, especially in small halls, was to create the best possible experience for their audience. They wanted everyone to hear all the voices and instrumentation clearly, for they were. . . . The Band!"

ABOVE LEFT: Promo card announcing the April 13, 2017, date for The Last Waltz 40 Tour at the Orpheum Theatre in Los Angeles.

BELOW: Etching of The Band by William Scheele.

CODA

The song "It Makes No Difference" from *Northern Lights–Southern Cross* is playing on the local hipster college radio station as these words are being written. The tune's rueful portrait of love's high cost contrasts sharply with the station's usual parade of alt singer-songwriters, whose earnest, fuzz-faced rhymes are weak tea compared to the Promethean standards of The Band. It's hard to believe that beneath their facial shrub and riverboat grins, The Band's members were once young men themselves, ambition rooted in their quaintly courteous, wary ways.

Robbie was just a boy when the Hawk snagged him. But Robbie could pull those Telecaster strings like an Olympic archer, letting fly with one stinging lead after another. Richard, whose wolfish exterior belied an anguished, aching spirit, conjured a voice that cut through the fug of life like a windswept lighthouse beacon. Garth, quiet and brooding, was a man content to listen with all his senses so that his every utterance carried an inscrutable weight. And there was Levon, pounding the skins, a rebel with a yell that echoed from deep within a rascally, rebellious soul, a man who cut to the chase in the first act. Levon told you how it was gonna be and you'd be a damn fool not to pay heed.

They arrived on the scene with a volley of buckshot in 1968. *Music from Big Pink* set a new standard, extending further the innovations of their musical confederates. Groups like Traffic, Procol Harum, and even the Rolling Stones laid tracks that echoed The Band's majestic mountains. One can just hear Richard's searing croak do justice to Traffic's gripping "No Time to Live" or perhaps Levon's roadhouse take on Procol's "Shine on Brightly," and Rick could be singing instead of Mick with that forlorn swagger on "No Expectations." It was a period rife with chaos and it brought the best out of the artists who were most willing to dig deep to wrest three minutes of honest feeling from the craziness.

After *The Last Waltz*, one more Band studio album was released, in March 1977. Called *Islands*, it was mostly previously unreleased tracks from a variety of recording sessions dating back to 1972 (see page 178). A few solo albums followed as well as session work, and a smattering of reunion tours, sans Robbie. Levon enjoyed a brief, but acclaimed turn as an actor, including his role as Loretta Lynn's father in the 1980 award-winning film *Coal Miner's Daughter*. But the shadow never seemed to fade far enough away. It engulfed Richard first, whose harrowing end had a grim inevitability to it; Rick, beat down by the ravages of a life lived large and hard, went next. Levon valiantly carried on until 2012, his barnstorming rambles keeping the carnival aloft. Garth soldiers on with characteristic steadfastness, surfacing occasionally with his Merlinesque sonic elixirs. Robbie also did a short turn as an actor, in the 1980 film *Carny*. He was the music producer of numerous film soundtracks, including many Scorsese projects (also composing the music for *The Color of Money*). He continues to record as a solo artist, and his 2016 autobiography *Testimony* was a *New York Times* best seller.

At their best, The Band brought a cauldron of sound—rockabilly and southern comfort, midtown pop and uptown jazz, old country twang and urban blues—to a lip-smacking boil, in the most joyous, authentic way possible. They succeeded beyond their wildest reckoning, forever and always-faithful servants to the music.

The Band's *Last Waltz*.

ACKNOWLEDGMENTS

The Kubernik brothers would like to offer gratitude and special thanks to: At Sterling Publishing, dream team collaborator—our editor Barbara Berger, the first responder, who developed our concept and journey, photo editor Linda Liang, for the precise visual placements, and production editor Scott Amerman, as well as cover designer Igor Satanovksy for the beautiful cover, cover director Elizabeth Lindy, interior art director Christine Heun, creative operations director Kevin Ullrich, and designer Bruce McKillip; Kevin Baier for the stunning interior design; the Gary and Greg Strobl infield combo at the Henry Diltz photography studio for visual library and technical support; trusted copy editor Joseph McCombs; John Simon; Larry LeBlanc; Martin Mulhuish; John Donabie; Tom Wilson; Gary Pig Gold; Elliott Lefko; Rob Bowman; Sharry Wilson; John Brower; Andrew Loog Oldham; third base coach William Scheele; John Scheele; Katelyn O'Neil; Quinn Martin; Jennifer Ballantyne; Jeff Rosen; Peter Alan Roberts; Barney Hoskyns and www.rocksbackpages.com; Michael Hacker; Jim Kaplan at *Record Collector News* magazine; Greil Marcus; David and Adam Tenenbaum; Richard Williams; Ray Coleman; Steven Van Zandt; Tom Cording; Patti Wright; David Kessel and www.cavehollywood.com; Rodney Bingenheimer; Jim Roup; Dave Love; Jerry Leiber; Sherry Hendrick; James Cushing and Celeste Goyer; Robbie Robertson; Jared Levine; Bob Dylan; Travis Pike; Jason Elzy; Jim Trombetta; Peter Knobler; Michael Simmons; Bob Sherman; Mike Stoller; Peter Stoller; Brad Elterman; Roger Steffens; Jackie DeShannon; Paul Body; Robert Marchese; Nick DeRiso; Stephen J. Kalinich; Benmont Tench; Bob Kushner; Peter Piper; Rosemarie Patronette; Al Kooper; Bruce Gary; Ringo Starr; Jim Keltner; Sarah Kramer; Miles Davis; Alanna Rizzo; Helen Hoey; John Coltrane; Bob Marley; Bobby Womack; Jack DeJohnette; Paul LaRaia; Brian Auger; Gene Aguilera; Cary Baker; Pooch; Andrew Solt and Greg Vines at SOFA Entertainment; the *Ed Sullivan Show*; Mark Nardone; Jim Delehant; *Hit Parader*; Gary Schneider; Mike Stax; Lisa Gizara; Buddy Collette; Kirk Silsbee; David and Eva Leaf; Heather Harris; Richard Bosworth; Nastasia Besman and Jeff Greenberg at the Village Studios; Justin Pierce; Parker Fishel; West Los Angeles College Library; Greg Franco; Hal Lifson; Harry E. Northup; Daniel Weizmann; Vivian Sisskin; Alan Kleinfeld; Michael Tiberi; Bill Graham; UCLA Music Library; Stephen Weiss Temple; Chris Darrow; Mark Guerrero; Juliette Jagger; Don Was; Charlie Watts; Denny Bruce; Rick Danko; Peter Aaron; John Niven; Ron Lando; Ray Randolph; Ram Dass; Eli Attie; Kent Kotal; Jeff Goldman; Stan Ross; Larry Levine and Dave Gold at Gold Star Studio; *Rolling Stone*; Elvis Costello; Ian Hunter; Michael Macdonald; David N. Pepperell; Steph Curry; Enrique Hernandez; Elliot Kendall; Rob Hill; D. A. Pennebaker; Wallichs Music City; the Frigate; Aron's Records; the Ash Grove; Arcade Music; Lewin Record Paradise; Tower Records; the Groove Company; Free Press Bookstore and Kazoo; Headquarters; the Psychedelic Supermarket; Barb and Greg Hall; Cake; Dean Dean; the Taping Machine; Rod Serling; Ralph Nader; Julia Holland; Harlan Ellison; Stirling Silliphant; George Harrison; and especially Marshall and Hilda Kubernik.

THE BAND: A SELECTED DISCOGRAPHY

ALBUMS

Music from Big Pink
(Capitol, July 1968; reissued as box set August 2018)
Producer: John Simon

Side One
1. "Tears of Rage"
2. "To Kingdom Come"
3. "In a Station"
4. "Caledonia Mission"
5. "The Weight"

Side Two
6. "We Can Talk"
7. "Long Black Veil"
8. "Chest Fever"
9. "Lonesome Suzie"
10. "This Wheel's on Fire"
11. "I Shall Be Released"

2000 CD Reissue Bonus Tracks
12. "Yazoo Street Scandal"
13. "Tears of Rage" (Alternate take)
14. "Katie's Been Gone"
15. "If I Lose"
16. "Long Distance Operator"
17. "Lonesome Suzie" (Alternate take)
18. "Orange Juice Blues (Blues for Breakfast)"
19. "Key to the Highway"
20. "Ferdinand the Imposter"

The Band
(Capitol, September 1969)
Producer: John Simon

Side One
1. "Across the Great Divide"
2. "Rag Mama Rag"
3. "The Night They Drove Old Dixie Down"
4. "When You Awake"
5. "Up on Cripple Creek"
6. "Whispering Pines"

Side Two
7. "Jemima Surrender"
8. "Rockin' Chair"
9. "Look Out Cleveland"
10. "Jawbone"
11. "The Unfaithful Servant"
12. "King Harvest (Has Surely Come)

2000 CD Reissue Bonus Tracks
13. "Get Up Jake (Outtake; stereo mix)"
14. "Rag Mama Rag (Alternate vocal take; rough mix)"
15. "The Night They Drove Old Dixie Down (Alternate mix)"
16. "Up on Cripple Creek (Alternate take)"
17. "Whispering Pines (Alternate take)"
18. "Jemima Surrender (Alternate take)"
19. "King Harvest (Has Surely Come) (Alternate performance)"

Stage Fright
(Capitol, released August 1970)
Producer: The Band

Side One
1. "Strawberry Wine"
2. "Sleeping"
3. "Time to Kill"
4. "Just Another Whistle Stop"
5. "All La Glory"

Side Two
6. "The Shape I'm In"
7. "The W.S. Walcott Medicine Show"
8. "Daniel and the Sacred Harp"
9. "Stage Fright"
10. "The Rumor"

Cahoots
(Capitol, released September 1971)
Producer: The Band

Side One
1. "Life Is a Carnival"
2. "When I Paint My Masterpiece"
3. "Last of the Blacksmiths"
4. "Where Do We Go from Here?"
5. "4% Pantomime"

Side Two
6. "Shoot Out in Chinatown"
7. "The Moon Struck One"
8. "Thinkin' Out Loud"
9. "Smoke Signal"
10. "Volcano"
11. "The River Hymn"

2000 CD Reissue Bonus Tracks

12. "Endless Highway (Early studio take)"
13. "When I Paint My Masterpiece (Alternate take)"
14. "Bessie Smith (Outtake)"
15. "Don't Do It (Outtake–Studio version)"
16. "Radio Commercial"

Rock of Ages (live album)
(Capitol, August 1972)
Producer: The Band

Side One

1. "Introduction by Robertson"
2. "Don't Do It"
3. "King Harvest (Has Surely Come)"
4. "Caledonia Mission"
5. "Get Up Jake"
6. "The W.S. Walcott Medicine Show"

Side Two

7. "Stage Fright"
8. "The Night They Drove Old Dixie Down"
9. "Across the Great Divide"
10. "This Wheel's on Fire"
11. "Rag Mama Rag"

Side Three

12. "The Weight"
13. "The Shape I'm In"
14. "The Unfaithful Servant"
15. "Life Is a Carnival"

Side Four

16. "The Genetic Method"
17. "Chest Fever"
18. "(I Don't Want to) Hang Up My Rock and Roll Shoes"

2000 CD Reissue Bonus Tracks

19. "Loving You Is Sweeter Than Ever"
20. "I Shall Be Released"
21. "Up on Cripple Creek"
21. "The Rumor"
22. "Rockin' Chair"
23. "Time to Kill"
24. "Down in the Flood"
25. "When I Paint My Masterpiece"
26. "Don't Ya Tell Henry"
27. "Like a Rolling Stone"

Moondog Matinee
(Capitol, released October 1973)
Producer: The Band

Side One

1. "Ain't Got No Home"
2. "Holy Cow"
3. "Share Your Love (With Me)"
4. "Mystery Train"
5. "Third Man Theme"

Side Two

6. "Promised Land"
7. "The Great Pretender"
8. "I'm Ready"
9. "Saved"
10. "A Change Is Gonna Come"

2001 CD Reissue Bonus Tracks

11. "Didn't It Rain (Outtake)"
12. "Crying Heart Blues (Outtake)"
13. "Shakin' (Outtake)"
14. "What Am I Living For (Outtake)"
15. "Going Back to Memphis (Outtake)"
16. "Endless Highway (Studio version)"

Northern Lights–Southern Cross
(Capitol, released November 1975)
Producer: The Band

Side One

1. "Forbidden Fruit"
2. "Hobo Jungle"
3. "Ophelia"
4. "Acadian Driftwood"

Side Two

5. "Ring Your Bell"
6. "It Makes No Difference"
7. "Jupiter Hollow"
8. "Rags and Bones"

2001 CD Reissue Bonus Tracks

9. "Twilight (Early alternate version)"
10. "Christmas Must Be Tonight (Alternate version)"

Islands
(Capitol, released March 1977)
Producer: The Band

Side One

1. "Right as Rain"
2. "Street Walker"
3. "Let the Night Fall"
4. "Ain't That a Lot of Love"
5. "Christmas Must Be Tonight"

Side Two

6. "Islands"
7. "The Saga of Pepote Rouge"
8. "Georgia on My Mind"
9. "Knockin' Lost John"
10. "Livin' in a Dream"

2001 CD Reissue Bonus Tracks

11. "Twilight (Single version)"
12. "Georgia on My Mind (Alternate take)"

The Last Waltz (soundtrack)
(Warner Bros., released April 1978; reissued as box set April 2002)
Producer: Robbie Robertson
(Singer[s]/Guest Performer[s] Noted)

Side One
1. "Theme from The Last Waltz"
2. "Up on Cripple Creek" (Levon Helm)
3. "Who Do You Love?" (Ronnie Hawkins)
4. "Helpless" (Neil Young)
5. "Stage Fright" (Rick Danko)

Side Two
6. "Coyote" (Joni Mitchell)
7. "Dry Your Eyes" (Neil Diamond)
8. "It Makes No Difference" (Rick Danko)
9. "Such a Night" (Dr. John)

Side Three
10. "The Night They Drove Old Dixie Down" (Levon Helm)
11. "Mystery Train" (Paul Butterfield, Levon Helm)
12. "Mannish Boy" (Muddy Waters)
13. "Further on Up the Road" (Eric Clapton)

Side Four
14. "The Shape I'm In" (Richard Manuel)
15. "Down South in New Orleans" (Bobby Charles, Dr. John)
16. "Ophelia" (Levon Helm)
17. "Tura Lura Lural (That's An Irish Lullaby)" (Van Morrison, Richard Manuel)
18. "Caravan" (Van Morrison)

Side Five
19. "Life Is a Carnival" (Levon Helm, Rick Danko)
20. "Baby, Let Me Follow You Down" (Bob Dylan)
21. "I Don't Believe You" (Bob Dylan)
22. "Forever Young" (Bob Dylan)
23. "Baby, Let Me Follow You Down (Reprise)" (Bob Dylan)
24. "I Shall Be Released" (Bob Dylan, Richard Manuel)

Side Six
"The Last Waltz Suite"
 i. "The Well" (Richard Manuel)
 ii. "Evangeline" (Rick Danko, Emmylou Harris, Levon Helm)
 iii. "Out of the Blue" (Robbie Robertson)
 iv. "The Weight" (Levon Helm, Mavis Staples, Pops Staples, Rick Danko)
 v. "The Last Waltz Refrain" (Richard Manuel, Robbie Robertson)
 vi. "Theme from The Last Waltz"

Anthology (2-LP compilation)
(Capitol, released 1978)
(Original album source noted)

Volume 1
1. "The Weight" (*Music from Big Pink*, 1968)
2. "Chest Fever" (*Music from Big Pink*)
3. "I Shall Be Released" (*Music from Big Pink*)
4. "Rag Mama Rag" (*The Band*, 1969)
5. "The Night They Drove Old Dixie Down" (*The Band*)
6. "Up on Cripple Creek" (*The Band*)
7. "King Harvest (Has Surely Come)" (*The Band*)
8. "Stage Fright" (*Stage Fright*, 1970)
9. "The Shape I'm In" (*Stage Fright*)
10. "Daniel and the Sacred Harp" (*Stage Fright*)

Volume 2
1. "Life Is a Carnival" (*Cahoots*, 1971)
2. "When I Paint My Masterpiece" (*Cahoots*)
3. "This Wheel's on Fire" (*Rock of Ages*, 1972; originally from *Music from Big Pink*)
4. "The Great Pretender" (*Moondog Matinee*, 1973)
5. "Mystery Train" (*Moondog Matinee*)
6. "Ophelia" (*Northern Lights–Southern Cross*, 1975)
7. "It Makes No Difference" (*Northern Lights–Southern Cross*)
8. "Acadian Driftwood" (*Northern Lights–Southern Cross*)
9. "Right as Rain" (*Islands*, 1977)
10. "Livin' in a Dream" (*Islands*)

The Band: A Musical History
(111 tracks over 5 CDs and one DVD)
(Capitol, released September 2005)
Producers: Henry Glover, Jan Haust, Bob Johnson, Cheryl Pawelski, Robbie Robertson, Andrew Sandoval, John Simon, Peter J. Moore

SINGLES
(All Capitol)
"The Weight" b/w "I Shall Be Released" (1968)
"Up on Cripple Creek" b/w "The Night They Drove Old Dixie Down" (1969)
"Rag Mama Rag" b/w "The Unfaithful Servant" (1969)
"Time to Kill" b/w "The Shape I'm In" (1970)
"Life Is a Carnival" b/w "The Moon Struck One" (1971)
"Don't Do It" b/w "(I Don't Want to) Hang Up My Rock 'n' Roll Shoes" (1972)
"Ophelia" b/w "Georgia" (1976)

WITH BOB DYLAN

The Bootleg Series Vol. 12: Bob Dylan The Cutting Edge 1965–1966
(Columbia/Legacy, released 2015)

A Tribute to Woody Guthrie (soundtrack)
(Warner Bros., released 1976)

Self-Portrait
(Columbia, released June 1970; reissued as box set 2013)
Producer: Bob Johnston

Planet Waves
(Asylum, released January 1974)
Producer: Rob Fraboni

Before the Flood (live)
(Asylum: released June 1974)
Producers: Bob Dylan and The Band

The Basement Tapes
(Columbia, released June 1975; reissued as box set 2014, *The Bootleg Series Vol. 11: The Basement Tapes Complete*)
Producers: Bob Dylan and The Band

The Bootleg Series Vol. 4: Bob Dylan Live '66 The "Royal Albert Hall Concert"
(Columbia/Legacy, released October 1998)
Producer: Jeff Rosen

Live 1962–1966: Rare Performances from the Copyright Collections
(Columbia/Legacy, released July 2018)
Producers: Steve Berkowitz and Jeff Rosen

WITH RONNIE HAWKINS

Mr. Dynamo—Ronnie Hawkins and the Hawks
(Roulette, released 1960)

Ronnie Hawkins and the Hawks—The Roulette Years
(Sequel, released 1994)

CANADIAN SQUIRES

"Leave Me Alone" b/w "Uh-Uh-Uh"
(Apex, Canada; Ware, US, 1965)

LEVON AND THE HAWKS

"The Stones I Throw" b/w "He Don't Love You (And He'll Break Your Heart)"
(Atco, Canada and US; Atlantic UK, 1965)

DISCOGRAPHY

SHOW LIST 1960–1976

Compiled by Jerry Tenenbaum.
Courtesy of the Jerry Tenenbaum Archives.
Additional dates for 1969–1971 supplied by William Scheele.

1960–62
7.11.60 (week) / Toronto, ON, CAN / Ronnie Hawkins & The Hawks (RH & The Hawks) / Le Coq d'Or
11.14.61 (week) / Toronto, ON, CAN / RH & The Hawks / Concord Tavern
11.27.61 (week) / Toronto, ON, CAN / The Hawks / Concord Tavern
Oct 1962? / New York, NY, USA / The Hawks / Peppermint Lounge

1963?
London, ON, CAN, RH & The Hawks / Brass Rail Tavern
Toronto, ON, CAN / RH & The Hawks / Le Coq d'Or
Toronto, ON, CAN / RH & The Hawks / Friar's Tavern
Toronto, ON, CAN / RH & The Hawks / Hawk's Nest
Toronto, ON, CAN, RH & The Hawks / Nickelodeon
Toronto, ON, CAN, RH & The Hawks / Embassy Tavern
Toronto, ON, CAN, RH & The Hawks / Town Tavern

1964
1964? / Toronto, ON, CAN / The Hawks / Concord Tavern
1964? / TX, USA / The Hawks
2.24.64 / London, ON, CAN, RH & The Hawks
4.14.64 / Port Dover, ON, CAN, RH & The Hawks / Pop Iveys
7.12.64 / Port Dover, ON, CAN / The Hawks / Pop Iveys
8.15.64 / Toronto, ON, CAN / The Hawks / Crang Plaza
8.17.64 (week) / Toronto, ON, CAN / The Hawks / Concord Tavern
9.4.64 (week) / Toronto, ON, CAN / The Hawks / Concord Tavern
10.17.64 (week) / Toronto, ON, CAN / The Hawks / Friar's Tavern
11.20.64 (week) / Toronto, ON, CAN / The Hawks / Friar's Tavern
12.8.64 (week) / Toronto, ON, CAN / The Hawks / Friar's Tavern
12.31.64 (week) / Toronto, ON, CAN, The Hawks / Friar's Tavern

1965
1965? / Oklahoma City, OK, USA / The Hawks / Onyx Club
Jan 1965? / London, ON, CAN / The Hawks / Brass Rail Tavern
6.5.65 / Dallas, TX, USA / The Hawks
Summer 1965 / Somers Point, NJ, USA / The Hawks / Tony Mart's
9.24.65 / Austin, TX, USA / Bob Dylan & the Hawks (BD & The Hawks) / Austin Municipal Auditorium
9.25.65 / Dallas, TX, USA / BD & The Hawks / Southern Methodist University, Moody Coliseum
10.1.65 / New York, NY, USA / BD & The Hawks / Carnegie Hall
10.2.65 / Newark, NJ, USA / BD & The Hawks / Mosque Theater
Oct 1965? / Baltimore, MD, USA / BD & The Hawks / Civic Center
Oct 1965?/ Princeton, NJ, USA / BD & The Hawks / Princeton University
10.8.65 / Knoxville, IN, USA / BD & The Hawks / Knoxville Civic Coliseum
10.9.65 / Atlanta, GA, USA / BD & The Hawks / City Auditorium
10.16.65 / Worcester, MA, USA / BD & The Hawks / Memorial Auditorium
10.22.65 / Providence, RI, USA / BD & The Hawks / Rhode Island Gymnasium
10.23.65 / Burlington, VT, USA / BD & The Hawks / University of Vermont, Patrick Hall
10.24.65 / Detroit, MI, USA / BD & The Hawks / Cobo Hall
10.29.65 / Boston, MA, USA / BD & The Hawks / Back Bay Theatre

10.30.65 / Hartford, CT, USA / BD & The Hawks / Bushnell Memorial Auditorium
10.31.65 / Boston, MA, USA / BD & The Hawks / Back Bay Theatre
Nov 1965? / Madison, WI, USA / BD & The Hawks / Orpheum Theater
Nov 1965? / Yellow Springs, OH, USA / BD & The Hawks / Antioch College
11.5.65 / Minneapolis, MN, USA / BD & The Hawks / Minneapolis Auditorium
11.6.65 / Ithaca, NY, USA / BD & The Hawks / Cornell University, Barton Hall
11.12.65 / Cleveland, OH, USA / BD & The Hawks / Music Hall
11.14.65 / Toronto, Ont., Canada, BD & The Hawks / Massey Hall
11.15.65 / Toronto, ON, CAN, BD & The Hawks / Massey Hall
11.18.65 / Cincinnati, OH, USA / BD & The Hawks / Music Hall
11.19.65 / Columbus, OH, USA / BD & The Hawks / Veterans Memorial Auditorium
11.20.65? / Buffalo, NY, USA / BD & The Hawks / Kleinhans Music Hall
11.20.65 / Rochester, NY, USA / BD & The Hawks
11.21.65 / Syracuse, NY, USA / BD & The Hawks / Onondaga County War Memorial
11.26.65 / Chicago, IL, USA / BD & The Hawks / Arie Crown Theater
11.27.65 / Chicago, IL, USA / BD & The Hawks / Arie Crown Theater
11.28.65 / Washington, DC, USA / BD & The Hawks / Washington Coliseum
12.1.65 / Seattle, WA, USA / BD & The Hawks
12.3.65 / Berkeley, CA, USA / BD & The Hawks / Community Center
12.4.65 / Berkeley, CA, USA / BD & The Hawks / Community Center
12.5.65 / San Francisco, CA, USA / BD & The Hawks / Masonic Hall
12.7.65 / Long Beach, CA, USA / BD & The Hawks / Civic Auditorium
12.8.65 / Santa Monica, CA, USA / BD & The Hawks / Civic Auditorium
12.9.65 / Pasadena, CA, USA / BD & The Hawks / Civic Auditorium
12.10.65 / San Diego, CA, USA / BD & The Hawks / Community Center
12.11.65 / San Francisco, CA, USA / BD & The Hawks / Masonic Memorial Auditorium
12.12.65 / San Jose, CA, USA / BD & The Hawks / Civic Auditorium
12.18.65 / Pasadena, CA, USA / BD & The Hawks / Civic Auditorium
12.19.65 / Santa Monica, CA, USA / BD & The Hawks / Civic Auditorium

1966

February 1966? / New Haven, CT, USA / BD & The Hawks
2.4.66 / Louisville, KY, USA / BD & The Hawks /
2.5.66 / White Plains, NY, USA / BD & The Hawks / Westchester Community Center
2.6.66 / Pittsburgh, PA, USA / BD & The Hawks / Syria Mosque
2.10.66 / Memphis, TN, USA / BD & The Hawks / Ellis Auditorium
2.11.66 / Richmond, VA, USA / BD & The Hawks / Shrine Mosque
2.13.66 / Norfolk, VA, USA / BD & The Hawks / Norfolk Municipal Auditoriu,
2.19.66 / Ottawa, ON, CAN / BD & The Hawks / Ottawa Auditorium
2.20.66 / Montreal, QC, CAN / BD & The Hawks / Place des Arts
? / Vancouver, BC, CAN / BD & The Hawks / PNE Agrodome
2.24.66 / Philadelphia, PA, USA / BD & The Hawks / Academy of Music
2.25.66 / Philadelphia, PA, USA / BD & The Hawks / Academy of Music
2.26.66 / Hampstead, NY, USA / BD & The Hawks / Island Garden
3.3.66 / Miami Beach, FL, USA / BD & The Hawks / Convention Hall
3.5.66 / Jacksonville, FL, USA / BD & The Hawks / Jacksonville Coliseum
3.11.66 / St. Louis, MO, USA / BD & The Hawks / Kiel Opera House
3.12.66 / Lincoln, NE, USA / BD & The Hawks / Lincoln Memorial Auditorium
3.13.66 / Denver, CO, USA / BD & The Hawks / Denver Auditorium Arena

3.19.66 / Los Angeles, CA, USA / BD & The Hawks / Hollywood Bowl
3.20.66 / Santa Monica, CA, USA / BD & The Hawks
3.21.66 / San Jose, CA, USA / BD & The Hawks
3.22.66 / San Francisco, CA, USA / BD & The Hawks
3.23.66 / Portland, OR, USA / BD & The Hawks / Paramount Theatre
3.24.66 / Tacoma, WA, USA / BD & The Hawks
3.25.66 / Seattle, WA, USA / BD & The Hawks / Center Arena
3.26.66 / Vancouver, BC, Canada, BD & The Hawks / PNE Agrodome
4.9.66 / Honolulu, HI, USA / BD & The Hawks / Honolulu International Center
4.13.66 / Sydney, AU / BD & The Hawks / Sydney Stadium
4.15.66 / Brisbane, AU / BD & The Hawks / Festival Hall
4.16.66 / Sydney, AU / BD & The Hawks / Sydney Stadium
4.19.66 / Melbourne, AU / BD & The Hawks / Festival Hall
4.20.66 / Melbourne, AU / BD & The Hawks / Festival Hall
4.22.66 / Adelaide, AU / BD & The Hawks / Palais Royal
4.23.66 / Perth, AU / BD & The Hawks / Capitol Theatre
4.29.66 / Stockholm, Sweden / BD & The Hawks / Konserthus
5.1.66 / Copenhagen, Denmark / BD & The Hawks / K.B. Hallen
5.2.66 / Dublin, IRE / BD & The Hawks / Adelphi Theatre
5.6.66 / Belfast, IRE / BD & The Hawks / ABC Theatre
5.10.66 / Bristol, ENG / BD & The Hawks / Colston Hall
5.11.66 / Cardiff, Wales, BD & The Hawks / Capitol Theatre
5.12.66 / Birmingham, ENG / BD & The Hawks / Odeon Theatre
5.14.66 / Liverpool, ENG / BD & The Hawks / Odeon Theatre
5.15.66 / Leicester, ENG / BD & The Hawks / Demontfort
5.16.66 / Sheffield, ENG / BD & The Hawks / Caumont Theater
5.17.66 / Manchester, ENG / BD & The Hawks / Free Trade Hall
5.19.66 / Glasgow, SCOT / BD & The Hawks / Odeon Theatre
5.20.66 / Edinburgh, SCOT / BD & The Hawks / ABC Theatre
5.21.66 / Newcastle, ENG / BD & The Hawks / Odeon Theatre
5.24.66 / Paris, France / BD & The Hawks / L'Olympia
5.26.66 / London, ENG / BD & The Hawks / Royal Albert Hall
5.27.66 / London, ENG / BD & The Hawks / Royal Albert Hall

1968

1.20.68 / New York, NY, USA / BD & The Hawks / Carnegie Hall
1.20.68 (second show) / New York, NY, USA / BD & The Hawks / Carnegie Hall

1969

1969? / Pasadena, CA, USA / The Band / Pasadena Civic Auditorium
1969? / Chicago, IL, USA / The Band / Auditorium
1969 ? / MN, USA / The Band / open air show
1969? / Bethlehem, PA / Lehigh University
4.17.69 / San Francisco, CA, USA / The Band / Winterland
4.18.69 / San Francisco, CA, USA / The Band / Winterland
4.19.69 / San Francisco, CA, USA / The Band / Winterland
5.9.69 / New York, NY, USA / The Band / Fillmore East
5.9.69 (second show) / New York, NY, USA / The Band / Fillmore East
5.10.69 / New York, NY, USA / The Band / Fillmore East
5.10.69 (second show) / New York, NY, USA / The Band / Fillmore East
6.21.69 / Toronto, ON, CAN / The Band / Toronto Pop Festival

7.14.69 / Edwardsville, IL, USA / The Band / Southern Illinois University, Mississippi River Festival
7.14.69 / Edwardsville, IL, USA / BD & The Band / Southern Illinois University, Mississippi R. Festival
8.17.69 / Bethel, NY, USA / The Band / Woodstock Festival
8.31.69 / Isle of Wight, ENG / The Band / BD & The Band / Isle of Wight Festival
9.7.69 / Vancouver, BC, CAN / The Band / Capilano Park?
10.11.69 / Brooklyn, NY, USA / The Band / Opera House, Brooklyn Academy of Music
10.26.69 / Philadelphia, PA, USA / The Band / Academy of Music
10.27.69 / Washington, DC, USA / The Band / Constitution Hall
10.31.69 / Boston, MA, USA / The Band / Symphony Hall
10.31.69 (second show) / Boston, MA, USA / The Band / Symphony Hall

11.2.69 / New York, NY, USA / The Band / *The Ed Sullivan Show*
11.12.69 / Detroit, MI, USA / The Band / Eastown Theatre
11.14.69 / Detroit, MI, USA / The Band / Grand Riviera Theater
11.15.69 / Detroit, MI, USA / The Band / Grand Riviera Theater
11.21.69 / Chicago, IL, USA / The Band / Auditorium
12.1.69 / Buffalo, NY, USA / The Band / Kleinhans Music Hall
12.26.69 / New York, NY, USA / The Band / Madison Square Garden
12.26.69 (second show) / New York, NY, USA / The Band / Madison Square Garden
12.27.69 / New York, NY, USA / The Band / Madison Square Garden
12.27.69 (second show) / New York, NY, USA / The Band / Madison Square Garden
12.29.69 / Hollywood, FL, USA / The Band / Sportatorium

1970

1970? / Tuscaloosa?, AL, USA / The Band / University of Alabama
Early 1970? / Hollywood, FL, USA / The Band / Sportatorium
1.1.70 / New York, NY, USA / The Band / Queen's Collage
1.16.70 / Guelph, ON, CAN, The Band / University of Guelph
1.17.70 / Toronto, ON, CAN, The Band / Massey Hall
1.18.70 / Hamilton, ON, CAN, The Band / McMaster University
1.23.70 / San Diego, CA, USA / The Band / San Diego Concourse
1.25.70 / Sacramento, CA, USA / The Band
1.24.70 / Pasadena, CA, USA / The Band / Civic Auditorium
1.31.70 / Berkley, CA, USA / The Band / Community Center
1.31.70 (second show) / Berkeley, CA, USA / The Band / Community Center
2.1.70 / Santa Barbara, CA, USA / The Band / UC Santa Barbara
2.6.70 / Long Beach, CA, USA / The Band
2.7.70 / Las Vegas, NV, USA / The Band
2.13.70 / Charlottesville, VA, USA / The Band / University of Virginia
2.14.70 / Binghamton, NY, USA / The Band / Harpur College
2.15.70 / Lowell, MA, USA / The Band / Lowell Technological Institute
2.20.70 / Waterville, ME / The Band / Colby College
2.21.70 / Boston, MA, USA / The Band / Boston College
2.22.70 / Bethlehem, PA, USA / The Band / Lehigh University
3.6.70 / East Orange, NJ, USA / The Band / Upsala College
3.7.70 / Hartford, CT, USA / The Band / Trinity College
3.7.70 (second show) / Hartford, CT, USA / The Band / Trinity College

3.8.70 / Kingston, RI, USA / The Band / University of Rhode Island
3.13.70 / Chicago, IL, USA / The Band
3.14.70 / Cleveland, OH, USA / The Band / Cleveland Music Hall
3.15.70 / Cincinnati, OH, USA / The Band
3.20.70 / St. Louis, MO, USA / The Band / Kiel Opera House
3.21.70 / Des Moines, IA / The Band
3.22.70 / Minneapolis, MN / The Band / Guthrie Theater
4.24.70 / Providence, RI, USA / The Band / Brown University
6.22.70 / Cambridge, MA, USA / The Band / Harvard University
6.27.70 / Toronto, ON, CAN / The Band / CNE Grandstand
6.28.70 / Toronto, ON, CAN / The Band / CNE Grandstand
6.29.70 / New York, NY, USA / The Band / Central Park
7.1.70 / Winnipeg, MB, CAN / The Band / Winnipeg Stadium
7.4.70 / Calgary, AB, CAN / The Band / McMahon Stadium
7.5.70 / Calgary, AB, CAN / The Band / McMahon Stadium
7.1.70? / CA, USA / The Band

7.10.70 / Los Angeles, CA, USA / The Band / Hollywood Bowl
7.11.70 / Mountaindale, NY, USA / The Band
Aug 1970? / Toronto, ON, CAN / The Band

Aug 1970? / Columbia, MD, USA / The Band / Merriweather Post Pavilion
8.1.70 / Toronto, ON, CAN / The Band / Canada Festival
8.11.70 / IL, USA / The Band
8.13.70 / Holmdel, N.J, USA / The Band / Garden State Arts Center
8.15.70 / New York, NY, USA / The Band / Forest Hills Stadium
Nov 1970? / Lewisburg, PA, USA / The Band / Bucknell University
11.1.70 / Pittsburgh, PA, USA / The Band / Syria Mosque
11.5.70 / Medford, MA, USA / The Band / Tufts University
11.7.70 / Worcester, MA, USA / The Band / Worcester Polytechnic Institute
11.8.70 / Philadelphia, PA, USA / The Band / Spectrum
12.10.70 / Atlanta, GA, USA / The Band / Municipal Auditorim
11.21.70 / Syracuse, NY, USA / BD & The Hawks / Onondaga County War Memorial
11.27.70 / Bloomington, IN, USA / The Band / University Assembly Hall
11.27.70 (second show) / Bloomington, IN, USA / The Band / University Assembly Hall
11.28.70 / San Francisco, CA, USA / The Band / Civic Auditorium
Nov or Dec 1970 / Madison, WI, USA / The Band / Coliseum
12.4.70 / Dallas, TX, USA / The Band / Texas Memorial Stadium
12.5.70 / Houston, TX, USA / The Band
12.6.70 / New Orleans, LA, USA / The Band / Warehouse
12.10.70 / Atlanta, GA, USA / The Band / Municipal Auditorium
Dec 1970? / Jacksonville, FL, USA / The Band
Dec 1970? / Miami, FL, USA / The Band

1971

1971? / Columbia, MD, USA / The Band / Merriweather Post Pavilion
4.16.71 / San Francisco, CA, USA / The Band / Civic Auditorium
5.18.71 / Hamburg, W. Germany / The Band / Musikhalle
5.19.71 / Munich, W. Germany / The Band / Cirkus Krone
5.20.71 / Frankfurt, W. Germany / The Band / Jahrhunderthalle
5.22.71 / Vienna, Austria / The Band / Wiener Konzerthaus
5.25.71 / Paris, France / The Band / L'Olympia
5.27.71 / Copenhagen, Denmark / The Band / K.B. Hallen
5.28.71 / Stockholm, Sweden / The Band / Konserthus
6.2.71 / London, ENG / The Band / Royal Albert Hall
6.3.71 / London, ENG / The Band / Royal Albert Hall
6.5.71 / Amsterdam, The Netherlands / The Band / Concertgebouw
6.5.71 (second show) / Amsterdam, The Netherlands / The Band / Concertgebouw
6.6.71 / Rotterdam, The Netherlands / The Band / De Doelen
6.22.71 / Columbia, MD / The Band / Merriweather Post Pavilion
6.26.71 / St. Paul, MN, USA / The Band / Open Air Celebration, Midway Stadium
6.30.71 / New York, NY, USA / The Band / Central Park
7.1.71 / New York, NY, USA / The Band / Central Park
8.21.71 / Toronto, ON, CAN, The Band / Borough of York Stadium
9.4.71 / Trenton, NJ, USA / The Band
9.5.71 / Monticello, NY, USA / The Band
11.27.71 / San Francisco, CA, USA / The Band / San Francisco Civic Auditorium
12.1.71 / Chicago, IL, USA / The Band / Arie Crown Theater
12.5.71 / Baltimore, MD, USA / The Band / Baltimore Civic Center
12.6.71 / Boston, MA, USA / The Band / Boston Garden
12.8.71 / Philadelphia, PA, USA / The Band / Spectrum
12.28.71 / New York, NY, USA / The Band / Academy of Music
12.29.71 / New York, NY, USA / The Band / Academy of Music
12.30.71 / New York, NY, USA / The Band / Academy of Music
12.31.71 / New York, NY, USA / The Band / Academy of Music
12.31.71 / New York, NY, USA / BD & The Band / Academy of Music

1973

7.23.73 / Osaka, Japan / The Band
7.27.73 / Watkins Glen, NY, USA / The Band / Grand Prix Racetrack
7.28.73 / Watkins Glen, NY, USA / The Band / Grand Prix Racetrack
7.30.73 / Jersey City, NJ, USA / The Band / Roosevelt Stadium
7.31.73 / Jersey City, NJ, USA / The Band / Roosevelt Stadium
8.1.73 / Jersey City, NJ, USA / The Band / Roosevelt Stadium

SHOW LIST

1974

- 1.3.74 / Chicago, IL, USA / BD & The Band / Chicago Stadium
- 1.4.74 / Chicago, IL, USA / BD & The Band / Chicago Stadium
- 1.6.74 / Philadelphia, PA, USA / BD & The Band / Spectrum
- 1.6.74 (second show) / Philadelphia, PA, USA / BD & The Band / Spectrum
- 1.7.74 / Philadelphia, PA, USA / BD & The Band / Spectrum
- 1.9.74 / Toronto, ON, CAN / BD & The Band / Maple Leaf Gardens
- 1.10.74 / Toronto, ON, CAN / BD & The Band / Maple Leaf Gardens
- 1.11.74 / Montreal, QC, CAN / BD & The Band / Forum
- 1.12.74 / Montreal, QC, CAN / BD & The Band / Forum
- 1.14.74 / Boston, MA, USA / BD & The Band / Boston Garden
- 1.14.74 (second show) / Boston, MA, USA / BD & The Band / Boston Garden
- 1.15.74 / Largo, MD, USA / BD & The Band / Capital Centre
- 1.16.74 / Largo, MD, USA / BD & The Band / Capital Centre
- 1.17.74 / Charlotte, NC, USA / BD & The Band / Charlotte Coliseum
- 1.19.74 / Hollywood, FL, USA / BD & The Band / Sportatorium
- 1.19.74 (second show) / Hollywood, FL, USA / BD & The Band / Sportatorium
- 1.21.74 / Atlanta, GA, USA / BD & The Band / Omni Coliseum
- 1.22.74 / Atlanta, GA, USA / BD & The Band / Omni Coliseum
- 1.23.74 / Memphis, TN, USA / BD & The Band / Memphis Coliseum
- 1.25.74 / Fort Worth, TX, USA / BD & The Band / Tarrant County Convention Center
- 1.26.74 / Houston, TX, USA / BD & The Band / University of Houston, Hofheinz Pavilion
- 1.26.74 (second show) / Houston, TX, USA / BD & The Band / University of Houston, Hofheinz Pavilion
- 1.28.74 / Uniondale, NY, USA / BD & The Band / Nassau Community College
- 1.29.74 / Uniondale, NY, USA / BD & The Band / Nassau Community College
- 1.30.74 / New York, NY, USA / BD & The Band / Madison Square Garden
- 1.31.74 / New York, NY, USA / BD & The Band / Madison Square Garden
- 1.31.74 (second show) / New York, NY, USA / BD & The Band / Madison Square Garden
- 2.2.74 / Ann Arbor, MI, USA / BD & The Band / Crisler Arena
- 2.3.74 / Bloomington, IN, USA / BD & The Band / Assembly Hall
- 2.4.74 / St. Louis, MO, USA / BD & The Band / Missouri Arena
- 2.4.74 (second show) / St. Louis, MO, USA / BD & The Band / Missouri Arena
- 2.6.74 / Denver, CO, USA / BD & The Band / Denver Coliseum

2.6.74 (second show) / Denver, CO, USA / BD & The Band / Denver Coliseum
2.9.74 / Seattle, WA, USA / BD & The Band / Seattle Center Coliseum
2.9.74 (second show) / Seattle, WA, USA / BD & The Band / Seattle Center Coliseum
2.11.74 / Oakland, CA, USA / BD & The Band / Alameda County Coliseum
2.11.74 (second show) / Oakland, CA, USA / BD & The Band / Alameda County Coliseum
2.13.74 / Los Angeles, CA, USA / BD & The Band / The Forum
2.14.74 / Los Angeles, CA, USA / BD & The Band / The Forum
2.14.74 (second show) / Los Angeles, CA, USA / BD & The Band / The Forum
7.4.74 / Wentzville, MO, USA / The Band / Berry Park?
7.5.74 / Pittsburgh, PA, USA / The Band / Three Rivers Stadium
7.6.74 / Buffalo, NY, USA / The Band / Rich Stadium
7.9.74? / Seattle, WA, USA / The Band / Seattle Center Coliseum
7.10.74? / Vancouver, BC, CAN / The Band / PNE Coliseum
7.13.74 / Oakland, CA, USA / The Band / Oakland Stadium
7.14.74 / Oakland, CA, USA / The Band / Oakland Stadium
7.16.74? / Tempe, Ariz, USA / The Band / Tempe Stadium
7.19.74? / Kansas City, KS, USA / The Band / Royals Stadium
7.21.74? / Milwaukee, WI, USA / The Band / County Stadium
7.22.74? / St. Paul, MN, USA / The Band / St. Paul Civic Center
7.24.74? / Denver, CO, USA / The Band / Mile High Stadium
7.25.74 / Denver, CO, USA / The Band / Mile High Stadium
7.28.74? / Houston, TX, USA / The Band / Jeppeson Stadium
7.31.74? / Dallas, TX, USA / The Band / Texas Stadium
8.3.74 / Ontario, CA, USA / The Band / Ontario Motor Speedway
8.5.74? / Boston, MA, USA / The Band / Boston Garden
8.6.74? / Boston, MA, USA / The Band / Boston Garden
8.8.74? / Jersey City, NJ, USA / The Band / Roosevelt Stadium
8.9.74? / Atlantic City, NJ, USA / The Band / Atlantic City Racetrack
8.14.74? / Uniondale, NY, USA / The Band / Nassau Coliseum
8.15.74? / Uniondale, NY, USA / The Band / Nassau Coliseum
8.17.74? / Norfolk, VA, USA / The Band / Foreman Field
8.19.74? / Largo, MD, USA / The Band / Capital Centre
8.20.74? / Largo, MD, USA / The Band / Capital Centre
8.21.74? / Largo, MD, USA / The Band / Capital Centre
8.23.74? / Tampa, FL, USA / The Band / Tampa Stadium
8.25.74? / Memphis, TN, USA / The Band
8.27.74? / Chicago, IL, USA / The Band / Chicago Stadium
8.28.74? / Chicago, IL, USA / The Band / Chicago Stadium
8.29.74? / Chicago, IL, USA / The Band / Chicago Stadium
8.30.74 / Uniondale, NY, USA / The Band / Nassau Coliseum
8.31.74 / Cleveland, OH, USA / The Band / Municipal Auditorium
Sept 1974? / Westbury, NY, USA / The Band / Roosevelt Raceway
9.1.74? / Toronto, ON, CAN, The Band / Varsity Stadium
9.2.74? / Toronto, ON, CAN, The Band / Varsity Stadium
9.4.74 / Ithaca, NY, USA / The Band / Cornell University
9.6.74 / Landover, MD, USA / The Band / Capital Centre
9.7.74? / Seattle, WA, USA / The Band / Seattle Coliseum
9.8.74 / Des Moines, IA, USA / The Band / Iowa Fairgrounds
9.14.74 / London, ENG / The Band / Wembley Stadium

1975–76

1976? / Kentucky, USA / The Band
1976? / Missouri, USA / The Band /
3.23.75 / San Francisco, CA, USA / The Band / Kezar Stadium
4.19.76? / San Francisco, CA, USA / The Band
6.4.76 / Palo Alto, CA, USA / The Band / Stanford University, Frost Amphitheater
6.26.76 / Palo Alto, CA, USA / The Band / Stanford University, Frost Amphitheater
6.28.76 / Santa Barbara, CA, USA / The Band / County Bowl
July 1976 / Asbury Park, NJ, USA / The Band / Casino Arena
7.7.76 / Homewood, IL, USA / The Band / Washington Park Racetrack
7.9.76 / Milwaukee, WI, USA / The Band / Summerfest
7.13.76 / Tarrytown, NY, USA / The Band / Westchester Premiere Theatre
7.14.76 / Long Island, NY, USA / The Band / Long Island Arena
7.16.76 / Long Island, NY, USA / The Band / Long Island Arena
7.17.76 / Washington, DC, USA / The Band / Carter Barron Amphitheater
7.18.76 / Lennox, MA, USA / The Band / Music Inn
August 1976? / Essex Junction, VT, USA / The Band / Essex Fair
8.24.76 / Los Angeles, CA, USA / The Band / Greek Theatre
8.25.76 / Los Angeles, CA, USA / The Band / Greek Theatre
8.29.76 / Lennox, MA, USA / The Band / Music Inn
8.31.76 / Toronto, ON, CAN, The Band / CNE Bandshell
9.2.76 / Boston, MA, USA / The Band / Boston Music Hall
9.5.76 / Austin, TX, USA / The Band
9.12.76 / Hattiesburg, MS, USA / The Band / University of Southern Mississippi
9.17.76 / Philadelphia, PA, USA / The Band / Spectrum
9.18.76 / New York, NY, USA / The Band / Palladium
9.19.76 / New York, NY, USA / The Band / Palladium
9.21.76 / Pittsburgh, PA, USA / The Band / Syria Mosque
9.24.76 / Charlottesville, VA, USA / The Band / University of Virginia
10.30.76 / New York, NY, USA / The Band / *Saturday Night Live*, Rockefeller Center
11.25.76 / San Francisco, CA, USA / The Band / Winterland

SOURCES

Harvey Kubernik newly conducted interviews for *The Story of The Band* and previous Kubernik written and published magazine/periodicals/online and non-published sources. All incorporated Harvey Kubernik–penned magazine articles and excerpts from digital endeavors were utilized from the Harvey Kubernik archives except where noted.

Prologue

Denny Bruce: interviews, 2017 and 2018.

Robbie Robertson: interviews, 1975 and 1976, for "Across the Great Divide with Robbie Robertson," *Crawdaddy*, March 1976; interview, December 2016, for "Robbie Robertson Gives Testimony," *Record Collector News*, March 2017.

Rick Danko: 1977, for "Rick Danko: From Band to Band," *Melody Maker*, February 1978.

Chapter 1: Igloos, Eskimos, and Dogsleds

Excerpt of Bill Haley and the Comets review: Stanley Bligh, *Vancouver Sun*, June 28, 1956.

Mike Stoller and Jerry Leiber: interviews, *HITS*, November 1995 and *Goldmine*, April 1995.

Sharry Wilson: interview, 2017

Garth Hudson: Nick DeRiso interview with Garth Hudson for *Something Else!*, October 31, 2012, http://somethingelsereviews.com/2012/10/31/the-bands-garth-hudson-to-pay-tribute-to-fallen-voices-rick-danko-levon-helm-and-richard-manuel.

Larry LeBlanc: interview, 2017.

Tom Wilson: interview, 2016; and excerpt from forthcoming book: *I Am Tommy: Onstage and Backstage*.

Juliette Jagger: interview, 2018.

Chapter 2: The Hawk Spreads His Wings

Levon Helm: *The Band: The Authorized Video Biography*, DVD video, 2001, Courtesy of TH Entertainment LLC, http://thentertainment.com.

Larry LeBlanc: interviews, 2016 and 2017.

Ronnie Hawkins: Larry LeBlanc interview with Ronnie Hawkins for *Ajax News Advertiser*, 1965, and *Hit Parader*, October 1965.

Rick Danko, Robbie Robertson, and Ronnie Hawkins: Excerpted from Canadian television series *Yonge Street: Toronto Rock & Roll Stories*, Bell Broadcast and New Media Fund (produced with the participation of) David Brady Productions, 2011.

Tom Wilson: interview, 2016; and excerpt from forthcoming book: *I Am Tommy: Onstage and Backstage*.

Garth Hudson: Barney Hoskyns interview with Garth Hudson, 2012.

Robbie Robertson: interview, December 2016, for "Robbie Robertson Gives Testimony," *Record Collector News*, March 2017.

John Ware: interview, 2017.

Gary Pig Gold: interview, 2018.

Chapter 3: Leaving the Nest and Preparing to Fly

Robbie Robertson: interview, December 2016, for "Robbie Robertson Gives Testimony," *Record Collector News*, March 2017.

Mike Stoller: interview, 2017.

Excerpt from Levon Helm with Stephen Davis, *This Wheel's on Fire: Levon Helm and the Story of The Band*. New York: William Morrow and Company, 1993, 102.

Larry LeBlanc: interview, 2017.

Sharry Wilson: interview, 2017.

Levon Helm: *The Band: The Authorized Video Biography*, DVD video, 2001, Courtesy of TH Entertainment LLC, http://thentertainment.com.

Gary Pig Gold: interview, 2018.

Andrew Loog Oldham, interview, 2017.

D. A. Pennebaker: interview, 2003. Excerpted in *Goldmine*, 2004 and in Harvey Kubernik, *Hollywood Shack Job: Rock Music in Film and On Your Screen*. Albuquerque: University of New Mexico Press, 2006; and interview, 2012, excerpted in *Treats!*, 2012.

Anthony Scaduto: interview, 1974.

Jon Donabie: interview, 2017.

Andrew Solt: interview, 2017.

Paul Body: interview, 2017.

Frank Neilsen: interview, 2017.

David N. Pepperell: interview, 2017.

Review of the European leg of the Dylan and the Hawks 1966 world tour by Tony Barrow for *KRLA Beat* and *KYA Beat*, July 2, 1966. Courtesy of *KRLA Beat* archive: 1966. Provided by D.L. MacLaughlan-Dumes, curator of http://krlabeat.sakionline.net.

Peter Alan Roberts: interview, 2017.

James Cushing: interview, 2017.

Chapter 4: The Basement Tapes

Rick Danko: Dennis Loren interview with Rick Danko, for *RPM*, July/August 1985.

Robbie Robertson: interview, December 2016, for "Robbie Robertson Gives Testimony," *Record Collector News*, March 2017.

Jonathan Taplin: interview via e-mail, 2014.

Roger McGuinn, interview, 2010.

Chris Hillman: interview, 2011.

Kirk Silsbee: interview, 2014.

James Cushing: interview, 2014.

Brian Auger: Kenneth Kubernik interview with Brian Auger, 2017.

Levon Helm: *The Band: The Authorized Video Biography*, DVD video, 2001, Courtesy of TH Entertainment LLC, http://thentertainment.com.

John Ware: interview, 2017.

Harry E. Northup: interview, 2007.

Chapter 5: Which One Is Big Pink?

Robbie Robertson: interview, 1975, for "The Struggle Has Gone," *Melody Maker*, January 1976.

Richard Manuel: Caroline Boucher interview with Richard Manuel for "The Band—Or When the Booing Ended," *Disc and Music Echo*, May 1971.

Levon Helm: *The Band: The Authorized Video Biography*, DVD video, 2001, Courtesy of TH Entertainment LLC, http://thentertainment.com.

Robbie Robertson: interview, December 2016, for "Robbie Robertson Gives Testimony," *Record Collector News*, March 2017.

Rick Danko: Dennis Loren interview with Rick Danko, for *RPM*, July/August 1985.

Robbie Robertson: Rob Bowman interview, © 2001, Rob Bowman, for liner notes to the box set *The Band: A Musical History*, Capitol Records, September 2005.

John Simon: interview, 2017, and excerpts from *Truth, Lies, and Hearsay: A Musical Memoir of a Life in and Out of Rock and Roll*

Richard Bosworth: interview, 2017

Fred Catero: interview, 2014, excerpted in Harvey Kubernik, *Leonard Cohen: Everybody Knows*. Milwaukee, WI: Backbeat Books, 2014.

Al Kooper: interview, 2017.

Stan Ross: interview, 2000.

Jack Nitzsche: interview, 1988. Excerpted in *Goldmine*, 2000 and in Harvey Kubernik, *This Is Rebel Music: The Harvey Kubernik InnerViews*. Albuquerque: University of New Mexico Press, 2004.

Brian Wilson: interview, Official Programme Brian Wilson 2007.

Larry Levine: interview, 2000

Robbie Robertson: interview, 2002. Excerpted in *Goldmine*, 2002 and in Harvey Kubernik, *Hollywood Shack Job: Rock Music in Film and On Your Screen*. Albuquerque: University of New Mexico Press, 2006.

Excerpt from Robbie Robertson, *Testimony*. New York: Three Rivers Press/Crown, 2016, Page 310.

Chapter 6: Something Was Delivered

Andrew Loog Oldham: interview, 2017.

Chris Darrow: interview, 2017.

Robbie Robertson: interviews, 1975 and 1976, for "Across the Great Divide with Robbie Robertson," *Crawdaddy*, March 1976.

James Cushing: interview, 2017

Denny Bruce: interview, 2014.

Gene Aguilera: interview, 2017.

Don Was: interview, 2017.

Peter Lewis: interview, 2017.

John Donabie: interview, 2017.

Larry LeBlanc: interview, 2017.

John Brower: interview, 2017.

David N. Pepperell, interview, 2017.

Robbie Robertson: Richard Williams interview with Robbie Robertson for "A *Melody Maker* Band Breakdown," *Melody Maker*, May 1971. © 1971 Richard Williams

Bob Dylan: interview, 1976, for "Across the Great Divide with Robbie Robertson," *Crawdaddy*, March 1976.

Chapter 7: Faithful Servants

Robbie Robertson: interview, 2016.

John Simon: interview, 2017, and excerpts from *Truth, Lies, and Hearsay: A Musical Memoir of a Life in and Out of Rock and Roll*.

Levon Helm: *The Band: The Authorized Video Biography*, DVD video, 2001, Courtesy of TH Entertainment LLC, http://thentertainment.com.

Jim Keltner: interview, 2017

Greil Marcus, "We Can Talk About It Now," *Good Times*, April 23, 1969.

Andrew Solt: interview, 2017.

John Brower: interview, 2017.

James Cushing; interview, 2017.

David N. Pepperell: interview, 2017.

Henry Diltz: 1969 diary entry, provided to Harvey Kubernik 2018.

Excerpt from Levon Helm with Stephen Davis, *This Wheel's on Fire: Levon Helm and the Story of The Band*. New York: William Morrow and Company, 1993.

Robbie Robertson: interviews, 1975 and 1976, for "Across the Great Divide with Robbie Robertson," *Crawdaddy*, March 1976.

Richard Bosworth: interview, 2017.

Jerry Garcia: interview, *Melody Maker*, April 1976.

Graham Nash: interview, 2008, for *MOJO 1969* issue, 2009.

Grace Slick, interview for *HITS*, 2001, excerpted in Harvey Kubernik, *This Is Rebel Music: The Harvey Kubernik InnerViews*. Albuquerque. University of New Mexico Press, 2004.

Rick Danko: Richard Williams interview with Rick Danko for "A *Melody Maker* Band Breakdown," *Melody Maker*, May 1971. © 1971 Richard Williams

Elliot Mazer: interview, 2015.

Chapter 8: Right Creek, Right Paddle

Robbie Robertson: interviews, 1975 and 1976, for "Across the Great Divide with Robbie Robertson," *Crawdaddy*, March 1976.
James Cushing: interview, 2017.
Michael Macdonald: interview, 2017.
Eli Attie: interview, 2017.
Steven Van Zandt, excerpted from the documentary by Catherine Bainbridge and Alfonso Maiorana, *Rumble: The Indians Who Rocked the World*, Rezolution Pictures, 2017.
Paul Body: interview, 2017.
William Scheele: interview, 2017.
Robbie Robertson: Rob Bowman interview with Robbie Robertson, © Rob Bowman, 2001.
John Scheele: interview, 2017.
David Dalton: interview, 2017.
Jack DeJohnette: Kenneth Kubernik interview with Jack DeJohnette, 2017.
Robert Marchese: interview, 2017.

Chapter 9: Life Is a Sideshow

Jon Tiven, review of *Cahoots* for the *Phonograph Record*, December 1971.
Jack DeJohnette: Kenneth Kubernik interview with Jack DeJohnette, 2017.
Sarah Kramer: interview, 2017.
William Scheele: interview, 2017.
John Scheele: interview, 2017.
Robbie Robertson: interview quotes from the 2013 media press release serviced by Capitol/Ume label to announce *Live at the Academy of Music 1971*, a 4CD+DVD collection released on September 17, 2013 by Capitol/UMe.
Michael Simmons: interview, 2017.
James Cushing: interview, 2017.
Elvis Costello: Barney Hoskyns interview with Elvis Costello for "Heart & Soul: The Band," *MOJO*, January 1994.
Robbie Robertson: interviews, 1975 and 1976, for "Across the Great Divide with Robbie Robertson," *Crawdaddy*, March 1976.

Chapter 10: Out in Malibu with a Different View

Richard Bosworth: interview, 2017.
Robbie Robertson: interview, December 2016, for "Robbie Robertson Gives Testimony," *Record Collector News*, March 2017.
William Scheele: interview, 2017.
Robbie Robertson: interview, 2002. Excerpted in *Goldmine*, 2002 and in Harvey Kubernik, *Hollywood Shack Job: Rock Music in Film and On Your Screen*. Albuquerque: University of New Mexico Press, 2006.
James Cushing: interview, 2017.
Celeste Goyer: interview, 2017.
William Scheele: interview, 2017.
Roger Steffens: interview, 2017.
John Scheele: interview 2017.
Robbie Robertson: interview, 1975, for "The Struggle Has Gone," *Melody Maker*, January 1976.
Sarah Kramer: interview, 2017.

Chapter 11: The Band Has Left the Building

Robbie Robertson: interview, 2002. Excerpted in *Goldmine*, 2002 and in Harvey Kubernik, *Hollywood Shack Job: Rock Music in Film and On Your Screen*. Albuquerque: University of New Mexico Press, 2006.
Robbie Robertson: interview, December 2016, for "Robbie Robertson Gives Testimony," *Record Collector News*, March 2017.
Michael Hacker: interview, 2017.
John Donabie: interview, 2017.
Rick Danko: 1977, for "Rick Danko: From Band to Band," *Melody Maker*, February 1978.
Robbie Robertson: interview, December 2016, for "Robbie Robertson Gives Testimony," *Record Collector News*, March 2017.
Jack DeJohnette: Kenneth Kubernik interview with Jack DeJohnette, 2017.
Don Was: interview, 2017.
Mike Stoller: interview, 2017.
William Scheele: interview, 2018.

BIBLIOGRAPHY

Books

Helm, Levon with Stephen Davis. *This Wheel's on Fire: Levon Helm and the Story of The Band.* New York: William Morrow and Company, 1993.

Kubernik, Harvey. *This Is Rebel Music: The Harvey Kubernik InnerViews.* Albuquerque: University of New Mexico Press, 2004.

———. *Hollywood Shack Job: Rock Music in Film and On Your Screen.* Albuquerque: University of New Mexico Press, 2006.

———. *Leonard Cohen: Everybody Knows.* Milwaukee, WI: Backbeat Books, 2014.

Robertson, Robbie *Testimony.* New York: Three Rivers Press/Crown, 2016

Simon, John. *Truth, Lies, and Hearsay: A Musical Memoir of a Life in and Out of Rock and Roll.* Unpublished.

Wilson, Tom. *I Am Tommy: Onstage and Backstage.* Unpublished.

Magazine and Newspaper Articles

Barrow, Tony. Review of the European leg of the Dylan and the Hawks 1966 world tour for *KRLA Beat* and *KYA Beat,* July 2, 1966. Courtesy of *KRLA Beat* archive: 1966. Provided by D. L. MacLaughlan-Dumes, curator of http://krlabeat.sakionline.net.

Bligh, Stanley. Review of Bill Haley and the Comets, *Vancouver Sun,* June 28, 1956.

Boucher, Carolin. Interview with Richard Manuel for "The Band—Or When the Booing Ended," *Disc and Music Echo,* May 1971.

Hoskyns, Barney. Interview with Elvis Costello for "Heart & Soul: The Band," *MOJO,* January 1994.

LeBlanc, Larry. Interview with Ronnie Hawkins for *Ajax News Advertiser,* 1965.

———. Interview with Ronnie Hawkins for *Hit Parader,* October 1965.

Loren, Dennis. Interview with Rick Danko, for *RPM,* July/August 1985.

Kubernik, Harvey. Interview with Graham Nash, MOJO, 1969.

Kubernik, Harvey. "The Struggle Has Gone," *Melody Maker,* January 1976.

———. "Across the Great Divide with Robbie Robertson," *Crawdaddy,* March 1976.

———. Interview with Jerry Garcia: interview, *Melody Maker,* April 1976

———. "Rick Danko: From Band to Band," *Melody Maker,* February 1978.

———. Interview with Mike Stoller and Jerry Leiber, *HITS,* November 1995.

———. Interview with Mike Stoller and Jerry Leiber, *Goldmine,* April, 1995.

———. Interview with Jack Nitzsche, excerpted in *Goldmine,* 2000.

———. Interview with Grace Slick, *HITS,* 2001.

———. Interview with D. A. Pennebaker, *Goldmine,* 2004.

———. Interview with D. A. Pennebaker, *Treats!,* 2012.

———. "Robbie Robertson Gives Testimony," *Record Collector News,* March 2017.

Marcus, Greil. "We Can Talk About It Now," *Good Times,* April 23, 1969.

Tiven, Jon. Review of *Cahoots* for the *Phonograph Record,* December 1971.

Williams, Richard. Interview with Robbie Robertson for "A *Melody Maker* Band Breakdown," *Melody Maker,* May 1971.

Television and DVD

The Band: The Authorized Video Biography, DVD video, 2001, Courtesy of TH Entertainment LLC, http://thentertainment.com.

Live at the Academy of Music 1971, Capitol/Ume, September 17, 2013.

Rumble: The Indians Who Rocked the World, Catherine Bainbridge and Alfonso Maiorana, Rezolution Pictures, 2017.

Yonge Street: Toronto Rock & Roll Stories, Bell Broadcast and New Media Fund (produced with the participation of) David Brady Productions, 2011.

Websites

DeRiso, Nick. Interview with Garth Hudson, *Something Else!,* October 31, 2012. http://somethingelsereviews.com/2012/10/31/the-bands-garth-hudson-to-pay-tribute-to-fallen-voices-rick-danko-levon-helm-and-richard-manuel.

Harvey Kubernik Original Interviews

Gene Aguilera: interview, 2017.
Eli Attie: interview, 2017.
Paul Body: interview, 2017.
Richard Bosworth: interview, 2017.
John Brower: interview, 2017.
Denny Bruce: interview, 2014.
Fred Catero: interview, 2014.
James Cushing: interview, 2014, 2017.
David Dalton: interview, 2017.
Rick Danko, 1977.
Chris Darrow: interview, 2017.
Jon Donabie: interview, 2017.
Bob Dylan: interview, 1976.
Gary Pig Gold: interview, 2018.
Celeste Goyer: interview, 2017.

Michael Hacker: interview, 2017.
Chris Hillman: interview, 2011.
Juliette Jagger: interview, 2018.
Jim Keltner: interview, 2017.
Al Kooper: interview, 2017.
Sarah Kramer: interview, 2017.
Larry LeBlanc: 2016, 2017.
Larry Levine: interview, 2000.
Peter Lewis: interview, 2017.
Michael Macdonald: interview, 2017.
Robert Marchese: interview, 2017.
Elliot Mazer: interview, 2015.
Roger McGuinn, interview, 2010.
Frank Neilsen: interview, 2017.
Jack Nitzsche: interview, 1988.
Harry E. Northup: interview, 2007.
Andrew Loog Oldham, interview, 2017.
D. A. Pennebaker: interview, 2003.
David N. Pepperell: interview, 2017.
Peter Alan Roberts: interview, 2017.
Robbie Robertson: interview, 1975, 1976, 2002, December 2016.
Stan Ross: interview, 2000.
Anthony Scaduto: interview, 1974.
John Scheele: interview, 2017.
William Scheele: interview, 2017.
Kirk Silsbee: interview, 2014.

Michael Simmons: interview, 2017.
John Simon: interview, 2017
Andrew Solt: interview, 2017.
Roger Steffens: interview, 2017.
Mike Stoller: interview, 2017.
Jonathan Taplin: interview via e-mail, 2014.
John Ware: interview, 2017.
Don Was: interview, 2017.
Brian Wilson: Official Programme Brian Wilson 2007.
Sharry Wilson: interview, 2017
Tom Wilson: interview, 2016

Kenneth Kubernik Original Interviews

Brian Auger: interview, 2017.
Jack DeJohnette: interview, 2017.

Other Interviews and Texts

Rob Bowman: interview with Robbie Robertson, © 2001, Rob Bowman, published in liner notes to the box set *The Band: A Musical History*, Capitol Records, September 2005.
Henry Diltz: 1969 diary entry, provided to Harvey Kubernik 2018.
John Scheele: text provided to Harvey Kubernik and Sterling Publishing, 2018.

PICTURE CREDITS

Front cover: © Barrie Wentzell; texture: javaman3/iStock.
Back cover, clockwise from top right: courtesy of Peter Alan Roberts; standa-art/Shutterstock.com (flowers, leaves); © William Scheele; courtesy of Gary Pig Gold; courtesy of Kirk Silsbee; Shutterstock.com (brushstrokes).

Alamy: AF Archive: 186; Album: 183; Keystone Pictures USA: 112; Moviestore Collection, Ltd.: 182; Photo 12: 189 top; Pictorial Press Ltd.: 28, 58, 113, 146 right; RGR Collection: 189 bottom; United Archives GmbH: 185; Mike Walker: 114
Zee Amer: 139
© David Attie: 35 top, 122, 123, 124, 125
Courtesy of Brian Auger: 63, 64
Courtesy of BDMC Productions: 49, 54
Barbara Berger: Front endpaper spread, 71, 105
Rodney Bingenheimer: 32, 48
Jasper Daily/David Leaf Productions Inc.: 76
Courtesy of David Dalton: 132
Courtesy of Chris Darrow Archives: 27, 65
Jim Dickson/courtesy of Henry Diltz: 47 top
© Henry Diltz: v, 38, 60 left; 84, 85, 87, 91, 98, 99, 106, 107, 108, 109, 110, 111, 135 top
Copyright © 1968 Bob Dylan Courtesy Bob Dylan: 79
Everett Collection: 15; © AGIP/RDA/Everett Collection: 60 right
Courtesy of Gary Pig Gold Archives: iii left third down, 22, 30, 35 bottom, 95, 103
Greg Gattine: 86
Getty Images: Bettmann: 77; Blank Archives/Archive Photos: 181 inset; Pierre Fournier: 52; David Gahr: 66; Gijsbert Hanekroot/Redferns: 138, 144; Larry Hulst/Michael Ochs Archives: 181; Norman James/Toronto Star: 31; Frank Lennon: 18; Michael Ochs Archive: 8, 37, 42, 73; New York Post Archives: 81; Winfield Parks: 24; Ed Perlstein/Redferns: 187, 188; Jan Persson/Redferns: 56
Courtesy of Michael Hacker: vi, 2, 3, 47 bottom, 104, 178, 184, back endpapers spread
Heather Harris: 6
iStock: 12, 13
Courtesy of Harvey Kubernik: iv, 7 top right, 190 top, back endpaper single
Courtesy of Kenneth Kubernik: iii bottom middle, iv, 166, 190 top

© Elliott Landy: i, 59, 68, 70, 75, 82, 94, 101, 116
Paul LaRaia: 134, 146 left
Courtesy of Larry LeBlanc: 14, 20
Courtesy of Leiber and Stoller Archives: 11
Library of Congress: 97, 118
Frank Neilsen: 43
Harry E. Northup: 67
Courtesy of Pennebaker Hegedus Films: 41
Courtesy of David N. Pepperell: 89
Courtesy of Ray Randolph: 4 bottom
Courtesy of Peter Alan Roberts: iii top left, 36, 52 inset
Courtesy of Paul Rock and The Wild Honey Foundation: 7 bottom right
© Joann S. Scheele: 128
© 2018 John Scheele – All Rights Reserved: 127, 130, 131, 133, 136, 141, 142, 157, 169, 171, 173, 175, 192. Please see more of John's work on Facebook at "Photography by John Scheele."
© William Scheele: iii left second top, iii top right, 129, 148, 149, 150, 151, 152, 155, 158, 160, 161, 162, 163 bottom, 164, 165, 166, 167, 170 inset, 190 bottom, 205, 211
Gary Schneider/Open Mynd Collectibles: 89 inset, 126
Shutterstock.com: Samuel Germaine-Scrivens: 5; John Storey/AP/REX: 176; Leonard Zhukovsky: 34; design elements throughout: alorac, Archiwiz; Stefan Balaz; chainarong06; Digiselector, Fine Art Studio; jumpingsack; LiveWithArt, one And only; standa-art; Toluk
Courtesy of Kirk Silsbee: iii bottom left, 5 inset, 135 inset, 204
Courtesy of SOFA Entertainment: 120, 121
Roger Steffens: 159, 163 top
Courtesy of Gary Strobl: 4 top
Courtesy of The Village: 154
Guy Webster Photography: 40
Courtesy of Wikimedia Commons: Tony Hisgett: 92; National Archives: 170
Courtesy of Wild Honey Foundation: iii bottom right, 7 left
York University Libraries, Clara Thomas Archives & Special Collections in the York University Libraries: 10, 23; Peter Geddes/Toronto Telegram: 21; Toronto Telegram: front endpapers single, 16, 45

INDEX

Page numbers in *italics* include photo captions.

Academy of Music, New York City, *137*, 140–42, *141*
"Acadian Driftwood," 174, 184
"Across the Great Divide," 96, 140
Aguilera, Gene, 87
Alk, Howard, 55, 70
Allman Brothers, 148
Anderson, Eric, *133*
Aronowitz, Al, 80
Attie, David, 122, 124
Attie, Eli, 122, 125
Auger, Brian, 61, 62

"Baby, Let Me Follow You Down," 51, 184
Bailey, Pearl, 120
"Ballad of a Thin Man," 51
The Band. *See also* Bob Dylan and the Band; *The Last Waltz* farewell concert; *Music from Big Pink* (album)
    at Academy of Music shows, *137*, 140–42, *143*
    airplay in Australia, 89, 119
    at Bearsville Studio, 147
    Bob Peak drawing of, 124
    Canadian tour, 132
    concert ad with Miles Davis, 5
    at Concertgebouw, Amsterdam, *145*
    debut album, 74
    double-keyboard combination, 90
    early formation of, 34
    on *The Ed Sullivan Show*, 120
    on European tour, 140
    on the Festival Express train, 132
    at Fillmore East, *100–102*
    at Gold Star Studio, 76, 77
    at Hollywood Bowl, 134, *135*
    at Isle of Wight Festival, 112–14
    in *The Last Waltz*, 178–89
    Music from Big Pink, 74
    at Oakland–Alameda County Coliseum, 156, *159*
    at Big Pink, 58, 59, 69, *70, 71*
    at Pasadena Civic Auditorium, *126*
    recording at the Hit Factory, 103
    recording *Cahoots*, 137–38
    recording demo tape, 72
    recording *Moondog Matinee*, 147
    recording *Northern Lights–Southern Cross*, 170–72, *175*
    recording *Stage Fright*, 127–31
    resettling by the Pacific, 153
    with Rick Danko's vintage car, *69*
    at Roosevelt Stadium, 148, *151*
    at Sammy Davis Jr.'s studio, *94–97*
    second album reviews, 126
    at Shangri-La Recording Studio, 170–72, *175*
    studio photographs of, *122*
    TIME magazine cover story, 122–24
    at Watkins Glen, 148
    in West Saugerties, 58, 59, 70, 104
    William Scheele etching of, *190*
    William Scheele touring with, 128–29
    at Winterland Ballroom, *1, 2*, 100, *122, 177, 178, 179*, 180
    at Woodstock Festival, 106, *107, 108*, 109
    at Woodstock Playhouse, 127
    at Woody Guthrie Memorial Concert, *66, 67*
The Band (album), 96–97, 117–19, 122, 126
The Band: The Authorized Video Biography (documentary), 65
Barrow, Tony, 52
The Basement Tapes (recordings), 58, 59, 60, 61, 64, 172
Bearsville Studio, 147
The Beatles, 36
Before the Flood (album), 170
Big Pink (house), West Saugerties, New York, 58, 59, 69, *70, 71*
Bill Haley and the Comets, 9
Blackwell, Otis, 33
Blakley, Ronee, 185
Blood, Sweat & Tears, 106
Blue, David, 166
Bluenote dance club, 15
Blues music, 22
Bob Dylan and the Band. *See also* The Band; Dylan, Bob; Dylan and the Hawks
    Cher performing with, *167*
    concertgoers, *159*
    equipment inventory list, *161*
    at Fabulous Forum, Inglewood, *166*
    at Isle of Wight Festival, *114*
    Planet Waves (album), 5, *153,* 156–57, 184
    set list for Boston Garden, *160*
    Tour '74, *153, 155, 156,* 157–63, *166*
    Tour '74 schedule, 158
    William Scheele on, 158, 161, 163, 166
Body, Paul, 1, 7, 48, 126
The Bootleg Series, Vol. II: The Basement Tapes Complete (box set), 59
Bosworth, Richard, 72, 108, 154
Bowman, Rob, 70, 77, 131
Brian Auger and the Trinity, 61
Brill Building, 33, 34
British Invasion, 36
Brower, John, 89, 103
Brown, Jerry, 185
Bruce, Denny, 4, 87
Burke, Sonny, 76

Butterfield, Paul, 1, *188*
The Byrds, 47, 60, 61

Cage, Buddy, *133*
Cahoots (album), 137, 138, 139
Cannon, Geoffrey, 114
Capitol Records, 69, 77, 78, 186
Caravan of Stars concert, 15
Carter, Fred, Jr., 28
Catero, Fred, 72
Chad Allan and the Expressions, 14
Charles, Bobby, 1
Charles, Ray, 16
Cher, 5, 166, *167*
"Chest Fever," 74, 184, 185
CHUM-AM, 14, 35, 88, 103
Clapton, Eric, 1, 90, *182–83, 188*
Clark, Dick, 15
Clemons, Clarence, 98, 99
Coal Miner's Daughter (film), 191
Cocker, Joe, 106, 112
Cohen, Lester, 1
Coleman, Ray, 52
Columbia Records, 70, 72–73, 135, 172
Columbia/Legacy, 59, 114
Confederate soldiers, *118*
Cooder, Ry, 4
Cooke, Sam, *146*
The Corvettes, 65
Costello, Elvis, 146
Country Joe and the Fish, 106
The Crackers, 66, 69, 78
Crill, Chester, 85
Crosby, Stills & Nash (and Young), 106
Curtola, Bobby, 14
Cushing, James
    on Academy of Music shows, 142
    on *The Band* (album), 118
    on *The Basement Tapes*, 61
    on Bob Dylan, 55
    on Dylan–Band tour, 1966, 53
    on *Great White Wonder*, 104, 105
    on Hudson Valley environment influencing music, 86
    recording *Planet Waves*, 156

Dalton, David, 132, *132*
D'Angelo, Beverly, 7
Dangerfield, Rodney, 120
Danko, Rick
    automobile accident, 100
    on The Band's name, 78
    on *The Basement Tapes*, 61, 172
    birth of, 13
    on Cannonball [Adderley] period, 35
    at De Doelen concert center, *138*
    death of, 191
    during Dylan–Band tour, 1974, *153, 156, 158, 163, 169*
    Elvis Costello on, 146
    on the Festival Express train, *133*

headlining at the Roxy Theatre, 6
at Isle of Wight Festival, *112*
at *The Last Waltz* show, 1, 2, 177, 189
on *The Last Waltz* show, 186, 187
at Massey Hall, 44
outside of Big Pink, 59
photograph of, *169*
on recording of *The Band* (album), 98
recording "Rockin' Chair," 118
relocating to Woodstock, 58
with Ringo Starr & His All-Starr Band, 99
on Ronnie Hawkins, 21
Ronnie Hawkins on, 25
on sabbatical, 147
at Sammy Davis Jr.'s studio, 74
at Shangri-La Recording Studio, 172
on *Stage Fright*, 131
at Sydney Stadium, 51
at Watkins Glen, *149*
William Scheele on, 149
at Winterland Ballroom, *177, 189*
Woodstock Festival and, 108, 111
at Woodstock Playhouse, 130
Darrow, Chris, 65, 84, 85
Davis, Miles, 5, 134, *135*
Davis, Sammy, Jr., pool house studio, 5, 74, 93, 94, 95, 98, 103, 128
DeJohnette, Jack, 134, *135*, 188
Delaney & Bonnie and Friends, 132
Densmore, John, 6–7
Deriso, Nick, 14
DeShannon, Jackie, 2–5
"Desolation Row," 48
Di Prima, Diana, 2
Diamond, Neil, 1, *174*, 189
Diddley, Bo, 22
Diltz, Henry, 107
Donabie, John, 44, 88, 180
"Don't Do It," 126, 140
Dont Look Back (documentary), 41
Dr. John, 1, 98, 99, 189
Driscoll, Julie, 61, 62–64
Dwarf Music, 59
Dylan, Bob. *See also* Bob Dylan and the Band; Dylan and the Hawks
at Academy of Music shows, *141, 142*
ad for California shows, *47*
Albert Grossman and, 39
as artist for *Music from Big Pink* cover, 78
in Australia, 43, 49
The Basement Tapes cover shoot, 172
bootleg album, 104
with the Byrds, 47
at Ciro's, 47
during Dylan–Band tour, 1974, *153, 155, 157–63, 164, 165,* 166
on Dylan–Band tour, 1974, *164*
Eat the Document (documentary), 55
European leg of world tour, 52
as family man, 57–58

Guthrie's influence on, 66
Harry Northup on, 67
hearing *Music from Big Pink*, 80
at Isle of Wight Festival, *112, 113, 114*
at *The Last Waltz* show, 1, 2, *184, 185, 189*
living in Woodstock, 57–58
Mary Martin and, 36
motorcycle accident, 57
at Newport Folk Festival, *42, 43*
recording *Planet Waves*, 5, 153–57
Rick Danko on, 61
Robbie Robertson on, 156, 160
on Robertson's guitar playing, 90
at Santa Monica concert, 47
as songwriter, 60
in Studio A, *72*
at Village Recorder Studio, 153
watching Levon and the Hawks perform, 36
at Woody Guthrie Memorial Concert, 66, 67
Dylan and the Hawks. *See also* Bob Dylan and the Band; Dylan, Bob
in Australia, 43, 49–51
at Carnegie Hall, 43
European leg of world tour, 52–55
at K.B. Hallen, Copenhagen, 57
at Massey Hall, 44, *45*
at Pasadena Civic Auditorium, 48
at Santa Monica Civic Auditorium, 33, 48
Scheele on, 128
ticket to Capitol Theatre concert, 52
world tour, *49*
at world tour's end, 57–58

Eat the Document (documentary), 55
Eaton-Walker Associates, 132
Echo chambers, 76–77
The Ed Sullivan Show, 120
Egan, Jack, 102
Elliott, Jack, 66
Emmylou Harris and the Hot Band, 65
Epstein, Brian, 38

Fain, Sammy, 76
Farrell, Joe, 140
Felder, Wilton, 98
Feldthouse, Solomon, 85
Fender Telecaster, 29, 55, 100, 191
Ferlinghetti, Lawrence, 2, *184*
Ferry, Antony, 46
Festival Express (documentary), 132
Fieger, Doug, 87
Flying Burrito Brothers, 132
"Forbidden Fruit," 174
"Forever Young," 156
Foulk, Ray, *112*
Fraboni, Rob, 156, *170, 171*
Freed, Alan, 15
Fulford, Robert, 46

Garcia, Jerry, 108, *133*
Garth Hudson and the Wild Honey Orchestra, 6
Gary, Bruce, 4
Gate of Horn folk club, 39
Geer, Will, 66
Geffen, David, 153, 166
"Go Go Liza Jane," 35
Gold Star Studio, Hollywood, 76
Gomelsky, Giorgio, 62
Goyer, Celeste, 156, 174
Graham, Bill
at David Geffen's birthday party, 166
at *The Last Waltz* show, 2
at Monterey International Pop Festival, 38
pitching debut at Fillmore venues, 100
promoting concert tour, 157
on recording *The Last Waltz* show, 178
at Watkins Glen, 148
Grateful Dead, 132, 148
Great White Wonder (album), *104*
Great Writer Series, 6–7
Griffin, Paul, 46
Grossman, Albert
biography of, 38–39
discovering Bob Dylan, 39
Harvey Kubernik on, 6
John Brower on, 103
at *The Last Waltz* show, 185
Mary Travers and, 39
at Monterey International Pop Festival, 38
recording at Woodstock Playhouse, 130
relocating the Hawks to Woodstock, 58
in Studio A, 72
Guthrie, Arlo, 66
Guthrie, Woody, 66
Guy, Buddy, 132
Gzowski, Peter, 46

Hacker, Michael, 1, 180
Hahn, Don, 74
Hale, Barry, 46
Hanns, Jeff, 65
Harman, Mark, 140
Harris, Ed, 7
Harrison, George, 90
Haust, Jan, 12
Havens, Richard, 66, 112
Hawkins, Ronnie. *See also* Ronnie Hawkins and the Hawks
on Canadian rock-and-roll scene, 30
discipline of, 34
on Garth Hudson, 28
hit singles of, 33
at *The Last Waltz* show, 1, 189
at Le Coq d'Or Tavern, *19*, 23
on Levon Helm, 25
Levon Helm on, 21
moonwalking on television, 30

Hawkins, Ronnie *(cont.)*
    photograph of, *9, 20, 28*
    on Rick Danko, 25
    Rick Danko on, 21
    on Robbie Robertson, 21
    at Roulette Records, 33
Helm, Levon. *See also* Levon and the Hawks
    at Academy of Music shows, *141*
    as actor, 191
    The Basement Tapes cover shoot, *172*
    beat placement, 26
    during Dylan–Band tour, 1974, *155, 163, 165*
    early formation of, 20
    Garth Hudson on, 24
    as group's new leader, 34–35
    at Hollywood Bowl, *135*
    Jack DeJohnette on, 134
    Jim Keltner on, 4, 98–99
    at *The Last Waltz* show, 1, 2, *177, 188*
    on Mary Martin, 36
    outside of Big Pink, *59*
    photograph of, *9*
    on playing with Bob Dylan, 45
    on putting songs together, 72
    recording "Rockin' Chair," 118
    with Ringo Starr & His All-Starr Band, *99*
    Ronnie Hawkins on, 25
    at Roosevelt Stadium, *151*
    on sabbatical, 147
    at Sammy Davis Jr.'s studio, *74, 94*
    songwriting at Big Pink, *71*
    on *Spectacle: Elvis Costello with TV* series, 146
    at Turtle Creek Studio, 174
    at Watkins Glen, *149*
    William Scheele on, 149
    at Winterland Ballroom, *177, 188*
    Woodstock Festival and, *106, 107, 108*
Hendrix, Jimi, 106
Highway 61 Revisited (album), 46
Hillman, Chris, 60, *60*
Holmes, Odetta, 66
Hopkins, Lightnin', 22
Hudson, Garth
    autism benefit show, 6
    birth of, 13
    compiling *The Basement Tapes*, 60
    during Dylan–Band tour, 1974, *155, 158, 163*
    on *Highway 61 Revisited*, 46
    Jonathan Taplin on, 60
    Kenneth Kubernik on, 168–69
    at *The Last Waltz* show, 1, *185*
    on Levon Helm, 24
    Levon Helm on, 29
    at Massey Hall, 44
    to Nick Deriso, 14
    outside of Big Pink, *59*
    photograph of, *169*

on recording of *The Band* (album), 98
    recording "Rockin' Chair," 118
    relocating to Woodstock, 58
    singing voice of, 28
    on *Spectacle: Elvis Costello with TV* series, 146
    at Sydney Stadium, 51
    trained in classical music, 28
    William Scheele on, 128–29, 149
    at Winterland Ballroom, 1, *185*
    at Woodstock Festival, *108*
Hutton, Danny, 76

"I Don't Believe You," 51, 184
"I Shall Be Released," 80, 86, 89, 126, 184, *185*
"I Want You," 53
"In a Station," 89
Islands (album), 178, 191
Isle of Wight Festival, 112–14
"It Makes No Difference," 174

Jagger, Juliette, 15
Jahn, Mike, 103, 117
"Jawbone," 97
Jefferson Airplane, 106, *110*
Jeffrey, Nat, 170
"Jemima Surrender," 103
Joe Cocker and the Grease Band, 106
Johns, Glyn, 127
Johnson, Howard, 140, *143*
Jones, Mickey, 46, 51, 53
Jones, Willard "Pop," *9*
Joplin, Janis, 132, *133*
Judnich, John, 87
"Just Like Tom Thumb's Blues," 53

Kaleidoscope, 85
Kandel, Lenore, 2
Kasper, Edward, 147
Keeler, Freddie, 29
Keltner, Jim, 4–5, 98, *99*
Kemp, Louis, 166
Kennedy, Robert F., *84*
King, B. B., 22
"King Harvest," 97, 118
Klegerman, Alex, 13
Konikoff, Sandy, 46
Kooper, Al, 43, 74, 78
Kramer, Sarah, 139, 174
Kubernik, Harvey, 3, 6, 85, 168–69, 182–85
Kubernik, Kenneth, 168–169

Lampell, Millard, 66
Landy, Elliott, 59, 69, 71, 74, 78, 83, 94, *100*, 117
Lang, Michael, 106
The Last Waltz farewell concert
    acts billed at, 1
    Bill Graham at, 2
    Bob Dylan at, 2, 184, *185*, 189
    Bob Margolin at, 182
    Carl Radle at, 184

circular welcome handout of, *181*
    concertgoers at, *181*
    Dr. John at, 1, *189*
    Eric Clapton at, 182–83, *186*, 188
    Ferlinghetti, Lawrence, *184*
    group jam session, *183*, 188
    Harvey Kubernik on, 182–85
    Jack DeJohnette on, 188
    John Donabie on, 180
    Joni Mitchell at, 1, *183*, 189
    Levon Helm at, 1, 2, *177*, 188
    marquee, *1, 179*
    Michael Hacker on, 179
    Muddy Waters at, *187*
    Neil Diamond at, 1, *189*
    Neil Young at, *183*, 188, *189*
    Paul Butterfield at, 188
    photograph of, *192*
    Pinetop Perkins at, 182
    poetry reading at, 184
    postcard announcing, *190*
    Rick Danko at, 1, *2, 177*, 187, *189*
    Rick Danko on, 6
    Ringo Starr at, 184
    Robbie Robertson at, 1, *2, 185*, 187, *188, 189*
    Robbie Robertson on, 178–79
    Ronnie Hawkins at, 1, *189*
    Ronnie Wood at, 184
    song selection for, 178–79
    Thanksgiving dinner at, 180
    Van Morrison at, 1, 184, *189*
The Last Waltz (film), 186
The Last Waltz 40 Tour, 190
Laurel Canyon (album), 2
"Lay Lady Lay," 114
Le Coq d'Or Tavern, Yonge St., Toronto, 15, *16, 19, 20, 23, 25*
Leakage, defined, 72
"Leave Me Alone," 34–35
LeBlanc, Larry
    on The Band after Ronnie Hawkins, 35
    on Canadian radio of the '50s and '60s, 14
    on Dylan–Grossman partnership, 41
    interviewing Ronnie Hawkins, 22
    on *Music from Big Pink*, 88
    on musicians copying Levon and the Hawks, 29
    photograph of, *14, 20*
    on Ronnie Hawkins, 20
    on Yonge Street nightly entertainment, 25
Led Zeppelin, 5
Leiber, Jerry, *11*, 33, 35, 190
Leishman, Larry, 29
"Leopard-Skin Pill-Box Hat," 51
Leventhal, Harold, 66
Levine, Larry, 76, 77
Levon and the Hawks, 34–35, 37, 43. *See also* Bob Dylan and the Band; Helm, Levon
Levy, Morris, 33
Lewis, Peter, 88

"Life Is a Carnival," 138, 139
"Like a Rolling Stone," 53, 158
Linden, Colin, 29
Loesser, Frank, 76
Lofgren, Nils, 98, 99
London, John, 65
"Lonesome Suzie," 74
Long, Jack, 29
"Long Distance Operator," 76
"Look Out Cleveland," 97
Lovin' Spoonful, 72
"Loving You Is Sweeter Than Ever," 126
Lowrey organ, 44, 84, 129, 184, 185
Lowrey Organ Company, 129

MacDonald, Michael, 119
Manchester Free Trade Hall, 55
Mann, Manfred, 59, 61
Manuel, Richard
   birth of, 13
   boating accident, 177
   Bob Dylan and, 80
   death of, 191
   during Dylan–Band tour, 1974, *163*
   on *Highway 61 Revisited*, 46
   at *The Last Waltz* show, 1, *177*
   at Massey Hall, 44
   outside of Big Pink, 59
   photograph of, *169*
   on recording of *The Band* (album), 98
   recording "Rockin' Chair," 118
   relocating to Woodstock, 58
   at Roosevelt Stadium, *151*
   on sabbatical, 147
   singing voice of, 28
   songwriting at Big Pink, 71
   on *Stage Fright*, 131
   at Sydney Stadium, 51
   William Scheele on, 149
   at Winterland Ballroom, 1, *177*
   at Woodstock Festival, *108*
   at Woodstock Playhouse, *130*
   on working with Bob Dylan, 81
Maple Leaf Gardens arena, audience at, 10
Marchese, Robert, *135*
Marcus, Greil, 100, 101
Margolin, Bob, 182
Martin, Mary, 36
Martinez, Hirth, *171*, 174
Massey Hall performance, 44–46
May, Tony, 74, 78
Mayfield, Curtis, 86
Mazer, Eliot, 113, 185
McClure, Michael, 2
McGuinn, Roger, 60
McHugh, Jimmy, 76
McIntyre, Earl, 140
Mercer, Johnny, 76
MET Theatre, Los Angeles, 6–7
"The Mighty Quinn," 58, 59, 61, 114
Minnesota
   Dylan birthplace, 86, 156
   Dylan–Band recordings, 104, 105

Mitchell, Joni, 1, *183*, 189
Moondog Matinee (album), *146*, 147
Morrison, Van, 1, 184, *185*, 189
"Mr. Tambourine Man," 47
Music from Big Pink (album)
   Andrew Oldham on, 84
   Canada's impression of, 88–89
   Chris Darrow on, 84
   cover artwork, 78
   debut of, 74
   fiftieth anniversary of, 7
   John Simon on, 74, 78
   origins of, 58
   reissue, 76
   release of, 83–85, *84*
   reviews of, 84–89
   setting innovations, 191
   United Kingdom's impression of, 90
Music from Big Pink (Niven), 59

Nash, Graham, 108
Neilsen, Frank, 49
Neuwirth, Bobby, 166, 185
New Riders of the Purple Sage, 132
Nicholson, Jack, 166
"The Night They Drove Old Dixie Down," 96, 98, 118, 126, 140
Nitzsche, Jack, 4, 76, 87
Niven, John, 59
No Direction Home: Bob Dylan (documentary), 55
Northern Lights–Southern Cross (album), 5, *170*, 174, *175*, 191
Northup, Harry E., 67

Offord, Eddy, 64
Oldham, Andrew Loog, 38, *40*, 84
"One Too Many Mornings," 51
Ontario, Canada, 13
"Ophelia," 174
Orange Juice Blues, 76
Owens, Buck, 120

Parker, Colonel Tom, 22, 38
Parron, J. D., 140
Paul Butterfield Blues Band, 106
Paulman, Jimmy Ray "Luke," *9*, 22
Paxton, Tom, 66
Penfound, Jerry, *23*
Pennebaker, D.A., *41*, *41*, 55
Pepperell, David N., 50–51, 88, 89, 104
Peppermint Lounge, 35
Perkins, Carl, 22
Perkins, Pinetop, 182
Peter, Paul & Mary, *60*, 61
Peterson, Oscar, 16
Pig Gold, Gary, *31*, 37
Planet Waves (album), 5, 153, 156–57, 184
Playboy Jazz Festival, 134
Playboy magazine, 83
Pomus, Doc, 33
Pop filters, 76
"Positively Fourth Street," 51
Presley, Elvis, 10, *11*, 22, 38

Preston, Billy, 98, 99
Putnam, Bill, 154

Quinn, Gordon, 55
"Quinn the Eskimo (The Mighty Quinn)," 59. *See also* "The Mighty Quinn"

Radle, Carl, 5, 98, 184
"Rag Mama Rag," 96, 140
Ramone, Phil, 72, 74, 76, 77, 140, 170
Ringo Starr & His All-Starr Band, 98, 99
Robbie & the Robots, 34
Roberts, Peter Alan, 53
Robertson, Jim, 13
Robertson, Robbie
   at Academy of Music shows, *141*
   on Academy of Music shows, 141
   as actor, 191
   Albert Grossman and, 80
   on arrival of rock 'n' roll, 12
   in Australia, *49*
   on The Band's name, 71
   on band's piano-and-organ-group instrumentations, 90
   on *The Basement Tapes*, 58, 172
   birth of, 13
   Bob Dylan on, 90
   during Dylan–Band tour, 1974, *153*
   on Dylan–Band tour, 1974, 156, 160
   on expanding original songs, 144
   at Fillmore East, 100
   as film music producer, 191
   on The Band's formation, 25
   guitar theory, 90
   on importance of studio locations, 77
   at Isle of Wight Festival, *112*
   James Cushing describing, 53
   on *The Last Waltz* film, 186
   at *The Last Waltz* show, 1–2, *177*, *185*, *188*, *189*
   at Le Coq d'Or Tavern, *23*
   at Massey Hall, 44
   moving to Malibu, 154
   on *Northern Lights–Southern Cross*, 174
   on "Ophelia," 174
   outside of Big Pink, 59
   Peter Traynor teaching, 29
   playing style of, 28
   recording *Planet Waves*, 5, 156
   reflecting Dylan/Hawks stage relationship, 54
   on Ronnie Hawkins and the Hawks, 21, 25
   Ronnie Hawkins on, 21
   at Roulette Records, 33
   on sabbatical, 147
   at Sammy Davis Jr.'s studio, 74, 95
   at Shangri-La Recording Studio, 170, *171*
   on sharing *Music from Big Pink* with Bob Dylan, 80
   on song selection for *The Last Waltz*, 178–79

Robertson, Robbie (cont.)
   on songwriting, 119
   songwriting at Big Pink, 71
   songwriting skills of, 70
   at Sydney Stadium, 51
   on *Testimony* (autobiography), 7
   William Scheele on, 149
   at Winterland Ballroom, 177
   on *Woodstock* (documentary), 111
   Woodstock Festival and, 91, 106, 108, 109
   at Woodstock Playhouse, 130
   on writing "The Night They Drove Old Dixie Down," 118
Rock of Ages (album), 140, 142
Rockabilly, 22, 26, 67
"Rockin' Chair," 97, 118
Rockin' Revols, 34
Rockwood club, Fayetteville, Arkansas, 26
Ronnie Hawkins and the Hawks, 9, 20, 23, 178–89. *See also* Hawkins, Ronnie
Roosevelt Stadium, 148, 151
Ross, Stan, 76
Rundgren, Todd, 127, 130
Ryan, Robert, 66

Scaduto, Anthony, 41
Scheele, John
   on Academy of Music shows, 140
   on Festival Express, 133
   on Shangri-La Recording Studio, 170
   on *The Basement Tapes* cover shoot, 172
   photograph of, 127
Scheele, William
   on Academy of Music shows, 140
   on *The Basement Tapes* cover shoot, 172
   at Beverly Wilshire Hotel closing party, 166
   construction notes, 170
   on Dylan–Band tour, 1974, 158, 161, 163
   etching of *The Band*, 190
   impressions of band members, 149
   on *The Last Waltz* show, 190
   photograph of, 127
   recording *Planet Waves*, 155, 156
   at Shangri-La Recording Studio, 171
   as stage manager for The Band, 128–29
   at Woodstock Playhouse, 127
Schroeder, Aaron, 43
Scorsese, Martin, 55, 178, 180, 191
Seeger, Pete, 66
Sha Na Na, 106
Shangri-La Recording Studio, 5, 170–72
Shapiro, Benny, 38
Shepard, Sam, 7
Shuman, Mort, 33
Siebel, Paul, 126

Silsbee, Kirk, 61
Simmons, Michael, 142
Simon, John
   on Charles Lloyd, 70
   at Fillmore East, 100
   at *The Last Waltz* show, 185
   mixing *Music from Big Pink*, 78
   on recording *Music from Big Pink*, 74
   recording "Rockin' Chair," 118
   on recording *The Band* (album), 96–97
   on Robbie Robertson, 97
   at Sammy Davis Jr.'s studio, 74, 94, 95
   at Woodstock Playhouse, 127, 130
Slick, Grace, 110
Slim, Lightnin', 22
Smalls, Charlie, 98
Solomon, Rita, 67
Solt, Andrew, 47, 102
Stage Fright (album), 127–31
Starr, Ringo, 90, 98, 99, 166, 184, 189
Steffens, Roger, 159
Stills, Stephen, 185
Stoller, Mike, 11, 33, 35, 190
"The Stones I Throw (Will Free All Men)," 34–35
Stookey, Paul, 60
Stratton, Dayton, 26
Studio A (Columbia), 72
Studio A (Village Recorders), 154
Studio echo chambers, 76–77
Szelest, Stan, 28

Taplin, Jonathan, 60, 93, 140, 143, 178
Taylor, James, 65
"Tears of Rage," 74, 80, 96, 102
Ten Years After, 106
Testimony (Robertson), 7, 80, 191
"This Wheel's on Fire," 59, 61, 62–64, 74, 86, 104, 126
This Wheel's on Fire (Helm), 34, 107, 147
Thumper & the Trombones, 34
TIME magazine, 122–24
Tiomkin, Dimitri, 76
Tiven, Jon, 138
TMQ (Trademark of Quality), 104
"Too Much of Nothing," 61
Toronto, Canada, 12–16
Toronto Pop Festival, 103
Toussaint, Allen, 138
Travers, Mary, 39, 60
Traynor, Peter, 29
Traynor amps, 29
Troiano, Domenic, 29
Turner, Titus, 33
Tyson, Ian, 133
Tyson, Sylvia, 133

"Unfaithful Servant," 97
"Up on Cripple Creek," 96, 103, 120, 126, 127

Van Heusen, Jimmy, 76
Van Zandt, Steven, 126

Village Recorders Studio, West Los Angeles, 5, 153, 154
Walker, Ken, 103, 133
Wallichs Music City, Hollywood, 4, 83
Walsh, Joe, 98, 99
Ware, John
   inspired by Ronnie Hawkins, 25, 26
   on Levon Helm, 26, 65
   as Linda Rondstadt's drummer, 65
   meeting Levon Helm, 26
   in Oklahoma City, 26
   photograph of, 26, 65
   playing drums for Emmylou Harris, 65
Warner Bros. Records, 69
Was, Don, 87, 190
Waters, Muddy, 1, 182, 187
Watkins Glen, 148, 149
"We Can Talk," 74
"The Weight"
   Bob Dylan on, 80
   Chris Darrow on, 84
   David Peperell on, 89
   Gene Aguilera on, 87
   on KHJ playlist, 4
   at *The Last Waltz* show, 184
   as lead single, 88
   Mike Stoller on, 190
   Robbie Robertson on, 74
Weiss, Donna, 5
Weizmann, Daniel, 7
West Saugerties, New York, 58, 59, 70, 86, 104
"Whispering Pines," 103
The Who, 112
Williams, Richard, 90, 140
Wilson, Brian, 76, 77
Wilson, Sharry, 36, 46
Wilson, Tom, 15
Wind screens, 76
Winter, Johnny, 106
Winterland Ballroom, San Francisco, 1, 2, 100, 177, 178, 179, 181
Wood, Ronnie, 184, 188, 189
Woodstock (documentary), 111
Woodstock, New York, 57–58, 86
Woodstock Festival, 106–11
Woodstock Playhouse, 95, 130, 127
Woody Guthrie Memorial Concert, 66, 67

Yakus, Shelly, 74
Yarrow, Peter, 60, 70
Yonge Street, Toronto, 16, 16, 31
Yonge Street: Toronto Rock & Roll Stories (documentary), 12
Yorkville Sound, 29
Young, Neil, 1, 87, 183, 185, 188, 189
Young, Snooky, 140

THE LAST WALTZ 40 TOUR

A CELEBRATION OF THE 40TH ANNIVERSARY OF THE LAST WALTZ

WITH

ORIGINAL MEMBER OF THE BAND GARTH HUDSON

WARREN HAYNES · DR. JOHN · JAMEY JOHNSON

DON WAS · CYRIL NEVILLE · DAVE MALONE

BOB MARGOLIN · TERENCE HIGGINS · DANNY LOUIS

MARK MULLINS & VERY SPECIAL GUESTS

FEATURING THE ORIGINAL HORN ARRANGEMENTS OF ALLEN TOUSSAINT

ARTISTS SUBJECT TO CHANGE

LASTWALTZ40TOUR.COM #LASTWALTZ40TOUR

THURSDAY, APRIL 13

Bill Graham's WINTERLAND

THE BAND IN THE LAST WALTZ